BEACH BOYS A...
VOLUME 1

FOREWORD

You can't ever duplicate the environment in which the Beach Boys rose to popularity. The early 1960s were a more innocent, more prosperous time, without the worries of 10% plus unemployment, global warming and similar environmental catastrophes on the horizon.

Kids seemed to worry more about whether they had enough chrome on their cars and how to get the gas money so that they could drive around with their friends. Or at least that's our collective stereotype of the time...

And in those days, the Beach Boys appeared to be a harmonious group in all ways. We liked the fact that their personal lives seemed to be a mirror reflection of their singing harmonies.

In those days, the record companies, for the most part, were able to use the press to create the images they wanted their stars to have. And they did wherever they could, even becoming the publisher in some cases.

In this first volume of Beach Boys Archives, you'll find that the early magazine stories are typical of the time: big in PR and light on actual facts about the artists. That said, the pictures are fun even if they are mostly staged.

We've unearthed a variety of materials from the years up to 1976, including tour books, music publication ads, and press materials. There's a good chance that unless you are a rabin fan (and even if you are), you haven't seen some of this material previously. We hope you enjoy them.

Copyright 2013 White Lightning Publications

BEACH BOYS
FIFTH ANNUAL
THANKSGIVING TOUR
BUFFALO SPRINGFIELD
STRAWBERRY ALARM CLOCK
SOUL SURVIVORS
PICKLE BROTHERS
Thanks to These Stations for Their Cooperation on This
WKNR WEAM WMCA WRKO
WICE WDRC KDKA WBZ WCAO
WICC

BEACH BOYS

THE BEACH
Featuring
Complete parts for Lead Guitar, Rhythm Guitar and Bass
Words and Music to eleven of the Beach Boys greatest hits

BEACH BOYS
CONCERT

MUSIC AD 1965

BILLBOARD DECEMBER 1963

TOP TALENT OF 1963

Top Singles Artists for 1963

DESPITE *the fact that success in the singles field is generally followed up with action in albums, a check of the top 10 singles artists for 1963 discloses that only one act was also among the top 10 LP artists. Ray Charles, who hit No. 4 position in the singles ranks, was also No. 5 in the album classification. Leading singles act, The Beach Boys, showed up No. 14 on the album charts, while runner-up, Dion DiMuci, was No. 45 among album artists.*

1. THE BEACH BOYS
2. DION DiMUCI 
3. THE 4 SEASONS 
4. RAY CHARLES 
5. CHUBBY CHECKER 
6. RICK NELSON 
7. BOBBY VINTON 
8. PETER, PAUL AND MARY 
9. BRENDA LEE 
10. ROY ORBISON 

11. ELVIS PRESLEY
12. THE CRYSTALS
13. SAM COOKE
14. THE SHIRELLES
15. ANDY WILLIAMS
16. LESLEY GORE
17. SKEETER DAVIS
18. RUBY & THE ROMANTICS
19. THE CHIFFONS
20. NAT KING COLE
21. CONNIE FRANCIS
22. GENE PITNEY
23. PAUL & PAULA
24. THE DRIFTERS
25. THE MIRACLES
26. BROOK BENTON
27. AL MARTINO
28. BOBBY DARIN
29. STEVE LAWRENCE
30. TONY BENNETT
31. MARY WELLS
32. BOBBY VEE
33. THE TYMES
34. MARTHA & THE VANDELLAS
35. LOU CHRISTIE
36. THE ROOFTOP SINGERS
37. THE KINGSTON TRIO
38. THE ESSEX
39. JOHNNY MATHIS
40. DEE DEE SHARP
41. JOHNNY TILLOTSON
42. LITTLE STEVIE WONDER
43. NEIL SEDAKA
44. LITTLE PEGGY MARCH
45. THE ANGELS
46. LONNIE MACK
47. EYDIE GORME
48. JACKIE WILSON
49. THE CASCADES
50. BOBBY BLAND
51. MAJOR LANCE
52. KYU SAKAMOTO
53. THE DOVELLS
54. BARBARA LEWIS
55. THE SAFARIS
56. THE COOKIES
57. BOBBY BARE
58. DEL SHANNON
59. BILL ANDERSON
60. BOBBY RYDELL
61. THE REBELS
62. RICHARD CHAMBERLAIN
63. INEZ FOXX
64. TRINI LOPEZ
65. THE CHANTAYS
66. JOHNNY CASH
67. LITTLE EVA
68. RANDY & THE RAINBOWS
69. BOB B. SOXX & BLUE JEANS
70. JIMMY SOUL
71. ROLF HARRIS
72. GARNET MIMMS & THE ENCHANTERS
73. BEN E. KING
74. DARLENE LOVE
75. ETTA JAMES
76. THE RONETTES
77. THE NEW CHRISTY MINSTRELS
78. HENRY MANCINI
79. THE EXCITERS
80. THE MARVELETTES
81. JOHNNY CYMBAL
82. THE RAINDROPS
83. TIMI YURO
84. PAUL PETERSON
85. KAI WINDING
86. BILL PURCELL
87. THE JAYNETTES
88. THEOLA KILGORE
89. JIMMY GILMORE & THE FIREBALLS
90. NED MILLER
91. JAN BRADLEY
92. ROCKY FELLERS
93. THE IMPRESSIONS
94. JAMES BROWN & FAMOUS FLAMES
95. DORIS TROY
96. ALLAN SHERMAN
97. SUNNY & THE SUNGLOWS
98. FREDDIE SCOTT
99. WAYNE NEWTON
100. PAUL ANKA

Who's Who in the World of Music • Billboard • December 28, 1963

BEACH BOYS AD - BILLBOARD DECEMBER 1963

The BEACH

MOVIN' SINGLES—

"Be True To Your School"   "In My Room"
#5056

THE MOVIN' ALBUMS—

Who's Who in the World of Music • Billboard • December 28, 1963

Nation's Most Popular Group
BOYS

Many thanks to all who have helped us in our most successful year--

Personal Mgt.
MURRAY WILSON

Capitol RECORDS

Artist Booking
WM. MORRIS AGENCY

December 28, 1963 • Who's Who in the World of Music • Billboard

THE BEACH BOYS

Featuring , **Lead Guitar**

Complete parts for Lead Guitar, Rhythm Guitar and Bass

Words and Music to eleven of the Beach Boys greatest hits

Chord Symbols and Diagrams in Easy Keys for accompaniment

Photos of the Beach Boys and Special Tips on playing the guitar

BEACH BOYS - LEAD GUITAR MUSIC

A Note from the Publisher:

WE HAVE RECEIVED so many hundreds of letters from aspiring guitarists, not only from the teeners of the United States, but many countries around the world asking for this long awaited guitar folio book of The Beach Boys.

As parents, and as publishers of all of The Beach Boys' fantastic hits, it gives us great pleasure to publish this guitar folio featuring pictures of Carl Wilson and Al Jardine who plays on the front line in stage concerts, along with Brian Wilson, leader, who plays the fender bass guitar.

The success story of The Beach Boys starting from scratch and not knowing how to play instruments to any great degree, and to become one of the most famous all time rock and roll great instrumental and vocal groups is a success story in itself, but when one knows that Carl Wilson was only 14½ years old when he started to play a battered up six string guitar and who made so many bad mistakes in the fingering of tough chords, but who later practiced religiously from three to four hours each day, with firm determination; and the result was he established after beats and guitar rift runs which became what was known to the world as Surfin' guitar sounds and which actually helped The Beach Boys distinctive band style sound different. Carl was 15 when he made the fine runs on the instrumental brothers and The Beach Boys. You all remember the first record called "Surfin'" with his parts of records such as "Surfin' Safari", "409", "Shutdown", "In My Room"; "Surfer Girl" and many, many others including "Surf Jam" and "Carl's Big Chance" which he composed.

Most of these instrumental parts on The Beach Boys' records which featured Carl Wilson's guitar were composed at The Beach Boys' home three or four days before the session or were composed right in the recording studio under great pressure. Carl's favorite position while playing at home was lying down on his bed and it was just as funny to see Carl sitting on a soap box at the western recording studios in Hollywood, where he did most of his great guitar solos.

We hope that this book will be of great help to not only the young men of our nation but also the young gals who do play electric and standard guitars. We would appreciate hearing from some of you, letting us know what you think of this folio and we welcome any helpful criticism or suggestions because we will issue another folio in due time.

Of all guitar players on records around the world, Chuck Berry's records and the guitar playing on Berry's discs was Carl Wilson's greatest inspiration. He was quick to learn every arrangement as Chuck Berry's hits came out. The more Carl learned, the more he became known with his own unique style and his production ideas on The Beach Boys' records enhanced The Beach Boys' hits and gave them that extra punch, thus enabling Capitol Records to have hit after hit.

When we asked Carl how we could quote him about his guitar playing and his success, he said 'Gee, Dad, I guess you could tell 'em to practice a lot and keep up with the current trends and to develop good styles and runs and that it is a lot of kicks when you know you have done a good job." Then, laughingly he said, "you might also tell them to be sure and keep new spare strings in the guitar case at all times because it is very embarrassing when you break a string on stage and run out to the wings and find you don't have any spares!" In closing, he added "tell all our fans thanks a million for being so great to us".

MURRY G. WILSON, *dad*
Sea of Tunes Publishing Company

NOTE All fan letters to The Beach Boys MUST go to their fan club, P.O. Box 110, Hollywood, California. Simply because we do not have the staff to answer same. Thanks!!

BEACH BOYS - LEAD GUITAR MUSIC

THE BEACH BOYS *at play...*

BRIAN, CARL, ALAN — at Shindig rehearsal

ALAN and CARL — Staunch on Stage

CARL — Wailing — in Boston

THE BEACH BOYS — 1964

CARL WILSON — Smiling after TV Show

BEACH BOYS - LEAD GUITAR MUSIC

Two Great *BEACH BOYS Collections*

CONTENTS

BALLAD OF OLD BETSY, THE
BE TRUE TO YOUR SCHOOL
FARMER'S DAUGHTER, THE
"409"
FUN, FUN, FUN
HAWAII
IN MY ROOM
LITTLE DEUCE COUPE
LITTLE ST. NICK
LONELY SEA, THE
NO-GO SHOWBOAT
SHUT DOWN
SURFIN

Price $2.00 in U.S.A.

CONTENTS

DANCE, DANCE, DANCE
DO YOU WANNA DANCE?
DON'T WORRY, BABY
HELP ME, RHONDA
I GET AROUND
IN THE BACK OF MY MIND
LITTLE HONDA
MAN WITH ALL THE TOYS, THE
PLEASE LET ME WONDER
SHE KNOWS ME TOO WELL
WARMTH OF THE SUN, THE
WENDY
WHEN I GROW UP (To Be A Man)

Price $2.00 in U.S.A.

SEA OF TUNES PUBLISHING COMPANY • 9042 La Alba Drive, Whittier, California 90603
Sales and Shipping: Suite 611, 1841 Broadway, New York 23, N.Y.

BEACH BOYS - FOLIO INSERT PAGES

ALAN JARDINE

BEACH BOYS - FOLIO INSERT PAGES

BRIAN WILSON

CARL WILSON

BEACH BOYS - FOLIO INSERT PAGES

MIKE LOVE

DENNIS WILSON

BEACH BOYS - FOLIO INSERT PAGES

17

BEACH BOYS - FOLIO INSERT PAGES

BEACH BOYS - FOLIO INSERT PAGES

The Beach Boys in Rome, November, 1964. The boys were especially impressed with the beauty of Rome, and it was a highlight of their tour which included England, France, Germany, Sweden, Denmark, Italy. They went over well in Europe.

In Paris, middle-aged Frenchmen were screaming their heads off, right along with the teenagers and at one part of the concert, teeners stormed the stage and had to be driven off by Gendarmes.

BEACH BOYS - FOLIO INSERT PAGES

Another shot of the Beach Boys appearing in front of 12,000 fans in Melbourne, Australia. Note how exhausted Brian looks after 18 days of touring with an average of 5 hours sleep a night.

The Beach Boys signing autographs after a charity appearance in the Hollywood Bowl, early 1963. (Carl was on the right, out of the picture.)

The Beach Boys autographing in a large Department store. Carl, Al, Dennis & Mike, from left to right. (Brian was sitting at table next to Carl) August 1963.

Picture of Mike Love performing "Monster Mash" in Australia, January, 1963. Dig the Bella Lugosi Eyes. Mike is always exhausted after doing "Monster Mash" because he puts so much into it. Mike does a fantastic job as M.C. at all of their concerts and does most of the leads on the fast songs and can sing any one of four parts of harmony, like Brian, Carl, & Al. When the chips are down, Mike comes through. In Las Vegas, Mike went on stage with a 103 degree temperature, and with a strep throat and although he hardly could sing, he stood there and put out. This is one of the reasons The Beach Boys are so great.

BEACH BOYS - FOLIO INSERT PAGES

Chinatown U.S.A.
The Beach Boys waiting impatiently for breakfast.

Chinatown U.S.A.
The Beach Boys Marching Time.

Chinatown U.S.A.
The Beach Boys — Carl, Mike and Al giving moral support to Denny.

BEACH BOYS - FOLIO INSERT PAGES

Photo of Carl being crushed after concert on the East Coast. Note how Al Jardine is holding on to man in foreground. Also note how the glass door was bulging out from the crowd pushing. A little more and Carl could have been cut from the glass. This is a terrifying experience for all stars.

Chinatown U.S.A.
Mike and Denny on a Honda

Early 1963, Carl's Grand Prix

Chinatown U.S.A.
The Beach Boys making a decision...

All the boys

BEACH BOYS - FOLIO INSERT PAGES

Photo of Paul & Paula, Mike Love, and Denny. (Also Brisbane Airport). It was 102 degrees at the Airport, at the height of Australia's summer, (January, 1964)

Another shot of the fellows in front of the plane at Brisbane. There were over 3,000 fans waiting at the Airport for The Beach Boys, Roy Orbison, Paul & Paula, and The Surfaris.

The Beach Boys arriving in Brisbane, Australia, January 8, 1964. Denny lost his Kuala bear after lugging it around on seventeen airplanes.

When The Beach Boys recorded their Live Concert Album, #1 in the Nation in Sacramento, California, Mike drove a Honda on stage much to the surprise and roar of the crowd. Mike got a big bang out of doing this. Notice Brian's happy surprise that Mike didn't fall off. The Beach Boys asked us to be sure to tell the teeners in Sacramento how wonderful it has been to appear six times in their Civic Memorial Auditorium which holds 5,100 seats. The screams you hear on the live concert album were authentic and not doctored up in any way. The Beach Boys cannot praise Sacramento enough.

BEACH BOYS - WILMINGTON DELAWARE 1965 APPEARANCE

NEW YORK   BEVERLY HILLS   CHICAGO   LONDON   PARIS   ROME

WILLIAM MORRIS AGENCY
INC.
1740 BROADWAY
NEW YORK 19, N.Y.
TELEPHONE JUDSON 6-5100

April 2, 1965

Mr. Frank Giamboy
Am-Boy Productions
Box 214 Road 2
Chadds Ford, Pa.

Re: BEACHBOYS
    WILMINGTON, DELAWARE
    April 20, 1965

Dear Mr. Giamboy:

Would you be good enough to sign all copies of the enclosed contract and return them to us at your earliest convenience. After counter-signature by the artist, one copy will be sent to you for your records.

PLEASE NOTE: The reverse side of the contract must be filled out in full before we are able to forward this contract to the artist for signature. When this is done, the contract can then be fully executed.

With thanks for your cooperation and every good wish, we remain,

Sincerely yours,

WILLIAM MORRIS AGENCY, INC.

Ronnie Fried
Ronnie Fried, for
John Quinn

encl.

BEACH BOYS - WILMINGTON DELAWARE 1965 APPEARANCE

WILLIAM MORRIS AGENCY, INC.

SINCE 1898...THE AGENCY OF THE SHOW WORLD

THIS IS THE CORRECT BILLING ---- NO CHANGES ARE TO BE MADE.....

Presenting

T H E B E A C H B O Y S --- 100%

jan
11/64

1740 BROADWAY • NEW YORK 19, N. Y. • JUDSON 6-5100

BEACH BOYS - WILMINGTON DELAWARE 1965 APPEARANCE

From: Press Department　　　　　　　　　　　　THE BEACH BOYS
　　　　William Morris Agency, Inc.　　　　　　　　Page　　One

    In less than three years, the Beach Boys have climbed from zero to No. 1 spot on the annual pop music charts. Their original songs started three new nation-wide musical trends: surfing, hot rods and motor scooting. It all began in Hawthorne, a green grass town five miles from the Southern California beaches where the breakers roar, the surfers ride their wild boards and the sun-kissed bikini belles loll on the golden sands.

    Until 1961 there was nothing special to distinguish the small five-room Wilson home in Hawthorne. It looked like the other bungalows where families lived their typical suburban lives and clustered around their TV sets in the evenings.

    Here lived the three Wilson boys, Brian, Dennis and Carl, who seemed average guys, going to school, surfing, playing football, drag racing and dating town girls to dances, parties, weenie roasts and drive-in movies. They and their future partners, Mike Love, a cousin, and Al Jardine, a school chum, shared little in common and went their separate ways. Even Brian, Dennis and Carl, living under the same roof, saw little of each other.

    In college where Brian studied music, teachers pounded Bach, Brahms and Beethoven into student skulls and implied, not very subtly,

(More)

BEACH BOYS - WILMINGTON DELAWARE 1965 APPEARANCE

From: Press Department
William Morris Agency, Inc.

THE BEACH BOYS
Page   Two

that rock-'n-roll was lower than an elephant's instep. This burned Brian who said, "I wasn't going to sit there and let any guy tell me that pop music is bad. I love both." In defiance, Brian staged several groovy vocal jam sessions with Mike, Al and other pals in the school locker room which really put the burn on the snobocratic music teachers.

After he dropped out of school, Brian lived for the musical hours he spent with Mike Love and Mike's sister, Maureen. Their enthusiasm infected Carl, then 15, who could already thrum a gassy guitar, Dennis born with a beat in his blood, and Al, novice folksinger. The five cool cats began wailing in a group.

By the summer of 1961, the Wilson home was transformed into a den of do-it-yourself din-and-clamor. The walls quivered and quaked with terrible loud strange discordant noises that frightened the gophers out of their holes in the lawn and shut down the TV sets for blocks around. In time the noises became identifiable as vocal and instrumental harmonies with a hot rock beat. The Hawthorne hopefuls were now dreaming wild dreams of havong a rock-a-dandy musical combo that would set the world on fire -- or at least earn them a living.

"The most beautiful part of this whole story is the way this musical awkward squad pulled together to form a team and the significant part each one played in building the organization," says Brian who was the magnet pulling the five highly individualistic fellows together.

(More)

BEACH BOYS - WILMINGTON DELAWARE 1965 APPEARANCE

From: Press Department
      William Morris Agency, Inc.

THE BEACH BOYS
Page   Three

One day Dennis Hawthorne's champ surfriend raced in from the beach and sprung the idea on Brian to write a song themed on the great new surfing craze Brian's incendiary imagination caught fire and he with Mike began to sweat out the music and lyrics.

But Before they had time to write the number, chance stepped in with an off-beat break. A music publisher invited Al Jardine to come to his office to discuss a folk song recording. Al brought the others with him.

That did it. Instead of talking folksy-flavored country music, the five boys bent the publisher's ears with an enthusiastic description of the new surfad and theur song about it. He agreed to buy -- not knowing it hadn't been written yet.

Briam and Mike rushed home and wrote "Surfin'". The five young rookie artists waxed it at an obscure recoding studio at their own expense. Carl, the only one who could string a tune from a guitar, provided the only instrumental backing for the five untrained voices. It sold to the Canix label, and they were dubbed THE BEACH BOYS to fit the title of their song. "Surfin'", primitive though it was by their later standards, hit the hidh spots on the pop charts and the boys were shouting, "We're off!!!!"

"This early chapter of Beach Boy history has been buried under a landslide of subsequent smash hits, "says Brian. "Before long it was our forgotten period but in truth it was the somplest and most uncomplicated rise to popular stardom I've ever known or heard about. Consequently there is little to talk about our long, hard bitter struggle for success, which never happened that way."

BEACH BOYS - WILMINGTON DELAWARE 1965 APPEARANCE

From: Press Department
      William Morris Agency, Inc.

THE BEACH BOYS
Page   Four

    The Beach Boy sound fascinated a Capitol veepee, Voyle Gilmore, who inked them for an exclusive Cap wax pact. Their first Capitol single, "Surfin' U.S.A."/"Shut Down", was the smash of 1963 and their surfing album was the top-selling teen-angled LP of the year.

    Right from the start The Beach Boys had the urge to get around and meet the disk-buying fans who dug their raunchy rhythmic R&R sounds. Five really scared guys make their stage debut on New Year's Eve, 1961-2, at the Municipal Auditorium in Long Beach, California, with a galaxy of established entertainers. They fumbled through their entire repertoire of three songs and received, if not a thundering ovation, at least, a fair share of the applause.

    Thus encouraged, the lure of the tour beckoned the beach minstrels to scores of U.S. cities and something new was added to their presentation at nearly every stop. They began switching vocal styling and instruments: Brian from drums to bass guitar, Mike from sax to lead vocalist and emcee of the shows. Carl, always the most accomplished musician, plays lead guitar.

    Although noted basically for their vocal talents, The Beach Boys have acquired a very polished sound for recording and personal performance. They now use all the modern electronic techniques in needling the hot wax. Clinging to the outdoor image, they dress casually, usually slacks and striped, short-sleeved shirts, on stage. Their humor is spontaneous and no two concerts are exactly alike. Critics agree these five troubadors have improved 1000 per cent since the early days.

(MORE)

BEACH BOYS - WILMINGTON DELAWARE 1965 APPEARANCE

From: Press Department   THE BEACH BOYS
        Willaim Morris Agency, Inc.   Page   Five

The Beach Boys are trail blazers in teen tune stuff. Their surfing disks caused a tidal wave of surfsongs by scores of artists on a dozen labels. While still holding the surfing beach-head, their "Shut Down" fired off the starting gun on the roaring hot rod platter trend that won't stop. Then Brians' newie, "Little Honda", sent people racing to the recording studios to climb aboard the motor scooter fad.

Unlike some pop idols, The Beach Boys don't intend to split the teen scene and try to make out with the senior citizen set. They love nothing better than a roaring, howling, screaming teen-age music romp.

"For three straight years we've been hearing the screaming of live teen audiences and we've grown dependent on that sound," says Brian. "Believe me, nothing is better for the ego. Maybe it's too good. We live by it now."

-WMA-

BEACH BOYS - WILMINGTON DELAWARE 1965 APPEARANCE

THE BEACH BOYS   Personal Mgt.   Direction: THE WILLIAM MORRIS AGENCY, INC.
                     Cummins & Current

BEACH BOYS - WILMINGTON DELAWARE 1965 APPEARANCE

BEACH BOYS - WILMINGTON DELAWARE 1965 APPEARANCE

LICENSE No. 2

N.Y.

WILLIAM MORRIS AGENCY, INC.   B-2 6525
1740 BROADWAY • NEW YORK 19, N.Y.
JUDSON 6-5100 • CABLE ADDRESS: "WILLMORRIS"

435 N. MICHIGAN AVENUE
CHICAGO 11, ILLINOIS
TELEPHONE: 467-1744

151 EL CAMINO
BEVERLY HILLS, CAL.
TELEPHONE CRESTVIEW 1-6161 / BRADSHAW 2-4111

THIS CONTRACT for the personal services of musicians, made this **18** day of **MARCH** 19**65**, between the undersigned employer (hereinafter called the employer) and **FIVE(5) BEACHBOYS** musicians (hereinafter called employees) represented by the undersigned representative.

WITNESSETH, That the employer employs the personal services of the employees, as musicians severally, and the employees severally, through their representative, agree to render collectively to the employer services as musicians in the orchestra under the leadership of **CARL WILSON**, according to the following terms and conditions:

Name and Address of Place of Engagement: **THE ARMORY, WILMINGTON, DELAWARE**

Date(s) of Employment: **ONE DAY, APRIL 20, 1965**

Hours of Employment: **ONE SHOW AT 8:00 PM**

Type of engagement (specify whether dance, stage show, banquet, etc.): **STAGE SHOW**

PRICE AGREED UPON $ **SEE BELOW;**
(Terms and Amount)

This price includes expenses agreed to be reimbursed by the employer in accordance with the attached schedule, or a schedule to be furnished the employer on or before the date of engagement.

To be paid **SEE BELOW;**
(Specify When Payments Are to Be Made)

ADDITIONAL TERMS AND CONDITIONS

The employer shall at all times have complete control of the services which the employees will render under the specifications of this contract. On behalf of the employer the Leader will distribute the amount received from the employer to the employees, including himself, as indicated on the opposite side of this contract, or in place thereof on separate memorandum supplied to the employer at or before the commencement of the employment hereunder and take and turn over to the employer receipts therefor from each employee, including himself. The amount paid to the Leader includes the cost of transportation, which will be reported by the Leader to the employer. The employer hereby authorizes the Leader on his behalf to replace any employee who by illness, absence, or for any other reason does not perform any or all of the services provided for under this contract. Upon request by the Federation or the Local in whose jurisdiction the employees shall perform hereunder, the employer either shall make advance payment hereunder or shall post an appropriate bond.

The agreement of the employees to perform is subject to proven detention by sickness, accidents, or accidents to means of transportation, riots, strikes, epidemics, acts of God, or any other legitimate conditions beyond the control of the employees.

All employees covered by this agreement must be members in good standing of the Federation. However, the employment provided for hereunder is subject to the Labor-Management Relations Act, 1947, all employees, who are members of the Federation when their employment commences hereunder, shall be continued in such employment only so long as they continue such membership in good standing. All other employees covered by this agreement, on or before the thirtieth day following the commencement of their employment, or the effective date of this agreement, whichever is later, shall become and continue to be members in good standing of the Federation. The provisions of this paragraph shall not become effective unless and until permitted by applicable law.

To the extent permitted by applicable law, nothing in this contract shall ever be construed so as to interfere with duty owing by any employee hereunder to the Federation pursuant to its Constitution, By-Laws, Rules, Regulations and Orders.

Any employees who are parties to or affected by this contract, whose services hereunder or covered hereby, are prevented, suspended or stopped by reason of any lawful strike, ban, unfair list order or requirement of the Federation, shall be free to accept and engage in other employment of the same or similar character, or otherwise, for other employers or persons without any restraint, hindrance, penalty, obligation or liability whatever, any other provisions of this contract to the contrary notwithstanding.

The Business Representative of the Local of the Federation in whose jurisdiction the employees shall perform hereunder shall have access to the place of performance (except to private residences) for the purpose of conferring with the employees.

The performances to be rendered pursuant to this agreement are not to be recorded, reproduced, or transmitted from the place of performance, in any manner or by any means whatsoever, in the absence of a specific written agreement between the employer and the Federation relating to and permitting such recording, reproduction, or transmission.

The employer represents that there does not exist against him, in favor of any member of the Federation, any claim of any kind arising out of musical services rendered for any such employer. No member of the Federation will be required to perform any provisions of this contract or to render any services for said employer as long as any such claim is unsatisfied or unpaid, in whole or in part.

The employer in signing this contract himself, or having same signed by a representative, acknowledges his (her or their) authority to do so and hereby assumes liability for the amount stated herein.

To the extent permitted by applicable law, there are incorporated into and made part of this agreement, as though fully set forth herein, all of the By-Laws, Rules and Regulations of the Federation, and of any Local of the Federation in whose jurisdiction services are to be performed hereunder insofar as they do not conflict with those of the Federation.

If the employer breaches this agreement, he shall pay the employees, in addition to damages, 6% interest thereon plus a reasonable attorney's fee.

SPECIAL PROVISIONS:

RIDERS ATTACHED HERETO ARE PART OF THIS CONTRACT....

Name of Employer: **AM-ROY PRODUCTIONS / MR. FRANK G. GIAMBOY**
Street Address: **BOX 214 ROAD 2,**
City: **READING** State: **PA.**
Phone: **Glote 9-1040**

Accepted by Employer: *Frank G. Giamboy*
Accepted: *Carl Wilson* (Orchestra Leader)
CARL WILSON Local No. **47**
Approved by WILLIAM MORRIS AGENCY, INC.
(Agent for Employees)
By

If this contract is made by a licensed booking agent, there must be inserted on the reverse side of the contract the name, address and telephone number of the collecting agent of the local union in whose jurisdiction the engagement is to be performed.

Form B-2-12-64

Printed in U.S.A.

BEACH BOYS - WILMINGTON DELAWARE 1965 APPEARANCE

Collecting Agent of Local _____
Address _____ City _____ State _____
Telephone _____

NAMES OF EMPLOYEES	LOCAL NUMBER	S.S. NUMBER	WAGES
_____ (Leader)	_____	_____	$ _____

THE BEACH BOYS

PERSONNEL LIST

CARL WILSON (LEADER)	LOCAL NUMBER 47	SOCIAL SECURITY NUMBER	
DENNIS WILSON	" " 47	" " "
MIKE LOVE	" " 47	" " "
ALAN JARDINE	" " 47	" " "
BRIAN WILSON	" " 47	" " "

RIDER TO CONTRACT DATED _____MARCH 30, 1965_____ BETWEEN THE BEACH BOYS
AND _____AD-BOY PRODUCTIONS_____

1. It is agreed that as full compensation for the services of THE BEACH BOYS, Employer will pay to THE BEACH BOYS a sum equal to __60%__ of the gross box office receipts (exclusive of admission taxes, if any) with a minimum guarantee of __$4000.__ . A deposit, in the form of U.S. currency, certified check or bank draft, in the amount of $ __2000.__ shall be paid to William Morris Agency, Inc., __NOT LATER THAN 4/9/65__ _____. Balance of guarantee will be paid immediately prior to performance set forth herein. Percentage, if any, together with a duly certified statement of the gross box office receipts shall be due and payable no later than intermission of the performance set forth herein.

2. It is agreed that the "House" shall be scaled to not less than $ __12,500.__ with a minimum admission price of $2.00 per person and a maximum admission price of $5.00 per person. Employer agrees to submit to THE BEACH BOYS' representative a certified copy of the ticket manifest from the printer and agrees that THE BEACH BOYS' representative shall have the right to inspect ticket racks and all of the box office and other records with respect to such receipts, including unsold tickets and stubs of tickets sold for the purpose of verifying statements submitted by Employer. Employer further agrees that THE BEACH BOYS' representative will, upon request, be admitted to the box office at any and all times during sale of tickets for the engagement hereunder. It is further agreed that no complimentary admission tickets shall be distributed without THE BEACH BOYS' prior written consent, except to members of the press.

3. Employer agrees that no radio apparatus or transmitting or recording device, specifically including television, shall be used by him or by any one other than THE BEACH BOYS, if they so desire, in any manner or form to reproduce THE BEACH BOYS performance hereunder.

4. Employer agrees that THE BEACH BOYS shall receive sole headline billing in 100 percent size type in all advertising, lights, displays, programs and in any and all other advertising and publicity. No other act to receive equal size billing without prior written consent of THE BEACH BOYS.

5. Employer agrees to provide THE BEACH BOYS with a dressing room or dressing rooms capable of being locked, or in the alternative the Employer agrees to post a special security guard at the door of the dressing room or dressing rooms.

6. Employer agrees that he will not sell any products identified with THE BEACH BOYS at the place of performance or in any adjacent place under his control, nor will he license third parties to do so or authorize such sale by any third parties.

7. Employer agrees that he will not commit THE BEACH BOYS or any of them to any personal appearances or other promotion without the prior written consent of THE BEACH BOYS.

8. Employer agrees to provide at least three (3) microphones, all of which shall be equipped with a removable hand microphone for the performance herein.

9. Employer agrees to provide at least one (preferably two) follow spots of trouper arc or super trouper quality. These are to include at least three colored "gels" one to include green.

10. Employer agrees to provide and pay for two security guards from the time of THE BEACH BOYS arrival at place of engagement, to time of departure from place of engagement. Guards to be under supervision of THE BEACH BOYS or their representative.

11. THE BEACH BOYS shall have the right to sell souvenir programs, ballet books, photographs and records on the premises of the place(s) of performance without any participation in the proceeds by Employer subject, however, to concessioneer's requirements, if any.

BEACH BOYS - WILMINGTON DELAWARE 1965 APPEARANCE

12. Employer shall provide and pay for 2 chauffeured driven Cadillac limousines for use of Employees prior to and after the engagement.

13. Employer shall provide at Employer's cost a first rate sound and amplification system at the place of engagement.

14. Employer shall provide and pay for police protection consisting of a minimum of 12.

15. Employer agrees to provide and pay for all advertising (including radio advertising) in connection with the within engagement commencing three weeks prior to said engagement.

INITIAL HERE: _____   INITIAL HERE: _____

BEACH BOYS - WILMINGTON DELAWARE 1965 APPEARANCE

Make-believe beatniks
Beach Boys breeze into town

By JUDITH M. ROALES

Even offstage, the Beach Boys are like a three-ring circus.

Currently high among teen-age singing idols, the quintet blew into Wilmington yesterday aboard a regular commercial airline flight. If the other passengers weren't told, they must surely have wondered about the long-haired, lively group.

They were here for an appearance last night at the Wilmington Armory, 10th & Du Pont Sts.

The boys sang last night to a packed house. Approximately 3,500 screaming, worshipping teen-agers jammed the aisles, stood on chairs and waved signs pledging their devotion to the five.

DENNIS Wilson was first off the plane, and no one could have missed him. Barefooted and clad in bermudas and a sloppy shirt, he shook his bushy head and grinned to the assembled teen-agers, "I didn't expect anyone to meet us at the 'port."

The location of their motel was top-secret information. But for a dedicated fan, there are ways... and three young high schoolers found their way into the rooms.

When you see them there, although you know that they're still playing the role, the Beach Boys disappear and Mike Love, Dennis Wilson, Carl Wilson, Alan Jardine and Bruce Johnston come into view.

Mike, at 24, is the oldest and most serious-minded of the group. He's a tall, sandy-haired guy—with a normal haircut—who doesn't hurry and talks like the boy next door. Once in his motel room, he kicked off his shoes, loosened his tie and, with an infectuous grin, slouched into a chair.

THE others wandered in and out, Dennis striking the clowning note at once. Proudly, he reeled off a list of recent traffic violations collected by the group for everything from driving without a license to driving too slow. And to prove the latter, Mike displayed yellow carbon copies of the tickets.

Alan Jardine, the only married Beach Boy, stuck his head in to say hello, and then returned to his room next door and wife Linda.

Bruce Johnston, Mike explained, it replacing Brian Wilson, who took sick before the tour began. Brian writes 90 per cent of the group's songs.

"We surf in California, there's nowhere to do it right in the East," Dennis said in relating spare time activities. "But there's always swimming and skiing and boating anywhere."

LATER, Mike observed that the "surfing" would probably be a tag for them the rest of their careers. At least three of their albums now on the market have the word in the title.

Wilmington is supposedly a quiet spot on the schedule, but even so there were problems. "What, no drums?" Mike exploded into the phone. Sure enough, the drums and suitcases of performance clothes hadn't been loaded on the plane in Washington, D.C. "We'll cancel," one guy displaying the brash which they're so...

But, of course... The show...

Staff Photo by Bill Snead

BEACH BOYS Dennis (left) and Carl Wilson arrive yesterday at the Greater Wilmington Airport with the rest of their group, 35 pieces of luggage and a crew of eight assistants.

BEACH BOYS - WILMINGTON DELAWARE 1965 APPEARANCE

EVENING JOURNAL
WILMINGTON, DELAWARE

Wednesday, April 21, 1965

Staff Photos by John Peterson

HELLO, THERE — Policemen strain to hold back some of the 3,500 youngsters at the State Armory (above) who last night waved greetings to The Beach Boys. One of the boys (below) leaps high from the stage with a responding wave and shout.

'Beach Boys,

BEACH BOYS - WILMINGTON DELAWARE 1965 APPEARANCE

'We Love You,' 3,500 Scream

By JUDITH M. ROALES

About 3,500 screaming teen-agers packed the aisles, stood on chairs and frantically cheered their current No. 1 idols last night at the State Armory.

The Beach Boys, a quintet of popular singers, dashed on stage amid upstretched arms, paper airplanes saying "Dennis, we love you" or "All the way, boys" and a deafening roar of young voices.

THE roar never stopped. Fans cheered from the moment the rumor spread that the stars had entered the building until long after the last note died away. Every song was greeted with a new outburst atop the already resounding one.

Songs ranged from "Little Deuce Coupe" to the "Monster Mash," with Mike Love, oldest of the group, cavorting around the stage as a "monster," thrilling dozens of smitten girls as he reached out and touched their fingertips.

"I'll never wash it again," a starry-eyed blonde confessed, hugging her hand to her cheek.

Signs with warm greetings to the group, pictures and programs waved above the audience. Flashbulbs popped and pocket tape recorders whirred, but police kept ambitious autograph and souvenier seekers off the stage.

TWO officers intercepted determined miss___ crawled over ___ for Ab___ J___

As Dennis Wilson, on the borrowed drums, led into the song "Do Ya Wanna Dance?" tears streamed down the cheeks of infatuated females yelling "Yes, yes."

There was one other substitution on the program. Brian Wilson, the group's songwriter and one of the performers, missed the tour because of illness and was replaced by Bruce Johnston. But no one seemed to mind that either.

Fifth member of the group is Carl Wilson.

HOARSE and half deaf, the audience continued to clap and cheer 45 minutes later when the group escaped the stage, sheltered by a wall of uniformed police.

After spending the night in a Wilmington area motel, the Beach Boys today continue their tour into New Hampshire. They came here for Am-Boy Productions from an engagement in Orlando, Fla.

Also on the program were the Nebulas, six red-coated young men from Unionville, Pa., and the Sonics, five New Castle County lads.

39

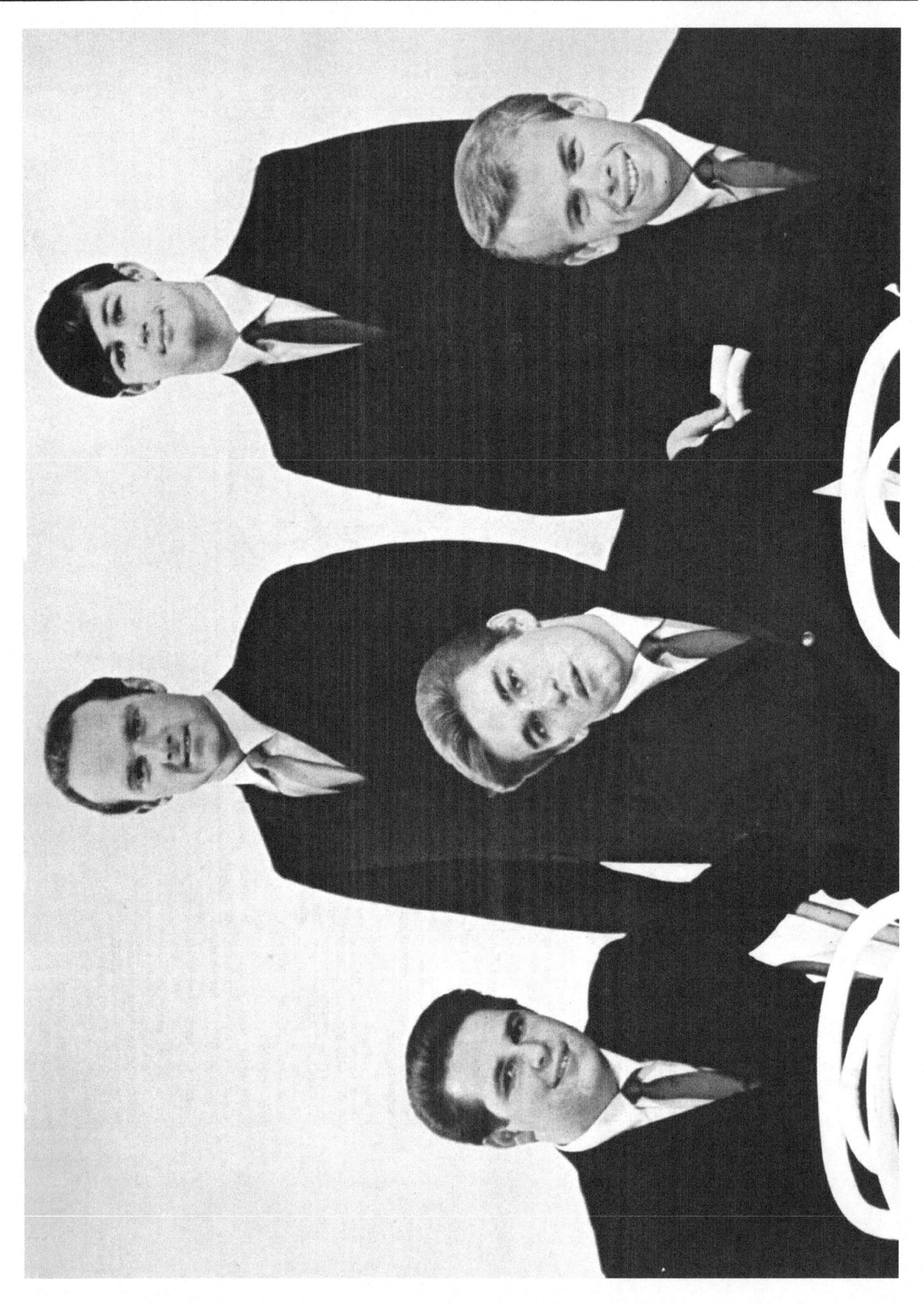

BEACH BOYS - PROMOTIONAL PHOTO

BEACH BOYS - 1965 TOURBOOK WITH AUTHENTIC SIGNATURES

BEACH BOYS - 1965 TOURBOOK WITH AUTHENTIC SIGNATURES

42

BEACH BOYS IN CONCERT

BEACH BOYS - 1965 TOURBOOK WITH AUTHENTIC SIGNATURES

THE BEACH BOYS

In less than three years, the Beach Boys have climbed from zero to No. 1 spot on the annual pop music charts. Their original songs started three new nation-wide musical trends: surfing, hot rods and motor scooting. It all began in Hawthorne, a green grass town five miles from the Southern California beaches where the breakers roar, the surfers ride their wild boards and the sun-kissed bikini belles loll on the golden sands.

Until 1961 there was nothing special to distinguish the small five-room Wilson home in Hawthorne. It looked like the other bungalows where families lived their typical suburban lives and clustered around their TV sets in the evenings.

Here lived the three Wilson boys, Brian, Dennis and Carl, who seemed average guys, going to school, surfing, playing football, drag racing and dating town girls to dances, parties, weenie roasts and drive-in movies. They and their future partners, Mike Love, a cousin, and Al Jardine, a school chum, shared little in common and went their separate ways. Even Brian, Dennis and Carl, living under the same roof, saw little of each other.

In college where Brian studied music, teachers pounded Bach, Brahms and Beethoven into student skulls and implied, not very subtly, that rock-'n-roll was lower than an elephant's instep. This burned Brian who said, "I wasn't going to sit there and let any guy tell me that pop music is bad. I love both." In defiance, Brian staged several groovy vocal jam sessions with Mike, Al and other pals in the school locker room which really put the burn on the snobocratic music teachers.

After he dropped out of school, Brian lived for the musical hours he spent with Mike Love and Mike's sister, Maureen. Their enthusiasm infected Carl, then 15, who could already thrum a gassy guitar, Dennis, born with a beat in his blood, and Al, novice folksinger. The five cool cats begain wailing in a group.

By the summer of 1961, the Wilson home was transformed into a den of do-it-yourself din-and-clamor. The walls quivered and quaked with terrible loud strange discordant noises that frightened the gophers out of their holes in the lawn and shut down the TV sets for blocks around. In time the noises became identifiable as vocal and instrumental harmonies with a hot rock beat. The Hawthorne hopefuls were now dreaming wild dreams of having a rock-a-dandy musical combo that would set the world on fire — or at least earn them a living.

"The most beautiful part of this whole story is the way this musical awkward squad pulled together to form a team and the significant part each one played in building the organization," says Brian who was the magnet pulling the five highly individualistic fellows together.

One day Dennis, Hawthorne's champ surfiend, raced in from the beach and sprung the idea on Brian to write a song themed on the great new surfing craze. Brian's incendiary imagination caught fire and he with Mike began to sweat out the music and lyrics.

But before they had time to write the number, chance stepped in with an off-beat break. A music publisher invited Al Jardine to come to his office to discuss a folk song recording. Al brought the others with him.

That did it. Instead of talking folksy-flavored country music, the five boys bent the publisher's ears with an enthusiastic description of the new surfad and their song about it. He agreed to buy — not knowing it hadn't been written yet.

44

BEACH BOYS - 1965 TOURBOOK WITH AUTHENTIC SIGNATURES

Brian and Mike rushed home and wrote "Surfin'." The five young rookie artists waxed it at an obscure recording studio at their own expense. Carl, the only one who could string a tune from a guitar, provided the only instrumental backing for the five untrained voices. It sold to the Candix label, and they were dubbed The Beach Boys to fit the title of their song. "Surfin'," primitive though it was by their later standards, hit the high spots on the pop charts and the boys were shouting, "We're off!!!"

"This early chapter of Beach Boy history has been buried under a landslide of subsequent smash hits," says Brian. "Before long it was our forgotten period but in truth it was the simplest and most uncomplicated rise to popular stardom I've ever known or heard about. Consequently there is little to talk about our long, hard bitter struggle for success, which never happened that way."

The Beach Boy sound fascinated a Capitol veepee, Voyle Gilmore, who inked them for an exclusive Cap wax pact. Their first Capitol single, "Surfin' U.S.A."/"Shut Down," was the smash of 1963 and their surfing album was the top-selling teen-angled LP of the year.

Right from the start The Beach Boys had the urge to get around and meet the disk-buying fans who dug their raunchy rhythmic R&R sounds. Five really scared guys made their stage debut on New Year's Eve, 1961-62, at the Municipal Auditorium in Long Beach, California, with a galaxy of established entertainers. They fumbled through their entire repertoire of three songs and received, if not a thundering ovation, at least a fair share of the applause.

Thus encouraged, the lure of the tour beckoned the beach minstrels to scores of U.S. cities and something new was added to their presentation at nearly every stop. They began switching vocal styling and instruments: Brian from drums to bass guitar, Dennis from vocals only to the skins, Al from stand-up bass to rhythm guitar, Mike from sax to lead vocalist and emcee of the shows. Carl, always the most accomplished musician, plays lead guitar.

Although noted basically for their vocal talents, The Beach Boys have acquired a very polished sound for recording and personal performance. They now use all the modern electronic techniques in needling the hot wax. Clinging to the outdoor image, they dress casually, usually slacks and striped, short-sleeved shirts, on stage. Their humor is spontaneous and no two concerts are exactly alike. Critics agree these five troubadors have improved 1000 per cent since the early days.

The Beach Boys are trail blazers in teen tune stuff. Their surfing disks caused a tidal wave of surfsongs by scores of artists on a dozen labels. While still holding the surfing beach-head, their "Shut Down" fired off the starting gun on the roaring hot rod platter trend that won't stop. Then Brian's newie, "Little Honda," sent people racing to the recording studios to climb aboard the motor scooter fad.

Unlike some pop idols, The Beach Boys don't intend to split the teen scene and try to make out with the senior citizen set. They love nothing better than a roaring, howling, screaming teen-age music romp.

"For three straight years we've been hearing the screaming of live teen audiences and we've grown dependent on that sound," says Brian. "Believe me, nothing is better for the ego. Maybe it's too good. We live by it now."

BEACH BOYS - 1965 TOURBOOK WITH AUTHENTIC SIGNATURES

BEACH BOYS - 1965 TOURBOOK WITH AUTHENTIC SIGNATURES

Dark-haired, hazel-blue-eyed, sturdy framed, tree-top-tall Brian Wilson is a genial genius and super song wrangler whose head constantly bubbles with new ideas and plans for the Beach Boys.

He served a short sentence as their business manager but soon realized his talents were more artistic than commercial. A professional management firm was hired, leaving Brian free to do what he loves most: learning new recording techniques, performing and creating new songs and sounds. He has the magic touch that turns wax into gold.

The other four boys generally accept Brian's judgments and decisions but they sound off loud when they don't see eye to eye with him. He readily gives in when a better idea is presented; he doesn't consider himself omniscient — a $64 word meaning all-wise, all-powerful, all-knowing and too doggoned smart to be human. Peace in the family and harmony in the group are more precious than rubies.

Starting in high school, he began organizing vocal and instrumental combos to entertain at parties and dances for peanuts and bread. The greatest of all he eventually found in his own home and neighborhood.

"In college I took a music appreciation course but the teachers were 100 percent against anything except operas, symphonies, cantatas, chamber and classical stuff," Brian recalls. "Well, I wasn't going to sit there and let any guy tell me that pop music is bad. I love both. After a year and a half, I became a college drop-out and I'm not sorry. My hunger for knowledge is very strong but I can learn more through self-study."

Brian's stiletto-sharp mind cuts through layers of confusion, disorder and double-talk to get at the meat of the matter at hand. Though inclined to be tense, serious and intellectual, he has a sense of humor that ranges from the whimsical to the way-out. His hearty laugh starts on the first floor of his diaphram and bellows out through the roof of the house.

BRIAN WILSON ************************

BEACH BOYS - 1965 TOURBOOK WITH AUTHENTIC SIGNATURES

MIKE LOVE ★★★★★★★★★★★★★★★

Born under the sign of Pisces (two fish), Mike Love, 23, has a complicated and dual personality.

He is both kind and sarcastic, neat and scruffy, carefree and cautious, idealistic and practical, sympathetic and impatient, playful as a puppy or serious as a tree full of owls. When he gets wound up, Mike is a non-stop laugh-getter and cut-up. When he turns on his brighter personality, he can charm the birds off the trees.

Most of the things he likes to do, he does well. If he can't make like an expert, his inferiority complex shows up like a walrus in a goldfish bowl. Dancing used to give him an inferiority complex that wouldn't stop. This bugged him so much he went all-out to become the best dancer around. Now he can dance the Monkey like a monkey wishes it could.

When he began with the Beach Boys, friends tell me, his voice resembled a gravel train with square wheels and he couldn't tell a guitar from his elbow. Today he sings both bass and tenor as lead vocalist of the group, emcees the stage shows and slaps a guitar around until it hollers for help. He wrote the lyrics for Fun Fun Fun, Surfin' and other songs. That's progress with a capital P.

Mike tells about himself:

"Travel, sports (track and football) are my favorite sports . . . Friends tell me my humor is often sarcastic but that stems from impatience, I think . . . When I'm out in public and feel a sneeze coming on, I let 'em have it . . . I'm a non-conformist and individualist but I'm not about to live in a cave in Griffith Park . . . Clothes are important to me . . . I love contrasting colors and textures that complement each other . . . The Beatles are okey but I like girls better . . . I have no problem keeping my nails clean as they are usually in my mouth . . ."

AVAILABLE NOW!

THE BEACH BOYS' FIRST LIVE ALBUM

You've seen the Beach Boys in-person. Did you ever think you could live that excitement all over again? You can. Here's a fabulous live-performance album recorded in the heart of Beach Boy Land (Sacramento, California). Hear the Boys do scream-backed versions of their own hits like **FUN, FUN, FUN; LITTLE DEUCE COUPE** and **IN MY ROOM**. Hear them do other big hits like **THE LITTLE OLD LADY FROM PASADENA** and **PAPA-OOM-MOW-MOW**. And, as an added bonus, this album features a whole potful of action photos of the **BEACH BOYS CONCERT**.

Naturally, The Beach Boys Record For *Capitol* RECORDS

Capitol RECORDS **...Your Choice For The Biggest Hits**

and here are the other albums that have made THE BEACH BOYS America's number one vocal group

I GET AROUND, LITTLE HONDA, WENDY – what a line-up. And it's only part of the great best-selling album: **ALL SUMMER LONG**

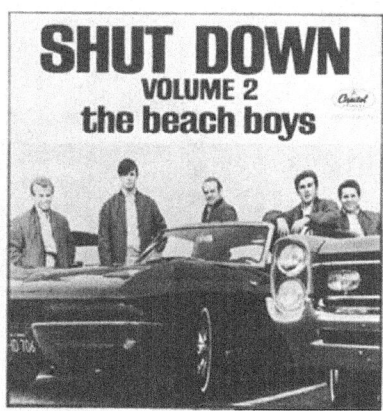

The original FUN, FUN, FUN; WHY DO FOOLS FALL IN LOVE?; DON'T WORRY BABY – all in one great hot-rodding album – **SHUTDOWN, VOL. TWO**

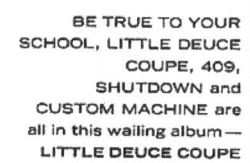

BE TRUE TO YOUR SCHOOL, LITTLE DEUCE COUPE, 409, SHUTDOWN and CUSTOM MACHINE are all in this wailing album – **LITTLE DEUCE COUPE**

SURFIN' USA is the title and the big tune in this Album that put surfin' music on the map (that's wherever the Beach Boys are).

SURFER GIRL and IN MY ROOM top the list of winners in this one – **SURFER GIRL**

SURFIN' SAFARI, TEN LITTLE INDIANS, LITTLE MISS AMERICA. No wonder this is the album that started the Beach Boys on their fantastic career – **SURFIN' SAFARI**

BEACH BOYS - 1965 TOURBOOK WITH AUTHENTIC SIGNATURES

Boyish dreams don't always come true. Once Al dreamed of yanking out molars for a living with a D.D.S. after his name. He was side-tracked when he met the Wilson clan. A possibly good dentist became a truly fine rhythm guitarist and chanter a la rock.

Alan has no regrets for his switched career because he likes his life as a Beach Boy. Though it does take him away from home more than he likes, his bank account is stuffed like a Christmas goose and he can afford to live the good life with his adorable wife.

Born in Lima, Ohio, 22 years ago, and raised in California, Al dragged his skull through El Camino College on the California coast. He is a devoted husband and wants to raise a family. When he's home he plays scrabble with his wife every night. Other hobbies: badminton, tennis, golf, ping-pong, bowling, surfing and building model airplanes. Although he and Mike both live in Manhattan Beach, they never see each other outside of work.

Other characteristics: Loves to dress in expensive jackets, tailored slacks and good casual clothes . . . Favorite color is red . . . Loves liver . . . Often eats dessert before the main course and otherwise change the usual order of dining . . . A very careful driver and has never nicked a fender or bashed in a headlight . . .

Al is quiet and pensive, reads books galore and loves to rack his brains on deep subjects. His inner strength and warm personality make him one of the most popular members of the group.

ALAN JARDINE ★★★★★★★★★★★★★★

BEACH BOYS - 1965 TOURBOOK WITH AUTHENTIC SIGNATURES

BEACH BOYS - 1965 TOURBOOK WITH AUTHENTIC SIGNATURES

BEACH BOYS - 1965 TOURBOOK WITH AUTHENTIC SIGNATURES

CARL WILSON ★★★★★★★★★★★★★★★

The youngest of the five, 17-year-old Carl was the only one who could twang a guitar when the Beach Boys made their recording debut in the fall of 1961.

While the other boys vibrated their tonsils in vocal harmonies, the then 14-year-old Carl alone carried the instrumental backing for the platter, Surfin', which launched their careers. He has a very sensitive ear and hopes some day to write songs for the group.

Carl is late in graduating from Hollywood Professional High, not that he's not bright, but because he's been absent so often on concert tours and recording dates. He won't get his sheepskin until June, almost a year after his classmates grabed theirs.

"I haven't learned anything in high school anyhow," he says. "Most of my learning has come from being with the Beach Boys. The music biz is like a college education."

Carl is generous, kind, affectionate, conscientious, cooperative and strongly attached to his home and family, especially to big brother Brian whom he worships.

Because he's so trustful, easy-going and good-natured, people often try to impose upon and take advantage of him. When he's had enough, his big infectious chipped-tooth grin vanishes, his face clouds over like a sudden summer squall and he can warn 'em: "Get off my back!"

Faithful and loyal, Carl comes on cool as a pool to the friends he knows. One day he said something to me that perhaps I shouldn't repeat (because it isn't exactly true) but it shows such sincere humility that I'll always remember it.

"Without the Beach Boys I'd be nothing," he declared.

55

BEACH BOYS - 1965 TOURBOOK WITH AUTHENTIC SIGNATURES

DENNIS WILSON ★★★★★★★★★★★★★★★

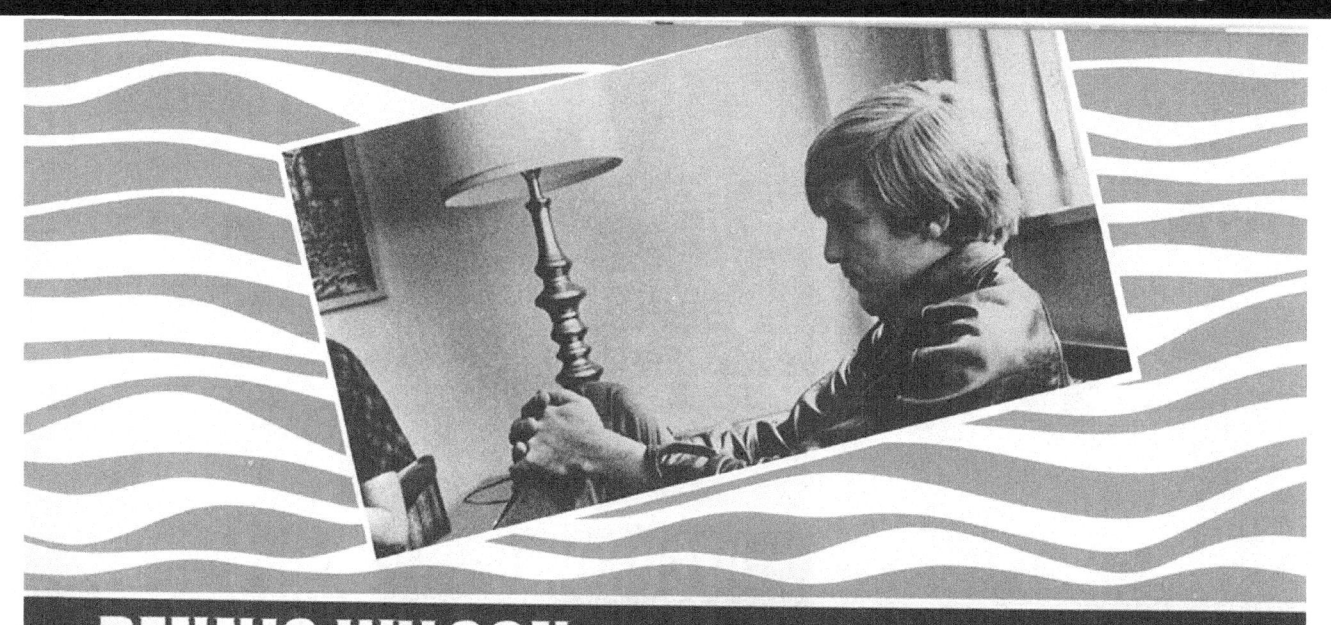

That's Dennis up there whipping those throbbing skins that feed the beat to the Beach Boy song. He always wanted to be a drummer. While all his little kid pals were playing on combs and yazoos, dinky Denny was beating out rhythms on his mother's pots and pans. Now 19, he plays the drums like the drums like to be played.

Dennis was the original surfer with dyed hair and knots on his feet who stirred up the surfin' excitement among his brothers and friends, leading to the formation of the Beach Boy Five. He's in the forefront of each new fad: hot rods, sports cars, drag racing, motor scooting, etc.

A complete out-going extrovert, blue-eyed blondish Dennis is the group's glad-hander, good-timer, mad-mixer and sex-pot. He loves to mill around with the mobs in the theater, flirt with the chickies and often brings them backstage to meet the other lads. Once he was nearly caught in the tender trap but now he plays the field. He loves to run barefoot through fields of flower-eating starlets. He intends to remain single as long as matrimony is not compulsory.

Answering a questionnaire, Dennis wrote:

"Most of my dreams are about money, cars and girls . . . Three of us are brothers and we naturally get into some pretty good scraps which blow over soon. There's no chance of the Beach Boys coming unglued, however . . . They tell me I'm the guy with the quick temper and the far-out temperament . . . When I look into the big baby blue eyes of a long-haired girl I can agree with anything she says . . ."

BEACH BOYS - 1965 TOURBOOK WITH AUTHENTIC SIGNATURES

RECORDING SESSION

TRAVELIN'

BEACH BOYS - 1965 TOURBOOK WITH AUTHENTIC SIGNATURES

SURFIN'

JOIN THE BEACH BOYS INTERNATIONAL FAN CLUB

To Show You Care...

THIS IS THE ONLY OFFICIAL AUTHORIZED BEACH BOYS FAN CLUB AND HAS COMPLETE CO-OPERATION OF THE ARTISTS

HERE'S WHAT'S IN IT FOR YOU!

- MEMBERSHIP CARD WITH PHOTO ON BACK
- AUTOGRAPHED PHOTO OF THE BEACH BOYS
- A BEACH BOYS NEWSLETTER SENT TO YOUR HOME EVERY 3 MONTHS

APPLICATION FOR MEMBERSHIP IN
THE BEACH BOYS INTERNATIONAL FAN CLUB

Name:_____ Date:_____

Address:_____

City:_____ State:_____

Birthdate:_____ Age:_____

Clip this application and send it today to THE BEACH BOYS, P.O. Box 110, Hollywood, California 90028. Make sure to include $2 to cover your yearly dues.

BEACH BOYS - 1965 TOURBOOK WITH AUTHENTIC SIGNATURES

BEACH BOYS - 1965 TOURBOOK WITH AUTHENTIC SIGNATURES

HOW IT IS WITH US!

By One of 'Em—MIKE LOVE

First, I've been asked to describe each of The Beach Boys. All I can do is try. So, here goes...

Dennis is an extrovert and a "fishamaniac." He does what he wants, moves at a furious pace and then relaxes by grabbing a pole and calmly fishing in a quiet lake for hours! In the same day, he can buy a Ferrari, zip around in it awhile and then go off hunting, forgetting about the cool car he just bought.

Al is the married one, who is strictly "familys-ville." He is a great talent and good guy, but he's also the quiet Beach Boy. Very reserved and intellectual, Al is never happy when he's on the road away from his family.

Carl is the best-dressed one of us. When those around him are wearing chinos and sweatshirts, he'll be dapper in a shirt and tie! A very cool character with a fantastic personality, Carl is one of those amazing people whom *everybody* likes!

Brian is the complex one of us, who does all our arranging. It takes a while to get to know him, but it's worth it. When he is about to write or arrange, he is moody, introspective and very quiet. But when everything's been worked out, his sense of humor breaks out and he laughs longer and louder than any of us!

Oh, yes! And then there's me... All I can tell you is that I'm a "way-out" guy who likes to joke around a lot.

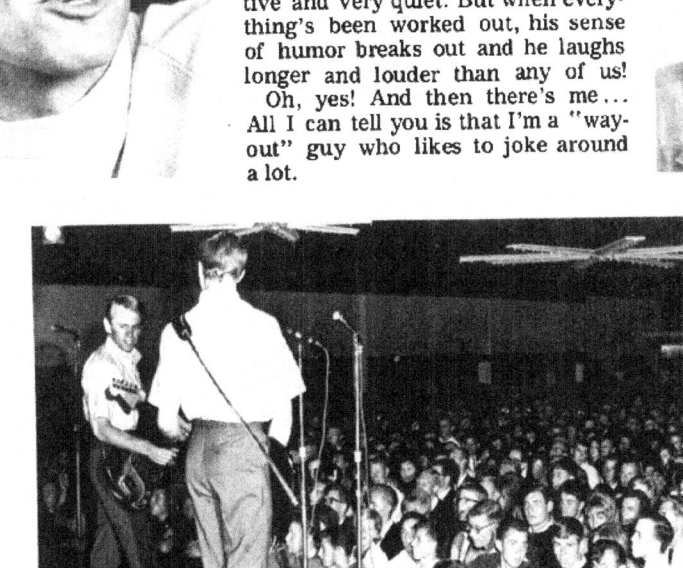

ALL ABOUT THE BEACH BOYS!

There is also a sixth sort of Beach Boy, Glen Campbell, who sometimes replaces Brian—when Brian is exhausted from working too hard or when he's working on our next record. Glen has quickly become one of us, filled with the spirit of the group.

Despite the fact that we work pretty hard because we travel so much, we try to lighten our load by having a good time wherever we may be. Sometimes we get more than we bargain for! Like the time Dennis was stopped by the police while waterskiing! Without knowing it, he'd skied in a Girl Scout swim area! Or the time Glen and I had a water fight which was spectacularly soggy while we were in Virginia.

Fans are fabulous except on those rare occasions when they get somewhat out of hand. In Buffalo, for instance, I was hit on the head with a soda bottle. That fan was trying to get me in stitches—but they were the wrong kind!

That's about all I can think of now. But I'd love to hear from you. If you'd like to write to me or Carl, Brian, Dennis or Al, FLIP has promised to collect all your mail for us!

BEACH BOYS PROMOTIONAL PHOTO

the teen set
VOLUME 1

THE BEACH BOYS

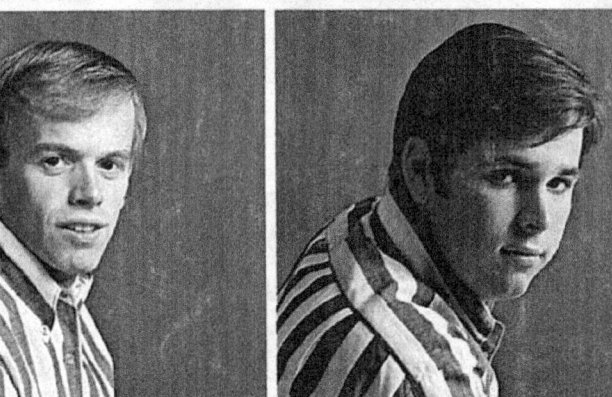

- Inside Story of America's No. 1 Group — by Earl Leaf!

- Contests! Win a Honda! Win a Hap Jacobs Surfboard! Win 100 Capitol Albums!

- Exclusive New Pix of Alan, Brian, Carl, Dennis & Mike!

- Special Feature: The Beach Boys Pick Their Mates!

- Learn How YOU Can Join The Teen Set!

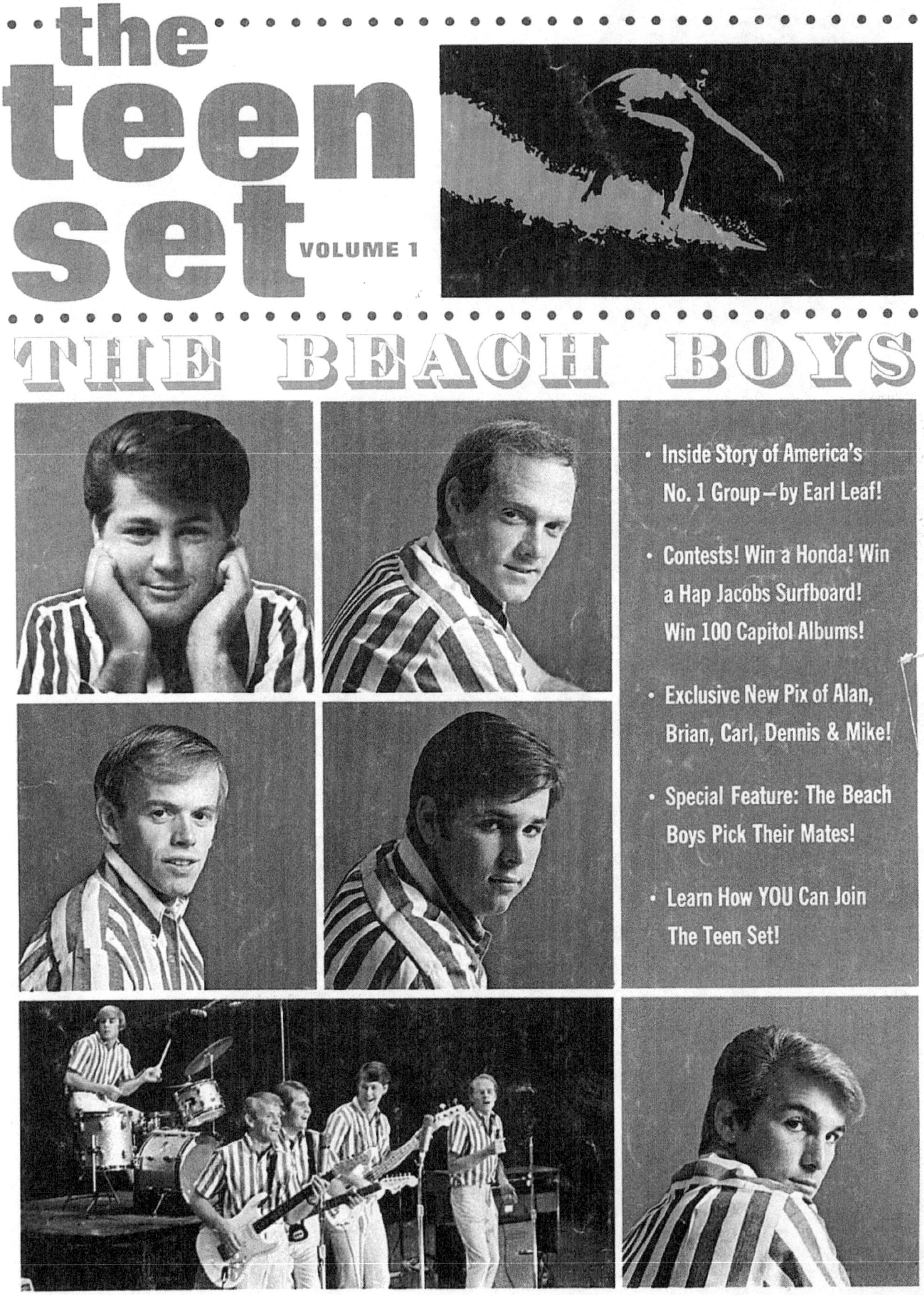

"**EARL SEZ**" We hope you dig this debut issue of THE TEEN SET because we wrote and published it especially for you, the millions of young fan-atic music lovers in this best of all possible teen worlds.

This first issue has been devoted entirely to the bright and bubbly Beach Boys, America's No. 1 singing group who have two terrif teen-angled albums topping the pack on the current music rack: *Beach Boys Concert* in a deluxe package, and the *Beach Boys Christmas* album. The BB's fan-onimal success is worth a book and a half. What the Beatles are to Britain, the Beach Boys are to the U.S.A.

In future issues of THE TEEN SET we'll present you with inside stories and exclusive photos on other fab teen raves such as Cilla Black, Wayne Newton, Donna Loren, Roy Clark, Nancy Wilson, Donna Lynn, Jerry Cole and his Spacemen, Dick Dale and the Deltones, Mr. Gasser and the Weirdos, Hub Kapp and his Wheels, the Peter and Gordon duo, the Lettermen trio, Beatle quads, more on the Beach Boy quints and gangs of other Capitol chart-grabbin' music-makers.

We'll have contests (see this issue) and other added attractions to spark your interest and keep the editorial pot perking.

The price is right on THE TEEN SET. It nicks your allowance nothing. Forthcoming issues will be tied to future cool Cap LP's, than which there is no better buy in your music shoppe.

So send your entries to the contest editor and win a sweet swingin' Honda or surf board or write and tell me which Caplatter songstars you'd like to see and hear about in later issues of THE TEEN SET.

EARL LEAF

CONTENTS

I. ORBITING WITH THE BEACH BOYS.
Like a tale out of a story book, the "five green idiots" from the California beaches are transformed into world famous gold record troubadours in two short years. Double-whammy hits on singles and super songs on albums have orbited them into the musical stratosphere.

II. NEEDLING THE WAX.
Mayhem and madness during a recording session where the cool sounds are etched on hot wax. Prying the boys away from their scooters and she-males for a siege in the studio. How they (don't really) need to rehearse the new songs.

III. BRIAN BIRTHS A SONG.
Writing a new song puts Brian Wilson through the wringer but he loves every minute of it. Seizures of inspiration strike him without warning. Beatles John Lennon and Paul McCartney sing praises of Brian's music and Beach Boy records.

IV. SWINGIN' THE SURFIN' SCENE.
Splashes from Beach Boy smashes shower the pop music field and start the surfing song trend that sweeps the world like a tidal wave. It all started when surfiend Dennis began to slingo the beach lingo around the family pad.

V. SCORCHED RUBBER AND MOTOR ROAR.
Hot rods and Hondas kick off new motor song trend with a roar. What wheels the Beach Boys themselves have the pinks on. Riding new fads to chartsville, followed by other groups hot on their trail.

VI. TREKS, TOURS AND TRAVELS.
Biggest thrill for the Beach Boys is the roaring and screaming of live audiences. Wild experiences around the land touring 35 cities on a wayward bus. Some cities are the gearest and others are like outsville.

VII. GIRLS GIRLS GIRLS = FUN FUN FUN.
What girlish charms appeal most to each lad. How the Beach Boys manage to meet and date sweet young things out of thousands of screamie-teenies they greet on tour. Romeo Mike and Lochinvar Dennis compete. Love and romance creeps into the lives and lyrics of the California chanters.

VIII. BEACH BOY PROFILES.
Personality sketches on the Fabulous Five: Brian Wilson, the creative one, Dennis Wilson, the sexy one, Carl Wilson, the cool one, Alan Jardine, the quiet one, Mike Love, the personality boy.

THE TEEN SET: P.O. Box 1271, Hollywood, Calif. 90028

STAFF:

Editor & Publisher	Brown Meggs
Managing Editor	Ron Tepper
Guest Editor	Earl Leaf
Art Director	George Osaki
Production Manager	Bob Bates
Special Consultants	Bill Frost
	Bob O'Neil
	Fred Rice
	Marvin Schwartz

Lyrics from *Fun, Fun, Fun, Little Deuce Coupe* and *I Get Around* reprinted by permission Murry Wilson, Sea of Tunes Publishing Co.

ORBITING WITH

Success is no hit or miss dealie with that colorful California quintette, the Beach Boys, whose platters are always toppers with young music-lovers of the world.

The five young troubadours—Brian, Dennis and Carl Wilson with Mike Love and Alan Jardine—plan it that way.

Every new singles release has goodies on both sides, not a funky beauty topside and a finky throw-away on the bottom deck. The Beach Boys have had more double-hit releases than any other aggregation on record.

Their first biggie for the Capitol label was the double-hitter *Surfin' U.S.A./Shut Down* and both sides begat albums of the same names. *Surfin' U.S.A.* was the largest selling single record and the surfing album was the hottest teen-angled LP of the entire year 1963. This year the boys have another double-whammy smash, *I Get Around/ Don't Worry, Baby*. The former already qualified as a gold record winner for the Beach Boys. Their first five albums have sold a total of well over a million.

Such popularity must be deserved!

Their successes were won by sheer merit alone, without the high-pressure publicity campaigns that have zoomed other record idols and groups to the top of the heap. While their records soared to the rarefied atmosphere of upper hits-ville, and they became America's hottest recording group, the boys themselves were still unknown as individuals. In a 'Teen Magazine article I once called them the Faceless Five. If you've seen their stage shows (as I later did) you know them as unique and highly distinctive personalities—a truly Fab Five.

The rapid rise of the Beach Boys is like a storybook tale. Three of the four Beatles were singing and performing together since 1958 but as late as 1961 four of the five Beach Boys couldn't even play an instrument. Yet a year later, 1962, they were so self-taught that they could strum guitars, beat the skins and blow the sax to accompany their socko-sound vocalizing on *Surfin' Safari*, their first Cap wax.

"We were five green idiots the first time we went

THE BEACH BOYS

into a recording studio," Brian recalls, "We had a song and a dream, thassal. We sang and played our song once through, paid the guy for the use of the hall and walked out with the demo record clutched tightly in our hot fist.

"With *Surfin' U.S.A.*, we developed grace and style. For the first time we used modern techniques, singing twice, the second time exactly on top of the first, perfectly synchronized. This gives a rather shrill and magical, much brighter, more gutsy and spectacular sound. Professionally we were coming of age."

A new thrill for the Beach Boys was making the album, *Beach Boys Concert*, recorded live at a frantic performance in Sacramento, California's state capital, before an exciting screamie-teenie audience. Here they couldn't use any of the technical advantages of studio recording—takes and re-takes, echo chambers, dual-tracking, over-dubbing and calculated effects.

"We were allowed one take on each number. It was a great experience for us, playing, singing, dancing, jumping around, making jokes and trying to look good at the same time. Man, that's a work-out!"

Another change of pace for the team was their Christmas album. One side is modern-traditional Xmas music backed by a 41-piece ork, the flip side is slightly-modified R&R with several up-tempo songs writ by Brian.

The boys intend to continue belting out rock-a-rhythmic foot-stompers laced with occasional romantic ballads and gassy novelties for stage performances, TV shows and platter parades.

One thing they don't want, they don't want to split the teen scene. They love nothing better than a roaring teen-age music romp. Many other pop idols hanker to ankle the young field and make out with the senior citizen set. Not our hip-hip-happy Beach Boys.

"For three straight years we've been hearing the screaming of live audiences and we've grown dependent on that sound," Brian admits. "Believe me, nothing is better for the ego. Maybe it's too good for the ego. We live by it."

OK, you ever-lovin' Beach Boy buffs, LET'S SCREAM!

NEEDLING THE WAX

*We had a hot recording date,
But I was two hours late,
So we blew all our studio time,
And that's the kind of guy I'm.*

A recording session with the Beach Boys always seems to reach a note of madness three octaves above chaos.

The five California minstrels amble into the studio anywhere from two minutes to two hours late and then begin horsing around like colts let out of the barn—as their studio time ticks away like a taxi meter. Usually they don't even begin their music-making until the studio crew are on double-time pay. That's why it takes a lot of bread to make a Beach Boy biscuit.

This is, I think, a backlash from the early days when Papa Wilson, as their manager, inflicted a system of fines ranging up to $500 for various infractions of group discipline such as tardiness and horseplay at concerts or recording sessions. Strangely enough, Brian, the rather serious-minded boss Beach Boy, remains as relaxed as spaghetti about their shenanigans.

Any place the boys gather turns into a nuthouse as they kid, tease, frolic, play practical jokes and practice miscellaneous mayhem on each other.

You get a dim idea of a typical B.B. recording katzenjammer in *Our Favorite Recording Sessions* which Capitol included in the scrumptilicious *All Summer Long* elpee. That bit of nonsense gave Beatle Paul McCartney a large charge. I happened to be with the Big B4 in their H-Town habitat when Paul first heard the piece on the record playing machine. He whooped and hollered with delight and called the other Liverpoolads to give it an 'earing.

"Them Beach Boy blighters go for gaggles of giggles just like we do when we record," laughed ring-fingered Ringo Starr.

"If you arsk me, that's the best way," John Lennon chirped. "I never yet sore a top rock group act like a bunch of bleedin' choir boys when they record."

Yeah, a sense of humor helps loads when you're with the Beach Boys. A Hollywood photographer hired to shoot publicity pictures of the BB5 told me, "I've had it! If those characters ever come to my studio again I'll charge them $500 apiece as they enter the door. They left my studio in shambles!"

The boys didn't deny it. "We weren't in the mood for having our pictures took that day," explained Brian. "We were bored."

A recent afternoon I spent with them on an expedition to Santa Monica Beach was a laff riot from beginning to end.

Yet with all their romping and running about, they get the job done better than somewhat. Brian explained their recording technique:

"When I come up with a new song that I'm excited about, I call the boys for a session. Sometimes I call them at the wrong time, they're not in the mood to work and I have a hard time prying them loose from their Hondas and chickies.

"So finally we all agree on a date. It usually takes about three hours to get everyone together in the studio. Once started we come on with perfect teamwork.

Continued on next page

"We've established such *rapport* that we rarely need rehearsals. They can read my mind, I read theirs, and we are as sensitive to each other as seismographs. The boys don't usually hear my new songs until we gather in the studio to record"

Carl interrupted: "I never even heard *I Get Around* until Brian played it in the studio. We rehearsed *Fun Fun Fun* only once before we needled it on wax."

Brian went on to say: "When I sit down at the piano and play a new song, the others can visualize the whole arrangement right away. We take the melody apart and work it out phrase by phrase. If they don't like my approach, they suggest another. If Carl doesn't dig my idea, I'll change it immijitly because Carl has exquisite musical taste. I trust it completely.

"The most important thing in our group venture is the kind of excitement we can create and express. When I'm excited about a new song, the boys catch it and we're off. We have a group spirit that won't stop."

The BB5 deliberately keep an untrained style. Formerly they kept their recording simple but lately they've progressed into dual-track and other mechanical sounds with greater production values.

"The boys are the greatest," Brian enthuses. "I couldn't be happier with any other combination of players-singers. Above all, we take enormous pride in our concerts and records. We intend to stay on top of the pop chart heap."

And he ain't just whistling Dixie.

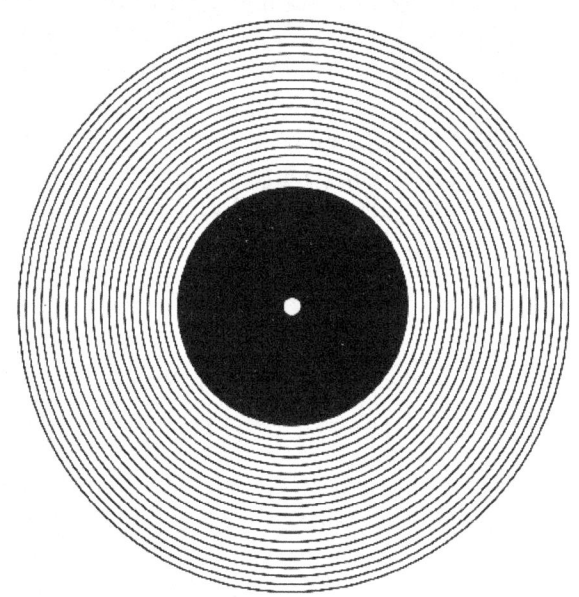

JOIN
THE BEACH BOYS
INTERNATIONAL FAN CLUB
To Show You Care...

THIS IS THE ONLY OFFICIAL AUTHORIZED BEACH BOYS FAN CLUB AND HAS COMPLETE CO-OPERATION OF THE ARTISTS

HERE'S WHAT'S IN IT FOR YOU!

- MEMBERSHIP CARD WITH PHOTO ON BACK
- AUTOGRAPHED PHOTO OF THE BEACH BOYS
- A BEACH BOYS NEWSLETTER SENT TO YOUR HOME EVERY 3 MONTHS

APPLICATION FOR MEMBERSHIP IN THE BEACH BOYS INTERNATIONAL FAN CLUB

Name:_____ Date:_____

Address:_____

City:_____ State:_____

Birthdate:_____ Age:_____

Clip this application and send it today to THE BEACH BOYS, P.O. Box 110, Hollywood, California 90028. Make sure to include $1 to cover your yearly dues.

BRIAN BIRTHS A NEW SONG

The birth of the blues,
Ain't no longer news now,
We sing a bright rock beat,
To make you stomp your feet now.

That husky, six-foot, ruggedly handsome but very fati-gued fellow slumped over a piano at four o'clock in the morning is Brian Wilson undergoing the birth pangs of a new song hit for the Beach Boys.

One hand fingers the ivories and the other scribbles symbols on a slice of music paper, weaving melody and words into a rhythmic-harmonic pattern that will be heard by young music-lovers throughout the world. Now and then he staggers to the kitchen and dumps a can of tuna on a thick hunk of bread and washes it down with a quart of grape juice.

At dawn when he needs toothpicks to prop his eyes open, he throws himself on a couch for a short order of shut-eye. Two hours later he returns to the piano and re-tackles the score sheet like a dog worrying a bone.

By noon the song is done and Brian is now so excited he can't sleep a wink. He dials the boys to tell them about it and set a recording date. But Carl is unscrambling Greek history dates at school. Dennis is in Redondo Beach with his toes on the nose of a fast-flying bile-green polka-dotted surfboard. Mike is eyeballing the girls on the golden sands of Malibu shores. Alan is chewing up the turf at an Orange County golf course.

The recording will be done sooner or latter. If a song isn't exactly right for the Beach Boys, Brian will give it to other artists. Five of his masterpieces, *Surf City, Drag City, Dead Man's Curve, Sidewalk Surfin'* and *New Girl In School* were etched on shellac by Jan and Dean.

Brian gets a seizure of inspiration at odd moments of the day or eve. It often hits him hard when he's driving.

"It's weird!" says Marilyn Rovell, one of Brian's fave femmes. "We'll be driving along chatting about something far removed from music. All of a sudden he stops talking and his mind soars off for songville. I see his head bobbing, his lips moving and his fingers thrumming a beat on the steering wheel. That's my cue to shut my mouth and let him think. He composed the music and lyrics to

Continued on next page

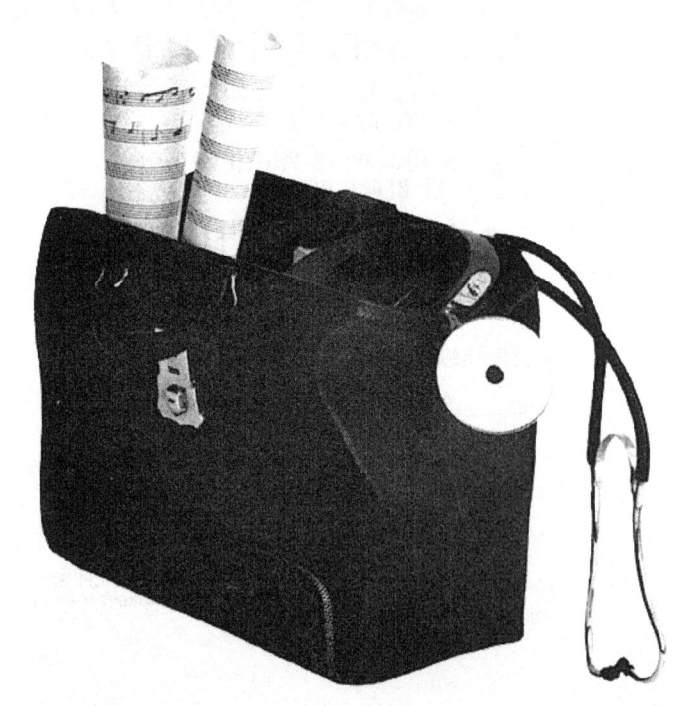

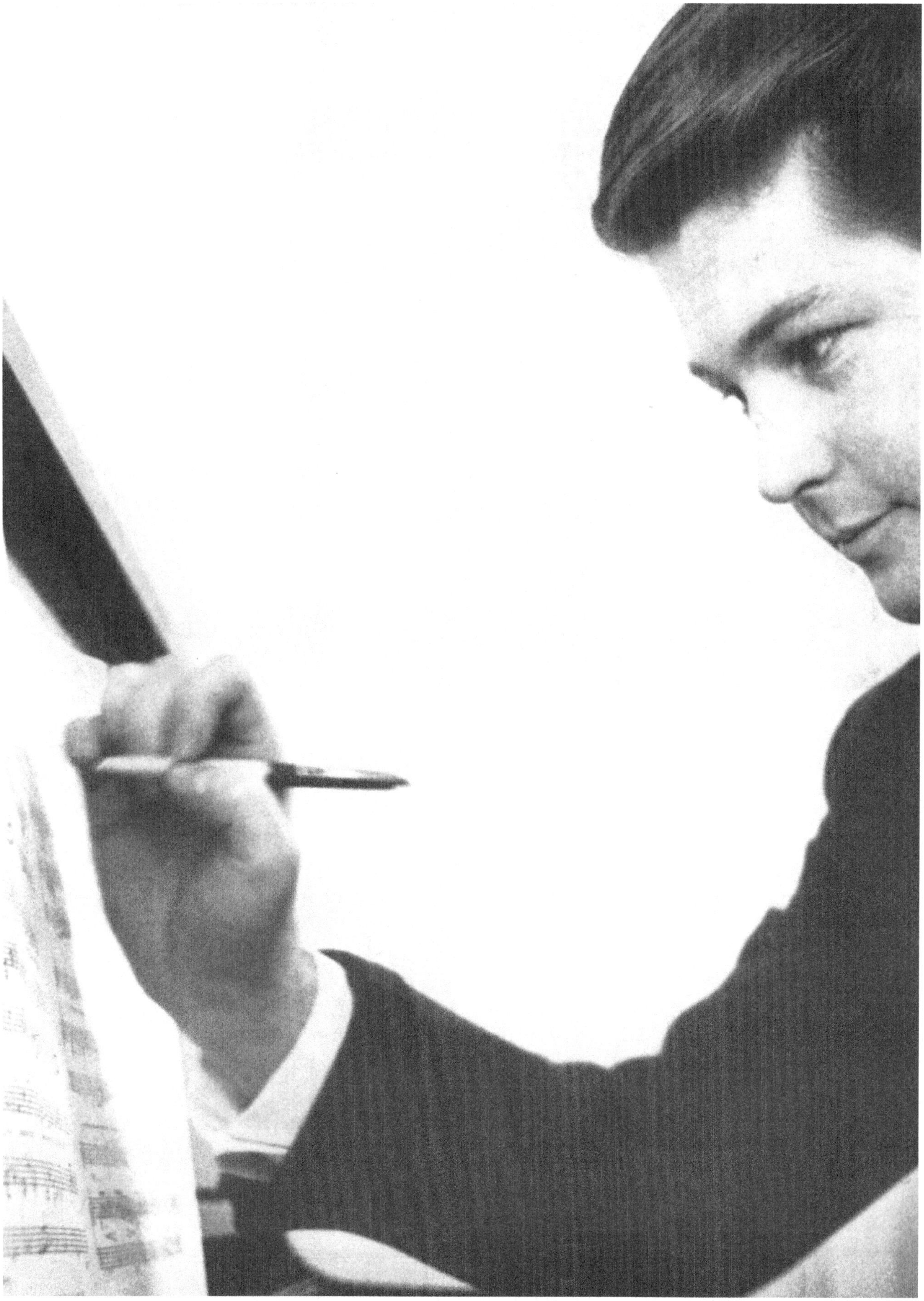

TEEN SET VOLUME 1

Other Beach Boys hear Brian's new song for first time when he plays it for them in recording studio.

Dennis and Mike like what they see on sheet of new arrangement.

Song wrangler Brian plucks magic music on strings of guitar.

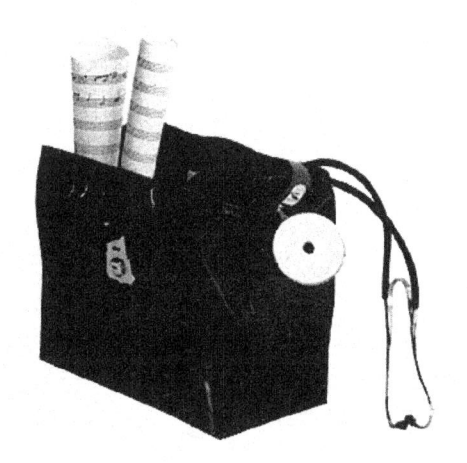

Mike Love plays guitars but sax is his favorite instrument.

Little St. Nick for the Christmas LP while we were driving to his mother's home in Hawthorne. He can remember every note and word until he puts it down on paper. Nearly all his music is head arrangements."

Among Brian Wilson's greatest admirers are Beatle tunesmiths John Lennon and Paul McCartney. Tall cool blonde Peggy Lipton, young H'wood actress, was with them one evening in their Bel Air hideout when they fell to talking about the Beach Boys whom she also knows. Peggy and Carl were classmates at Hollywood Professional School.

"Paul and John are infatuated with the Beach Boy sound, especially the harmonic variations in the upper registers," Peg reported. "They played the Beach Boys' LP *All Summer Long* all night long and asked me many questions about them. Paul and John were fascinated by Brian's style of composing and arranging. Paul went over to the music rack, picked up the album and studied Brian's picture for a long time."

Paul told her, "There's a bloke I really admire and would like very much to meet."

That makes it a mutual admiration society. Beach Boy Brian is also keen to meet the Beatles and have a long session with Paul and John. Brian and Paul, both 22-year-olds who write songs, play guitar and sing with a fabulous group, have more than a little in common—and that's saying a lot.

"The Beatle invasion really shook me up," Brian told me. "They eclipsed the whole musical world . . . total eclipse, you might say. Their fantastic record sales temporarily, at least, hurt all other artists. Many pop stars and groups held their own records off the market hoping Beatlemania would fade out. Of course it wouldn't. They are too great. In fact they are a shot in the arm to the entire recording industry."

Continued on page 27

75

SWINGIN' THE SURFIN' SCENE

You can rightly put the finger on the Beach Boys as the solid-sending tune stars who started the surfing song trend that swept the world like a tidal wave.

When their first Capitol disk click, *Surfin' USA*, created such a sensational stir in 1963, splashes showered all over the pop music world and scores of other rock-a-rhythm aggregations began writing and recording sound-alike songs. Surfing music was the new rage even in the arid regions where the only waves available were ripples in a bathtub. Some of the surfsingers were super-swingy (Dick Dale and the Deltones) and others were drippy as wet baggies.

Actually surf music is traditional rock with surfing titles, lyrics, album covers and sound effects—the roar of a green-water wall as great as the Taj Mahal and the calls of gulls looking for something fishy to eat.

It all started in 1961 when Dennis, then 17 and a surfiend since 13, began to slingo the surfing lingo around the family pad in Hawthorne, a green grass town near enough to the ocean to see the bikini'd beach bunnies on a clear day. Brother Brian and cousin Mike perked their ears to the fab vocab and began tinkering it to music and rhyme.

Their maiden effort, the *Surfin'* tune, really turned on the others, Dennis, Carl and pal Alan Jardine. In fact the five guys got all jazzed up about forming their own musical group, learning to play by ear on borrowed and rented instruments. Carl was the only one who could twang a guitar at that time. They practiced their vocalizing so long and hard that they all developed corns on the lungs, knots in the larynx, dents in the diaphragm and a tendency to bubble when they slept.

Nobody was more surprised than Pa Murry Wilson, himself a songwriter of the old school, when he and his Mrs. returned from a trip to Mexico and saw what his kith and kin were up to.

Continued on page 27

Surfin' still lures the Beach Boys on their days off.

She's got a competition clutch,
With four on the floor, yeah,
She purrs like a kitten,
Till the lake pipes roar . . .
She's my Little Deuce Coupe.

© 1963 BY SEA OF TUNES PUBLISHING COMPANY, HAWTHORNE, CALIFORNIA
INTERNATIONAL COPYRIGHT SECURED

The bright and breezy Beach Boys live amid roaring crowds, roaring surf, roaring motors. There's nothing boring about their roaring lives, that's for sure.

Gear-jammin' Dennis Wilson, the madman of the tracks, charges around town in his XKE or soup-job Sting Ray looking for other car cats to drag for the pink. He leaves ten feet of scorched rubber on the blacktop when the light turns green. The way Dennis expends their power and speed you'd think XKE's and SR's grew on trees. Yet you'll find him later tending, nursing, guarding and polishing them with a silken handkerchief like they were the crown jools.

Mike Love is jollied up about his high-strung iron, a blue Jag 3.8 sedan that impresses the ladies far more than somewhat. Al Jardine drives a neat wire-wheeled T-Bird which is "just for the looks, not the drags," as the song says.

Brian and Carl each drive a Grand Prix but Carl can't wait to transfer to a hairy foreign beast like a Lotus or Cobra. Brian probably will always drive a sedate crate.

As with surfing music, it was the Beach Boys who sent the hot rod music craze off to a roaring start. The first jalopy tune was that now-famous tailored-for-teeners single, *409*. Five albums and dozens of singles later, they kicked off a new motor scooter trend with the Caplatter winner *Little Honda*.

The Beach Boys are trail blazers in teen tune stuff.

Music Business, national music trade sheet, put it this way: "Capitol and the Beach Boys actually contrived to break the new hot rod trend while holding the surf beach-head at the same time. That happened with the single which coupled *Surfin' U.S.A.* and *Shut Down*. It's the *only* single in recent memory that ever spawned two separate hit albums. It also gave birth to a rash of hot rod albums from a rash of West Coast labels just as it happened at first with the surf scene."

Continued on page 30

SCORCHED RUBBER & MOTOR ROAR

THE BEACH BOYS

BRIAN WILSON
(The Creative One)

Dark-haired, hazel-blue-eyed, sturdy framed, treetop-tall Brian Wilson is a genial genius and super song wrangler whose head constantly bubbles with new ideas and plans for the Beach Boys.

He served a short sentence as their business manager but soon realized his talents were more artistic than commercial. A professional management firm was hired, leaving Brian free to do what he loves most: learning new recording techniques, performing and creating new songs and sounds. He has the magic touch that turns wax into gold.

The other four boys generally accept Brian's judgments and decisions but they sound off loud when they don't see eye to eye with him. He readily gives in when a better idea is presented; he doesn't consider himself omniscient—a $64 word meaning all-wise, all-powerful, all-knowing and too doggoned smart to be human. Peace in the family and harmony in the group are more precious than rubies.

Starting in high school, he began organizing vocal and instrumental combos to entertain at parties and dances for peanuts and bread. The greatest of all he eventually found in his own home and neighborhood.

"In college I took a music appreciation course but the teachers were 100 per cent against anything except operas, symphonies, cantatas, chamber and classical stuff," Brian recalls. "Well, I wasn't going to sit there and let any guy tell me that pop music is bad. I love both. After a year and a half, I became a college drop-out and I'm not sorry My hunger for knowledge is very strong but I can learn more through self-study."

Brian's stiletto-sharp mind cuts through layers of confusion, disorder and double-talk to get at the meat of the matter at hand. Though inclined to be tense, serious and intellectual, he has a sense of humor that ranges from the whimsical to the way-out. His hearty laugh starts on the first floor of his diaphragm and bellows out through the roof of the house.

MIKE LOVE
(The Personality Boy)

Born under the sign of Pisces (two fish), Mike Love, 23, has a complicated and dual personality.

He is both kind and sarcastic, neat and scruffy, carefree and cautious, idealistic and practical, sympathetic and impatient, playful as a puppy or serious as a tree full of owls. When he gets wound up, Mike is a non-stop laugh-getter and cut-up. When he turns on his brighter personality, he can charm the birds off the trees.

Most of the things he likes to do, he does well. If he can't make like an expert, his inferiority complex shows up like a walrus in a goldfish bowl. Dancing used to give him an inferiority complex that wouldn't stop. This bugged him so much he went all-out to become the best dancer around. Now he can dance the Monkey like a monkey wishes it could.

When he began with the Beach Boys, friends tell me, his voice resembled a gravel train with square wheels and he couldn't tell a guitar from his elbow. Today he sings both bass and tenor as lead vocalist of the group, emcees the stage shows and slaps a guitar around until it hollers for help. He wrote the lyrics for *Fun Fun Fun, Surfin'* and other songs. That's progress with a capital P.

Mike tells about himself:

"Travel, sports (track and football) are my favorite sports . . . Friends tell me my humor is often sarcastic but that stems from impatience, I think . . . When I'm out in public and feel a sneeze coming on, I let 'em have it . . . I'm a non-conformist and individualist but I'm not about to live in a cave in Griffith Park . . . Clothes are important to me . . . I love contrasting colors and textures that complement each other . . . The Beatles are okey but I like girls better . . . I have no problem keeping my nails clean as they are usually in my mouth . . ."

ALAN JARDINE
(The Quiet One)

Boyish dreams don't always come true. Once Al dreamed of yanking out molars for a living with a D.D.S. after his name. He was side-tracked when he met the Wilson clan. A possibly good dentist became a truly fine rhythm guitarist and chanter a la rock.

Alan has no regrets for his switched career because he likes his life as a Beach Boy. Though it does take him away from home more than he likes, his bank account is stuffed like a Christmas goose and he can afford to live the good life with his adorable wife.

Born in Lima, Ohio, 22 years ago, and raised in California, Al dragged his skull through El Camino College on the Cal. coast. He is a devoted husband and wants to raise a family. When he's home he plays scrabble with his wife every night. Other hobbies: badminton, tennis, golf, ping-pong, bowling, surfing and building model airplanes. Although he and Mike both live in Manhattan Beach, they never see each other outside of work.

Other characteristics: Loves to dress in expensive jackets, tailored slacks and good casual clothes . . . Favorite color is red . . Loves liver . . . Often eats dessert before the main course and otherwise change the usual order of dining . . . A very careful driver and has never nicked a fender or bashed in a headlight . . .

Al is quiet and pensive, reads books galore and loves to rack his brains on deep subjects. His inner strength and warm personality make him one of the most popular members of the group.

CARL WILSON
(The Cool One)

The youngest of the five, 17-year-old Carl was the only one who could twang a guitar when the Beach Boys made their recording debut in the fall of 1961.

While the other boys vibrated their tonsils in vocal harmonies, the then 14-year-old Carl alone carried the instrumental backing for the platter, *Surfin'*, which launched their careers. He has a very sensitive ear and hopes some day to write songs for the group.

Carl is late in graduating from Hollywood Professional High, not that he's not bright, but because he's been absent so often on concert tours and recording dates. He won't mitt his sheepskin until June, almost a year after his classmates grabbed theirs.

"I haven't learned anything in high school anyhow," he says. "Most of my learning has come from being with the Beach Boys. The music biz is like a college education."

Carl is generous, kind, affectionate, conscientious, cooperative and strongly attached to his home and family, especially to big brother Brian whom he worships.

Because he's so trustful, easy-going and good-natured, people often try to impose upon and take advantage of him. When he's had enough, his big infectious chipped-tooth grin vanishes, his face clouds over like a sudden summer squall and he can warn 'em: "Get off my back!"

Faithful and loyal, Carl comes on cool as a pool to the friends he knows. One day he said something to me that perhaps I shouldn't repeat (because it isn't exactly true) but it shows such sincere humility that I'll always remember it.

"Without the Beach Boys I'd be nothing," he declared.

DENNIS WILSON
(The Sexy One)

That's Dennis up there whipping those throbbing skins that feed the beat to the Beach Boy song. He always wanted to be a drummer. While all his little kid pals were playing on combs and yazoos, dinky Denny was beating out rhythms on his mother's pots and pans. Now 19, he plays the drums like the drums like to be played.

Dennis was the original surfer with dyed hair and knots on his feet who stirred up the surfin' excitement among his brothers and friends, leading to the formation of the Beach Boy Five. He's in the forefront of each new fad: hot rods, sports cars, drag racing, motor scooting, etc.

A complete out-going extrovert, blue-eyed blondish Dennis is the group's glad-hander, good-timer, mad-mixer and sex-pot. He loves to mill around with the mobs in the theater, flirt with the chickies and often brings them backstage to meet the other lads. Once he was nearly caught in the tender trap but now he plays the field. He loves to run barefoot through fields of flower-eating starlets. He intends to remain single as long as matrimony is not compulsory.

Answering a questionnaire, Dennis wrote:

"Most of my dreams are about money, cars and girls . . . Three of us are brothers and we naturally get into some pretty good scraps which blow over soon. There's no chance of the Beach Boys coming unglued, however . . . They tell me I'm the guy with the quick temper and the far-out temperament . . . When I look into the big baby blue eyes of a long-haired girl I can agree with anything she says . . ."

TEEN SET VOLUME 1

GIRLS GIRLS GIRLS=FUN FUN FUN

*Well, she got her daddy's car,
And she cruised through the
hamburger stand now,
Seems she forgot all about the library,
Like she told her old man now . . .
She'll have fun, fun, fun,
Till her daddy takes the T-Bird away.*

© 1964 BY SEA OF TUNES PUBLISHING COMPANY, HAWTHORNE, CALIFORNIA

Girls loom Very Big in the eyes of the Beach Boy Five. They think about girls, dream about 'em, talk about 'em and serenade all types of 'em —the *Car Crazy Cutie, Pom Play Girl, Farmer's Daughter, Little Miss America, Surfer Girl* and all the *Girls On The Beach.*

Why Do Fools Fall In Love? asks one of their most popular ballads. At one time or another they have all lost their fool heads to some chic chick but so far only one has marched up the aisle with a bride and promised to love, honor and take the consequences.

Those long 35-city one-nighter tours are murder on romance. The boys don't have half enough time to find some fun with the femmes.

"During that great tour last summer I had dates with only four girls," moans marvy Mike Love. "I do better at home in one week. It's not easy to pick out a date from, say, 10,000 or 20,000 wildly screaming dollies in the audience or among hundreds waiting for us at the stage door. I glimpse many I'd love to meet and date but I can't get to them with an invite. Anyhow hit-and-romance is for the birds. So often us guys have to go back to our hotel, send out for cheeseburgers and hit the sack early."

Asked what he notices first about a girl, Mike says, "Femininity has many alluring aspects, to say the least, but I'm crazy about extremely long hair."

Ducky Dennis Wilson has such a practiced perfect 20-20 eye for super-femininity that he can spot a sweetie at the 33rd floor window of a 44-story building while careening his Sting Ray 85 mph around a sharp curve in a pea-soup fog. On

Continued on next page

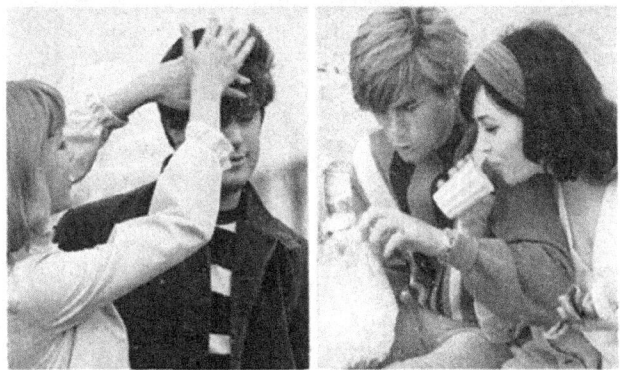

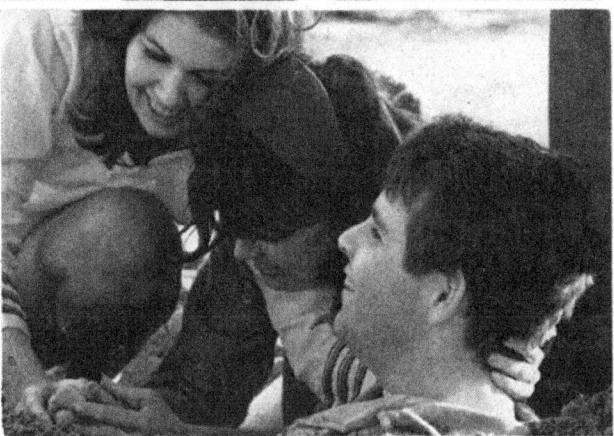

Girls spell fun to boys on holidays and vacations.

TEEN SET VOLUME 1

Cavorting in the sun, sand, surf and spray with bevies of beauties is their idea of having wonderful time.

84

GIRLS GIRLS GIRLS=FUN FUN FUN

stage he can gaze over a sea of 100,000 lovely faces and girlish figures in the audience, select the one of his choice and send her an RSVP message, via the language of the eyes, to meet him backstage after the show.

Man, that's communication!

Dennis doesn't miss a thing when he inventories a girl's charms but the feature that turns him on most is her mouth.

Carl has been a shy guy until now—after all he's just pushing 18—but he definitely shows signs of becoming a ladies' man par excellence. Some day he will give Dennis and Mike serious competition—with a difference. Instead of scattering his shots among many, he will concentrate on a choice few.

Carl follows the traditional school of amour, performing all the charming little courtship courtesies that went out with the waltz. Like he sends a girl candy, brings her flowers, surprises her with charming (and expensive) gifts, trots around and opens car doors, holds her chair when she sits down and even tips his hat when he wears one. Carl is the type to give up his seat in a bus or train and lead a little old blind lady across the street.

What appeals to Carl most in the ladies are "face, figure, eyes, legs, hair and personality, in

Continued on page 28

TREKS, TRIPS & TRAVELS

I get around from town to town,
I'm a real cool head,
   Making good bread,
I get around, round, round,
I get around . . . .

The sweetest music to Beach Boys ears is the roaring, thundering applause of their vast enthusiastic audiences in the theaters, music halls, auditoriums and amusement parks from Coolville, U.S.A. to Down Under, Australia, and across to Gay Paree.

Last summer they tooled the highways and byways in a chartered bus headlining shows in 35 cities on their third and gassiest annual barnstorming tour. Then they winged over the Big Damp to meet and entertain their fans in London, Paris and Rome where Beach Boy platters are seldom current pop tally absentees.

They want their fans everywhere to see 'em, know 'em and love 'em. They knock themselves out in performance no matter whether they're playing the Ed Sullivan TV show in New York Town or a hayloft in Prairie Hole, Wyo. In their eyes a cute 14½-year-old girl who spends her allowance on their disks and shows is as important as Mr. Big at Capitol Records.

"There's nothing more thrilling to us on tour than the pleasure of the audiences," Carl declared at a bull session in my pad one day. The others echoed the sentiments all the way. "Kids who pay $4.50 admission are entitled to the best we can give them. If they pay that much and go away disappointed, we are crushed. It hurts us personally and of course it would hurt our record sales, too.

"Like some animals are super-sensitive to the weather, we are sensitive to the moods of the crowds. As soon as we enter an auditorium we can tell what kind of a crowd we'll have. There's either a chilling silence or a mild roar even before the show starts."

As a true-blue fan of both the Beatles and the Beach Boys, I've noticed a large difference between the two types of audiences. Girls are screeching, screaming, moaning, hollering and yelling all the while the Beatles are singing and playing. One non-stop Beatlemaniac tearing her tonsils to tatters behind me at the Hollywood Beatle Bowl afterwards told me (hoarsely): "I

Continued on next page

can hear the Beatles any time on my transistor or hi-fi. I came here to *look* at 'em."

Audiences *listen* to the Beach Boys' patter, music and song and burst into wild acclaim when the number is finished.

"We learn all the time," Carl said. "Once we went on a filmed Dick Clark TV show without our instruments, doing a lip-sinc to records. Later when we saw how we looked, we each died a thousand deaths. It was awful. We'll never do that again!"

"Every city and every section of the country is different," Mike interrupted. "Los Angeles and Hollywood are the most apathetic places we've ever played, maybe because they see so many pop idols and movie stars. Any entertainer can tell you that. But the L. A. kids certainly weren't apathetic about the Beatles so maybe things won't be the same again. We'll know next time we play the Hollywood Bowl."

They all agree that Texas has the best and worst audiences. Those in Houston and Dallas are tremendously enthusiastic and appreciative, while Amarillo and San Antonio are the coldest they've ever seen. The kids there seem to be saying, "We dare you to entertain us!" The Beach Boys took the dare and sang their hearts out. It took the crowd a long time to warm up but the boys did get a loud and long ovation in the end.

Showfolk break out with clogged pores, irregularity, shingles, nervous tension and zits when they are booked to Amarillo or San Antonio. Another chart-grabbing songstar told me, "That Amarillo audience sat on their hands all night. I picked out a girl in the front row who had a look as cold as a pawnbroker's eye and I sang to her and flirted with her from the stage. She didn't even smile. Maybe she had bad teeth—but none of the other girls in the audience smiled either and I'm sure they don't all need dental care."

The Rolling Stones got the hook when they played San Antone last summer, reported their home-town paper, the London Daily Mirror. "Local singers were cheered wildly, a tumbling act and trained monkeys were recalled for encores but the long-haired boys from England were booed off the stage."

"The mid-west is the friendliest down-to-earth area we've ever appeared in," Brian stated. "Mil-

Continued on page 31

Autografans besiege the Beach Boys after concert at Hollywood Bowl. The boys love the excitement of it all.

Scene at Sacramento, Calif, where concert album was recorded.

Live shows give boys biggest thrill.

Drummer Dennis beats the skins and feeds the beat to the singers.

BRIAN BIRTHS A NEW SONG *Continued from page 12*

Brian finished off another glass of milk and continued: "I'll tell you something I wouldn't tell anyone else. When I hear really fabulous material by other groups I feel small as the dot over the *i* in nit. Then I just have to create a new song to bring me up on top.

"That's probably my most compelling motive for writing new songs—the urge to overcome an inferiority feeling. I have a powerful competitive spirit and do my best work when I am trying to top other songwriters and music-makers.

"An interviewer once asked me if money is my incentive to write music. The answer is no. I've never written one note or word of music simply because I think it will make money."

Brian is proud of the way the Beach Boys have expanded and enlarged their scope and versatility.

"We've evolved about 800 per cent since we started two years ago," he says proudly. "My ideas for the group are to combine music that strikes a deep emotional response among listeners and still maintains a somewhat untrained and teen-age sound. I depend upon harmonics more than before and fuse it with rhythm and a 1964-65 approach in production."

In the beginning record fans used to say the Beach Boys were sound-alikes to the Four Freshmen. That was no accident; the BB's took the FF's as their shining example of what a gear group should sound like. Now the BB's are creating new themes, trends and new cool sounds. Soon the fans may be saying that other groups sound like the Beach Boys.

"Brian is a dedicated genius," Carl says admiringly. "He composes all our material. He's had collaboration assists with some lyrics but he writes all the music and arrangements. I don't know how he finds time to do it all. He just calls us and says, 'I just wrote another song. Let's record it.'"

Says Brian: "Songwriting is the hardest work I know but I love it. The other guys can have the fun—and they do."

Yeah, they certainly do!

SWINGIN' THE SURFIN' SCENE *Continued from page 14*

Half of Hawthorne's youngfolk hung about the Wilson windows when the boys carried on their jam sessions.

When hip Pa felt the group was good and gassy, he bank-rolled a recording session in dear old Hollywood. Their first ditty, *Surfin'*, released by a minor label, excited even the jaded disk jockeys who began whirling it on the turntables for a swift ride to the suburbs of hitsville.

A Capitol Records exec, Voyle Gilmore, a cat with a golden ear, heard a new Beach Boy master and grabbed them pronto for an exclusive Cap wax pact. Their first release under that label, *Surfin' Safari* climbed the charts like a homesick angel in the fall of 1962. They've had nothing but smasherinos and no floperoos since then. That's the way they like it most.

"Success took us out of the surf," Dennis sighed. "We rarely get a chance to ride the wild waves now. The good old simmertime, the best surfing months, is our busiest season on tour."

"We blew that part of our image," Brian chipped in. "When the surf's up we are likely to be in Bonedry, Kansas, soaking in perspiration or wetting our hides under the showers."

The boys are home only a few scattered days all summer long. Mike and Al live in Manhattan Beach, dead center of the California surfing coast. Al and his wife like to settle down to a frantic game of scrabble but hot-dogger Dennis takes every chance to blast off to the beach with board and baggies when the surf is as high as an elephant's eye. 'Tween rides he likes nothing better than to eyeball the beach belles with boards but no boys. Man, that's something else, he says.

Surfing and surfing songs, the Beach Boys aver, will last until the last crashing, thundering, whitecapped wave breaks against the wild and windswept shore.

GIRLS, GIRLS, GIRLS, = FUN, FUN, FUN *Continued from page 22*

that order." That's a large order for one young container!

Al Jardine, happily wed to a childhood sweetheart, notices that the gals who flirt so brightly and merrily with Brian, Mike, Dennis and Carl don't mess around with him.

"They adopt a hands-off policy with me," Al reports. "I guess it's the same with the married Beatle, John Lennon, who has a sort of father image to the teen-age girls. The most important thing in my personal life is to concentrate on my marriage and make it a success."

This is not to say Al is blind to the charms of the dollings he meets on their treks and tours.

Continued on page 31

The Newest, Nicest, Noises Now Await You...

PEGGY LEE
MINK JAZZ
Swinging Peggy Lee steps out with her own jazz sound. The millions who already love her, and even those few who haven't heard her will love this album.
(S)T-1850

KYU SAKAMOTO
SUKIYAKI
The original hit single, and 3 of the top 5 on the Japanese Hit Parade are included in this delightful album by Kyu Sakamoto the cute little rising male star of the Orient.
(D)T-10349

STAN KENTON
ARTISTRY IN BOSSA NOVA
A quieter Kenton sound that Kenton fans and those who don't yet know him, will appreciate. The masterful manner of Kenton applied to the newest popular beat.
(S)T-1931

RAY ANTHONY
SMASH HITS OF '63
All the best sounds of this year by Ray Anthony, at his best.
(S)T-1917

These are but a few of the latest great albums we have for you now from Capitol RECORDS

Ask for these great LPs wherever you buy your records.

TEEN SET VOLUME 1

Brian, Mike and Dennis hug the curves at Santa Monica go-kart track.

Alan sneaks up on the competition.

Honda fun with Mike and Dennis.

Mike fights for lead near the finish line.

SCORCHED RUBBER & MOTOR ROAR *Continued from page 15*

"But now you don't see so many surfing and hot rod albums," says Brian. "Today it's the Honda scene. You've got to be on the motor scooter kick to be really *in*. Those baby motor bikes are really thrifty. You can drive all over town for a week on thirty cents."

Mike, Dennis and Carl, the three drag-minded Beach Boys, are now jazzed about the super-scooter Honda 90 ("First gear, all right; second gear, lean right; third gear, hang on tight.") They love to dig gravel on the side roads or barrel up the avenoos and thunder down the boulevards on their Hondas, hair streaming and jackets ballooning behind them.

What comes after scooters? Well, the Beach Boys are tuned to the teen wave-length and will be the first with a new rock-a-dandy record to match the next fad that catches on, whatever it may be.

"We aim to keep up with what young guys and dolls are doing and thinking," Brian promises. "It doesn't have to be specifically about surfing, hot rodding or motor scooting. We can't be too dedicated to current crazes because the pressure builds up on us to follow through until they die—and we with 'em.

"I don't like to plan our future more than a couple of months ahead. Meanwhile we'll do more beat-ballads like *I Get Around* and *When I Grow Up (To Be A Man)*. But when a new fad comes along we'll be the first to ride it."

Yeah, Brian, but what's the matter with some of the old familiar crazes? Gang rumbles are very popular among some circles. Eating is the thing with young fatsos. Russian roulette is *in* with adolescent nit-nuts. Pajama parties, drive-in movies and just plain girl-(or boy-) watching will always be a good scene among the junior jet set.

THE HOTTEST NEW RACING ALBUMS

THE HISTORY OF DRAG RACING
STAO-2145
Interviews with top drivers in the country, interviews with people who made the sport great, and recorded live racing... all backed by a brief history of the sport. The outstanding four-page, full-color photos on jacket make this a must for everyone who digs cars... plus photo insert.

THE BIG SOUNDS OF THE GO-KARTS
ST-2147
Here's a collection of the wild sounds of the go-karts... recorded live at the site of go-kart tracks.

THE BIG SOUNDS OF THE DRAGS, VOLUME 2
ST-2146
Because of the demand for the original THE BIG SOUNDS OF THE DRAGS Capitol has come out with an even more extensive volume recorded live at the leading drag spots in Southern California, in order to get the best sounds of the drags. This great LP includes terrific descriptive narration.

PLUS THESE OTHER GREAT ALBUMS

SCHOOL IS A DRAG by Gary Usher & The Super Stocks—ST-2190 • Here's a wayout album all about teachers, cars, and schools. A brand new collection of vocals and instrumentals by the rising young star, Gary Usher, with the able backing of The Super Stocks.

HOT ROD HIGH by The Knights—ST-2189 • A new Capitol group of rockin', wailin', wayout artists delivers a collection of new tunes and current hits. Tunes included are: Rock Around The Clock, Lonely Little Stocker, Midnight Auto, Ditch Day, Theme For Teen Love, Funny Mrs. Brown, Hot Rod High, Hot Rod U.S.A., Skippin' School, I Get Around, School Days, and Be True To Your School.

Ask for these great LPs wherever you buy your records.

Capitol RECORDS

GIRLS, GIRLS, GIRLS, = FUN, FUN, FUN *Continued from page 28*

"To me a girl's most appealing feature is her hair," he admits.

"Long live love!" cries Brian. "I believe in love even though I don't have much time for it. We are all pretty normal guys. Girls play a different role in each of our lives. Each has his own typical approach to the problems and delights of young love. Mike is the most intense girl-watcher. Dennis is a man of action. Carl is the dark horse that may pass the others yet."

TREKS, TRIPS & TRAVELS *Continued from page 25*

waukee is the wildest. Those Milwaukee gals are like hungry tigresses. They grabbed our feet while we were performing on stage and tore at our clothes on the streets. If many other cities were like Milwaukee we'd have to buy a wardrobe of breakaway suits."

"In Boston one trip," Denny recalled, "we were drowned in a surging sea of 4,000 hysterical girls. About 1,000 waited at the stage door when we came out and wrecked the taxi to get at us."

Whenever the Beach Boys are hop-skip-jumping around our grand land I always get a pail of mail from their feminine admirers telling me about the scene in various places.

"There was a fan-tastic mob of screaming girls at the Sacramento (California capital) airport when they arrived," wrote Beach Boy booster Su Green. "City officials presented them with a key to the city and there was a motorcade from the airport to their downtown hotel. The streets were lined with cheering teen-agers. The howling and screaming of the audience at their evening performance was not to be believed."

"The Beach Boys are America's answer to the British Beatles," wrote one teenstress from Indianapolis. "They are witty and charming on stage and off. They make funny cracks that the Beatles themselves would admire. The boys are very cool in a crisis also. The mike went dead on Brian twice but the show went on as though nothing had happened. Fifteen thousand fans can well explain this. It was hot and crowded and although Denny looked like he was going to faint any moment, he made it through the entire show. The conditions they played under were unbearable. The Beach Boys are so sweet and natural and I think they deserve much more attention than they have been getting. In fact, I just love them."

Who doesn't?

This is it! the teen set's fabulous Beach Boys Contest!

Contest Rules

1) Contest will be judged by The Teen Set Contest Board, as designated by Capitol.

2) Entries will be judged on originality, aptness and clarity of thought. Judges' decision will be final and no prize substitutions will be made.

3) Fill out and send in the official entry blank, or write your name, address, age and telephone number on a plain sheet of paper and complete this statement in 50 words or less: "I Like The Beach Boys Because...." Mail, postage prepaid, to Beach Boys' Contest, P.O. Box 1271, Hollywood, Calif. 90028.

4) Only one entry per person will be considered.

5) Offer void where prohibited by law.

6) Winners will be contacted by telephone by one of The Beach Boys. If winners cannot be contacted by phone they will be notified by mail.

7) This contest not open to employees of Capitol Records, Inc., its affiliates or subsidiaries.

8) List of winners will be furnished upon request if the request is accompanied by a self-addressed, stamped envelope.

9) Entries must be postmarked on or before Jan. 1, 1965, contest closing date.

10) Winners will be notified within six weeks of contest closing date.

Win one of these fantastic prizes: *Win one of these fantastic prizes:*

1ST PRIZE: A roaring, running Honda 50!

2ND PRIZE: A sleek, fiberglass, custom made HAP JACOBS Surfboard! *SURF BOARDS by JACOBS*

3RD PRIZE: 100 Capitol albums by The Teen Set's greatest recording stars, including THE BEACH BOYS, THE BEATLES, DICK DALE & THE DELTONES, PETER & GORDON, & many more!

Plus 25 additional winners will get 5 CAPITOL albums each — your choice of the "cream" of the greatest teen catalog of all! It's all for free and it's **easy**. All you have to do is finish this sentence in 50 words or less:

"I Like The Beach Boys Because..."

And dig this — One of The Beach Boys will personally notify each winner **by telephone**!!!

Don't wait — send in your entry blank today! **You** may receive a personal call from The Beach Boys saying that you've won a fabulous Honda, a super Hap Jacobs surfboard, or a stack of great Capitol albums!

---------- ENTRY BLANK ----------

"I Like The Beach Boys Because..." (in 50 words or less) _____

_____

_____

_____

Name _____ age ____ Address _____

City and State _____ Telephone Number _____ area code ____

TEEN SET VOLUME 1

AMERICA'S NUMBER ONE TEENAGE RECORDING ARTISTS ARE ON CAPITOL RECORDS

HERE ARE THE LATEST GREAT NEW SOUNDS

BEACH BOYS CONCERT — STAO 2198
FUN, FUN, FUN; THE LITTLE OLD LADY FROM PASADENA; LITTLE DEUCE COUPE; LONG, TALL TEXAN; IN MY ROOM; THE MONSTER MASH; LET'S GO TRIPPIN'; PAPA-OOM-MOW-MOW; THE WANDERER; HAWAII; GRADUATION DAY; I GET AROUND; and JOHNNY B. GOODE.

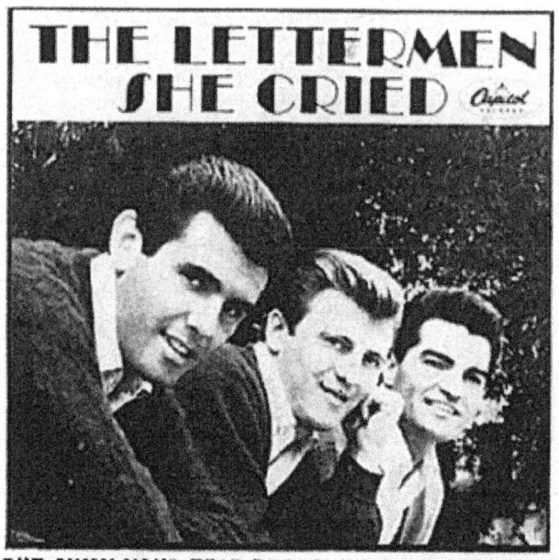

SHE CRIED — The Lettermen — ST 2142
PUT AWAY YOUR TEAR DROPS; TIME TO CRY; WALK ON BY; ARE YOU LONESOME TONIGHT; CRYING; RUN TO HIM; SHE CRIED; IT'S ALL IN THE GAME; DON'T LET THE SUN CATCH YOU CRYING; SEVENTH DAWN THEME; HEARTACHE OH HEARTACHE; and SOFTLY, AS I LEAVE YOU.

THE BEATLES Present SOMETHING NEW — ST 2108
I'LL CRY INSTEAD; THINGS WE SAID TODAY; ANY TIME AT ALL; WHEN I GET HOME; SLOW DOWN; MATCHBOX; TELL ME WHY; AND I LOVE HER; I'M HAPPY JUST TO DANCE WITH YOU; IF I FELL; and KOMM, GIB MIR DEINE HAND.

THE BEACH BOYS' CHRISTMAS ALBUM — ST 2164
LITTLE SAINT NICK; THE MAN WITH ALL THE TOYS; SANTA'S BEARD; MERRY CHRISTMAS, BABY; CHRISTMAS DAY; FROSTY THE SNOWMAN; WE THREE KINGS OF ORIENT ARE; BLUE CHRISTMAS; SANTA CLAUS IS COMIN' TO TOWN; WHITE CHRISTMAS; I'LL BE HOME FOR CHRISTMAS; and AULD LANG SYNE.

PLUS THESE OTHER GREAT CAPITOL "TEENAGE" LPS

ALL SUMMER LONG — The Beach Boys — ST 2110 — I Get Around; All Summer Long; Hushabye; Little Honda; We'll Run Away; Carl's Big Chance; Wendy; Do You Remember?; Girls On The Beach; Drive-In; Our Favorite Recording Sessions; and Don't Back Down.

SHUT DOWN, VOLUME 2 — The Beach Boys — ST 2027 — Fun, Fun, Fun; Don't Worry Baby; In The Parkin' Lot; "Cassius" Love vs "Sonny" Wilson; The Warmth Of The Sun; This Car Of Mine; Why Do Fools Fall In Love; Pom, Pom Play Girl; Keep An Eye On Summer; Shut Down, Part II; Louie, Louie; and Denny's Drums.

LITTLE DEUCE COUPE — The Beach Boys — ST 1998 — Little Deuce Coupe; Ballad Of Ole' Betsy; Be True To Your School; Car Crazy Cutie; Cherry, Cherry Coupe; 409; Shut Down; Spirit Of America; Our Car Club; No-Go Showboat; A Young Man Is Gone; and Custom Machine.

SURFER GIRL — The Beach Boys — ST 1981 — Surfer Girl; Catch A Wave; The Surfer Moon; South Bay Surfer; The Rocking Surfer; Little Deuce Coupe; In My Room; Hawaii; Surfer's Rule; Our Car Club; Your Summer Dream; and Boogie Woogie.

SURFIN' U.S.A. — The Beach Boys — ST 1890 — Surfin' U.S.A.; Farmer's Daughter; Misirlou; Stoked; Lonely Sea; Shut Down; Noble Surfer; Honky Tonk; Lana; Surf Jam; Let's Go Trippin'; and Finders Keepers.

SURFIN' SAFARI — The Beach Boys — DT 1808 — Surfin' Safari; County Fair; Ten Little Indians; Chug-A-Lug; Little Girl (You're My Miss America); 409; Surfin'; Heads You Win — Tails I Lose; Summertime Blues; Cuckoo Clock; Moon Dawg; and The Shift.

THE BEATLES' SECOND ALBUM — The Beatles — ST 2080 — Roll Over Beethoven; Thank You Girl; You Really Got A Hold On Me; Devil In Her Heart; Money (That's What I Want); You Can't Do That; Long Tall Sally; I Call Your Name; Please Mister Postman; I'll Get You; and She Loves You.

MEET THE BEATLES — The Beatles — ST 2047 — I Want To Hold Your Hand; I Saw Her Standing There; This Boy; It Won't Be Long; All I've Got To Do; All My Loving; Don't Bother Me; Little Child; Till There Was You; Hold Me Tight; I Wanna Be Your Man; and Not A Second Time.

THE BEATLES SONG BOOK — The Hollyridge Strings — ST 2116 — From Me To You; I Saw Her Standing There; Please Please Me; P.S. I Love You; Love Me Do; I Want To Hold Your Hand; Can't Buy Me Love; All My Loving; A Taste Of Honey; Do You Want To Know A Secret?; and She Loves You.

THE BEACH BOYS SONG BOOK — The Hollyridge Strings — ST 2156 — I Get Around; Don't Worry Baby; She Knows Me Too Well; Fun, Fun, Fun; In My Room; Little Saint Nick; Surfin' U.S.A.; The Warmth Of The Sun; Wendy; Shut Down; and Girls On The Beach.

SUMMER SURF — Dick Dale And His Del-Tones — ST 2111 — Summer Surf; Feel So Good; Surfin'; Spanish Kiss; The Star (Of David); Banzai Washout; Glory Wave; Surfin' Rebel; Never On Sunday; Mama's Gone Surfin'; Tidal Wave; and Thunder Wave.

MR. ELIMINATOR — Dick Dale — ST 2053 — Mr. Eliminator; 50 Miles To Go; Flashing Eyes; Taco Wagon; The Squirrel; The Victor; Blond In The 406; Firing Up; My XKE; Nitro Fuel; and Hot Rod Alley.

A WORLD WITHOUT LOVE — Peter And Gordon — ST 2115 — Lucille; Five Hundred Miles; If I Were You; Pretty Mary; Trouble In Mind; A World Without Love; Tell Me How; You Won't Have To Tell Me; Leave My Woman Alone; All My Trials; and Last Night I Woke.

THE BIG HITS FROM ENGLAND & U.S.A. — VARIOUS — DT 2125 — Can't Buy Me Love, The Beatles; I Get Around, The Beach Boys; A World Without Love, Peter And Gordon; You Can't Do That, The Beatles; Don't Worry Baby, The Beach Boys; Nobody I Know, Peter And Gordon; I Don't Want To Be Hurt Anymore, Nat King Cole; Suffer Now I Must, Cilla Black; Tears And Roses, Al Martino; People, Nat King Cole; You're My World, Cilla Black.

THE LETTERMEN LOOK AT LOVE — The Lettermen — ST 2983 — Go Away, Little Girl; Sincerely; Forget Him; Till Then; Through A Long And Sleepless Night; The Shelter Of Your Arms; Secret Love; Only You; All I Have To Do Is Dream; Love Letters In The Sand; and Blue Moon.

BIG SOUNDS OF THE DRAGS, VOL. II — ST 2146
BIG SOUNDS OF THE GO-KARTS — ST 2147

ASK FOR THESE GREAT LPS WHEREVER YOU BUY YOUR RECORDS

Capitol RECORDS

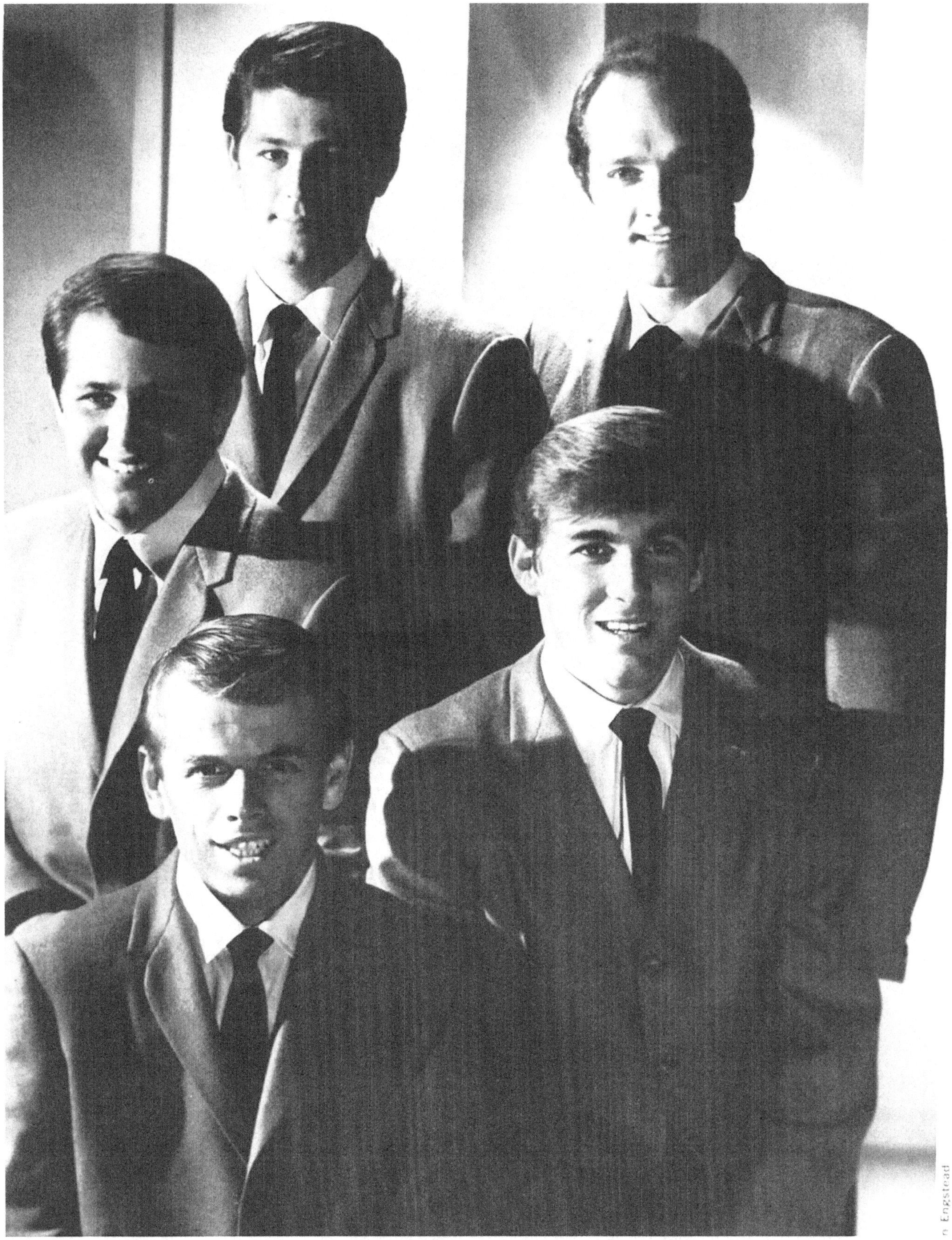

TEEN SET VOLUME 1

AMERICA'S NUMBER ONE SINGING GROUP
THE BEACH BOYS
offer you two great new LPs

THE BEACH BOYS' CHRISTMAS ALBUM ST-2164

In this LP The Beach Boys have chosen holiday greetings ranging all the way from their own light-hearted seasonal hit "Little Saint Nick" to beautiful traditional favorites done with a forty piece orchestral background. On the flip of the album cover you'll find an attractive autographed black & white photo Christmas card from The Beach Boys. The selections from this LP included are: LITTLE SAINT NICK; THE MAN WITH ALL THE TOYS; SANTA'S BEARD; MERRY CHRISTMAS, BABY; CHRISTMAS DAY; FROSTY THE SNOWMAN; WE THREE KINGS OF ORIENT ARE; BLUE CHRISTMAS; SANTA CLAUSE IS COMIN' TO TOWN; WHITE CHRISTMAS; I'LL BE HOME FOR CHRISTMAS; and AULD LANG SYNE.

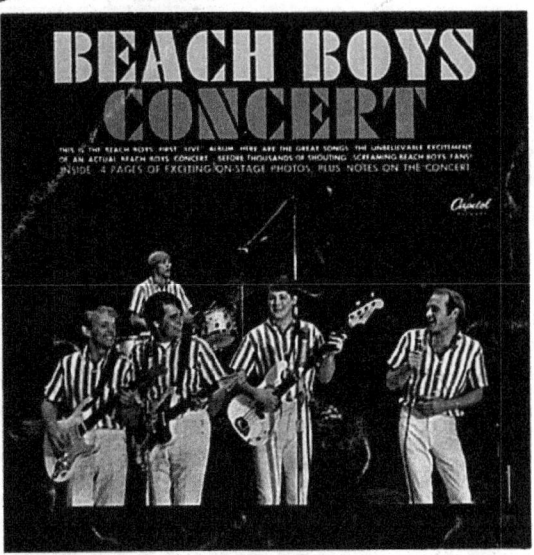

BEACH BOYS CONCERT / STAO-2198

Here's your front row center seat to a wild, rocking, live, in-person concert by The Beach Boys. The screams are for real... As you know if you've ever been to a Beach Boys' concert. But, there's more here than just great music. There are four pages of photos of The Beach Boys in action PLUS a full-color cover, inside and out, of great photos of The Beach Boys in concert. It's the next best thing to being there yourself. You'll hear The Beach Boys deliver these songs just as they do on stage: FUN, FUN, FUN; THE LITTLE OLD LADY FROM PASADENA; LITTLE DEUCE COUPE; LONG, TALL TEXAN; IN MY ROOM; THE MONSTER MASH; LET'S GO TRIPPIN'; PAPA-OOM-MOW-MOW; THE WANDERER; HAWAII; GRADUATION DAY; I GET AROUND; and JOHNNY B. GOODE.

BE SURE YOUR BEACH BOY COLLECTION INCLUDES THESE OTHER SMASH LPs

All Summer Long—ST-2110—I Get Around, All Summer Long, Hushabye, Little Honda, We'll Run Away, Carl's Big Chance, Wendy, Do You Remember?, Girls On The Beach, Drive-In, Our Favorite Recording Sessions; Don't Back Down.

Surfer Girl—ST-1981—Surfer Girl, Catch A Wave, The Surfer Moon, South Bay Surfer, The Rocking Surfer, Little Deuce Coupe, In My Room, Hawaii, Surfer's Rule, Our Car Club, Your Summer Dream, and Boogie Woogie.

Surfin' Safari—DT-1808—Surfin' Safari, County Fair, Ten Little Indians, Chug-A-Lug, Little Girl (You're My Miss America), 409, Surfin', Heads You Win—Tails I Lose, Summertime Blues, Cuckoo Clock, Moon Dawg, and The Shift.

Shut Down, Volume 2—ST-2027—Fun, Fun, Fun; Don't Worry Baby; The Warmth Of The Sun; This Car Of Mine; Why Do Fools Fall In Love; Pom, Pom Play Girl; Keep An Eye On Summer; Shut Down, Part II; Louie, Louie; Denny's Drums; others.

Little Deuce Coupe—ST-1998—Little Deuce Coupe; Ballad of Ole' Betsy; Be True To Your School; Car Crazy Cutie; Cherry, Cherry Coupe; 409; Shut Down; Spirit of America; Our Car Club; No-Go Show-Boat; A Young Man Is Gone; and Custom Machine.

Surfin' U.S.A.—ST-1890—Surfin' U.S.A., Farmer's Daughter, Misirlou, Stoked, Lonely Sea, Shut Down, Noble Surfer, Honky Tonk, Lana, Surf Jam, Let's Go Trippin', and Finders Keepers.

This is your chance to bring your Beach Boy collection up to date. Drop by your record dealer today and pick up these two great new LPs by The Beach Boys. And while you're there ask to see the other fine Beach Boy LPs pictured above and make sure you've got each and every one of them.

Capitol RECORDS

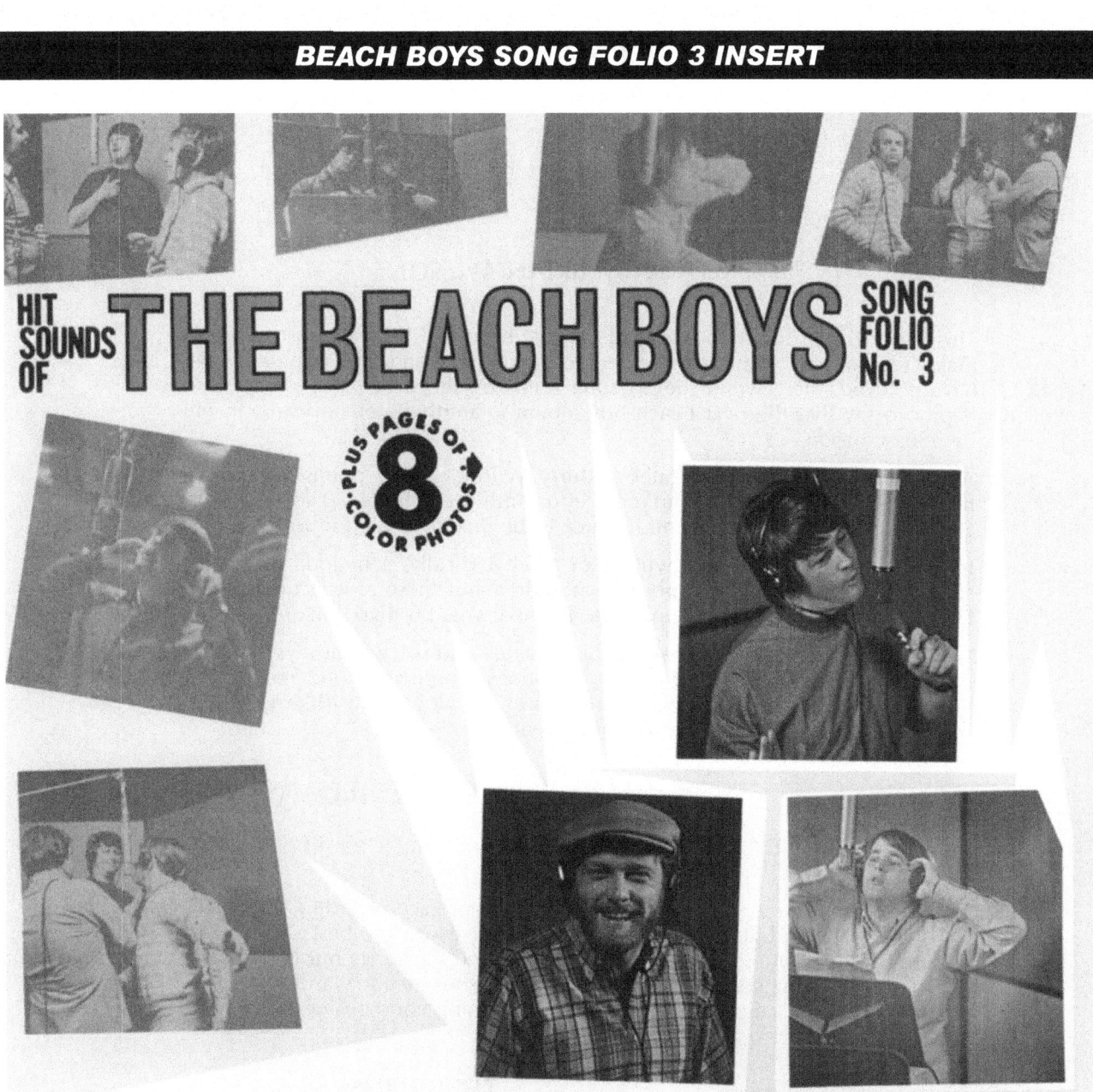

BEACH BOYS SONG FOLIO 3 INSERT

HIT SOUNDS OF THE BEACH BOYS
SONG FOLIO No. 3

PLUS 8 PAGES OF COLOR PHOTOS

BEACH BOYS SONG FOLIO 3 INSERT

PREFACE by BRIAN WILSON

This is our third song folio. I'm glad that we have had more opportunities to make records, for without these records and the wonderful popularity we have enjoyed, there would be no song folios by the Beach Boys. I am also happy to say that the next Beach Boy album is another step forward. It will be released soon.

As many of you know, our father, Murry Wilson, is our publisher and he told us that he was going to put more effort into the Folio No. 3 for you fans, and we see now what he meant. It's nice to be included in good productions.

If you have a talent for songwriting or more basically, a melodic or lyrical sense, I hope you develop a positive attitude about these artistic qualities — I'm one of those fortunate people who learned what positive thinking can do.

We thank you all again for making this possible and we will always strive to do our best regarding our writing of the songs, producing good records for the radio audience, and brothers Dennis and Carl along with Mike Love and Al Jardine still enjoy being Beach Boys in concert.

Brian Wilson

EDITORS NOTE

There is not much more one can say after Brian's preface regarding the SONG HIT FOLIO NO. 3, but we again have tried to give you the best selection of pictures, to be of interest to you fans. Brian picked the songs out himself and our way of thanking you for the blessings of our sons, nephew and Al Jardine, is try to give you a value unheard of in the publishing trade business. We hope you like it.

THE PUBLISHER

MURRY G. WILSON

BEACH BOYS SONG FOLIO 3 INSERT

BEACH BOYS SONG FOLIO 3 INSERT

Carl Wilson

BEACH BOYS SONG FOLIO 3 INSERT

You are looking at more than a group of guys in a recording studio. These are the Beach Boys in production with their 12th album. They truly felt the importance of this project.

BEACH BOYS SONG FOLIO 3 INSERT

Brian and Bruce talking to friends

Brian, the producer and leader, cracking the whip

Mike giving his "all" on a solo

Al, tense while under pressure

Dennis singing with emotion

Brian and Bruce resting after "Pet Sounds" album session

Mike happy with a hit sound — "dig the beard"

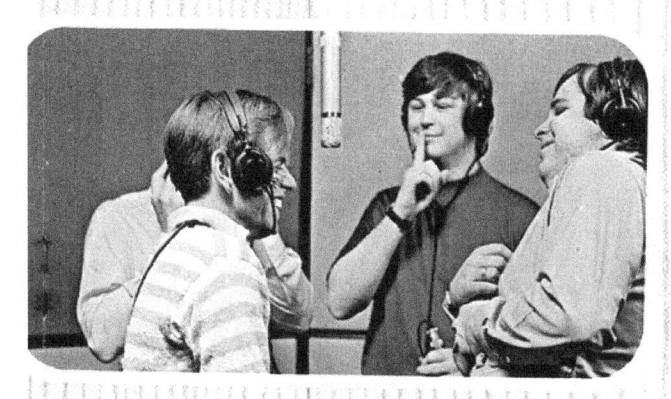

BEACH BOYS SONG FOLIO 3 INSERT

Brian cautions the fellows after a good take on song

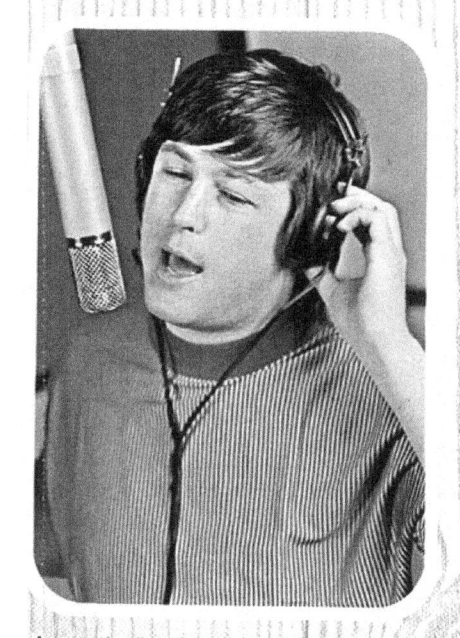

rian, enjoying his solo part of a record

Carl "cooling it" after a take

Bruce Jonston — fills in for Brian on most concerts. Does a grand job.

Brian in the control booth with recording engineer

Brothers Brian and Carl listening to "Pet Sounds" album

105

BEACH BOYS SONG FOLIO 3 INSERT

Dennis Wilson

BEACH BOYS SONG FOLIO 3 INSERT

Alan Jardine

BEACH BOYS SONG FOLIO 3 INSERT

Mike Love

FLIP MAGAZINE MARCH 1966

THE GROUPS Part I
March 1966

FREE with FLIP Magazine

FOR GEAR GROUPERS ONLY

PUBLISHED AND PRODUCED BY THE EDITORS OF FLIP MAGAZINE

THE BEACH BOYS DO IT AGAIN!
And You Are There!

Because Brian, Carol, Dennis, Mike and Al won't put a note on record until they've got satisfaction... it takes a lot of heat to produce that cool California sound which belongs to The Beach Boys. And we added to that heat by popping lots of flashbulbs during their latest recording session at a studio in Hollywood.

Brian, the "boss" Beach Boy, takes charge of the session with a sense of excitement and anticipation. "No matter how often you record and no matter how many hits you've been lucky enough to have," he says, "you're nervous all over again every time you get inside the studio." But Brian doesn't let it show, and he checks out all the details so thoroughly that he probably loses ten pounds every time the group cuts a record!

Mike is intensely looking over the music, Carl is tuning his temperamental guitar, Al is testing the microphone levels, and Dennis is watching it all while tapping a bongo drum and getting the "feel" of the song. All of them are keeping their fingers crossed, and none of them will uncross them until the verdict is in. Then, Brian gives the word... the studio falls silent... the engineer inside the booth clicks the tape machine... the producer says, "Beach Boys, take one"... and the special sounds of The Beach Boys fill the studio with incredible excitement!

Another hit has just been born. To see how it happened, check out the exclusive pictures on this pop page!

Brian and Mike go over the music for the last time! But chances are Brian will have another look just before they cut the record.

Al strums and hums a little to see if the microphone can pick everything up.

Dennis keeping his eye on the whole scene from the best seat in the studio.

Carl concentrating on only one thing: his guitar. It was a little off, but he adjusted it in time for the session.

BEACH BOYS THANKSGIVING CONCERT POSTER

BEACH BOYS
FIFTH ANNUAL THANKSGIVING TOUR

- BUFFALO SPRINGFIELD
- STRAWBERRY ALARM CLOCK
- SOUL SURVIVORS
- PICKLE BROTHERS

Thanks to These Stations for Their Cooperation on This Tour.

WKNR	WEAM	WMCA	WRKO
WNDR	WDRC	KDKA	WICE
WKBW	WICC	WBZ	WCAO

And Thanks to All the Stations for Your Support Throughout the Year.

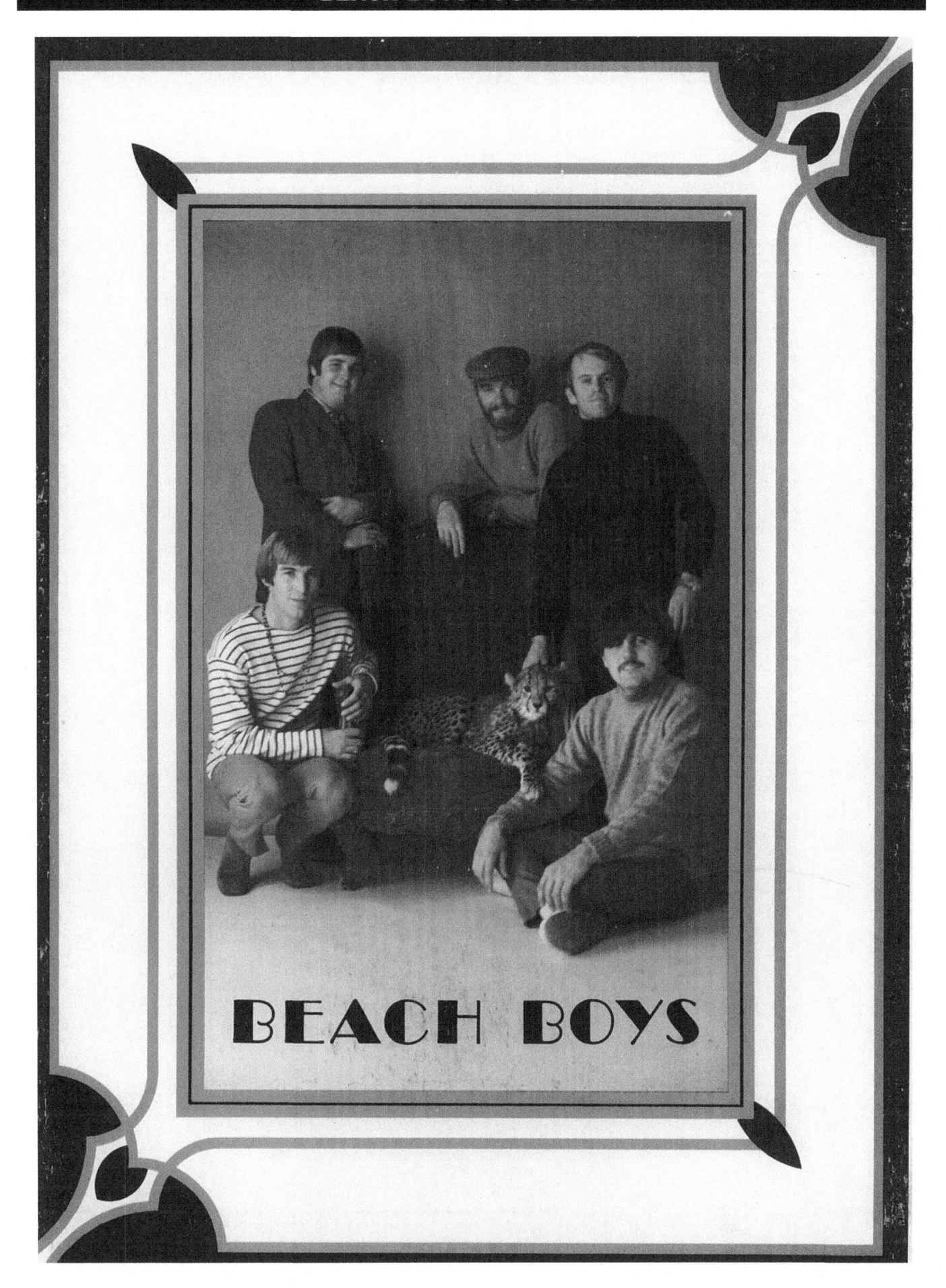

BEACH BOYS TOUR BOOK

BEACH BOYS

Capitol
REG US PAT OFF
RECORDS

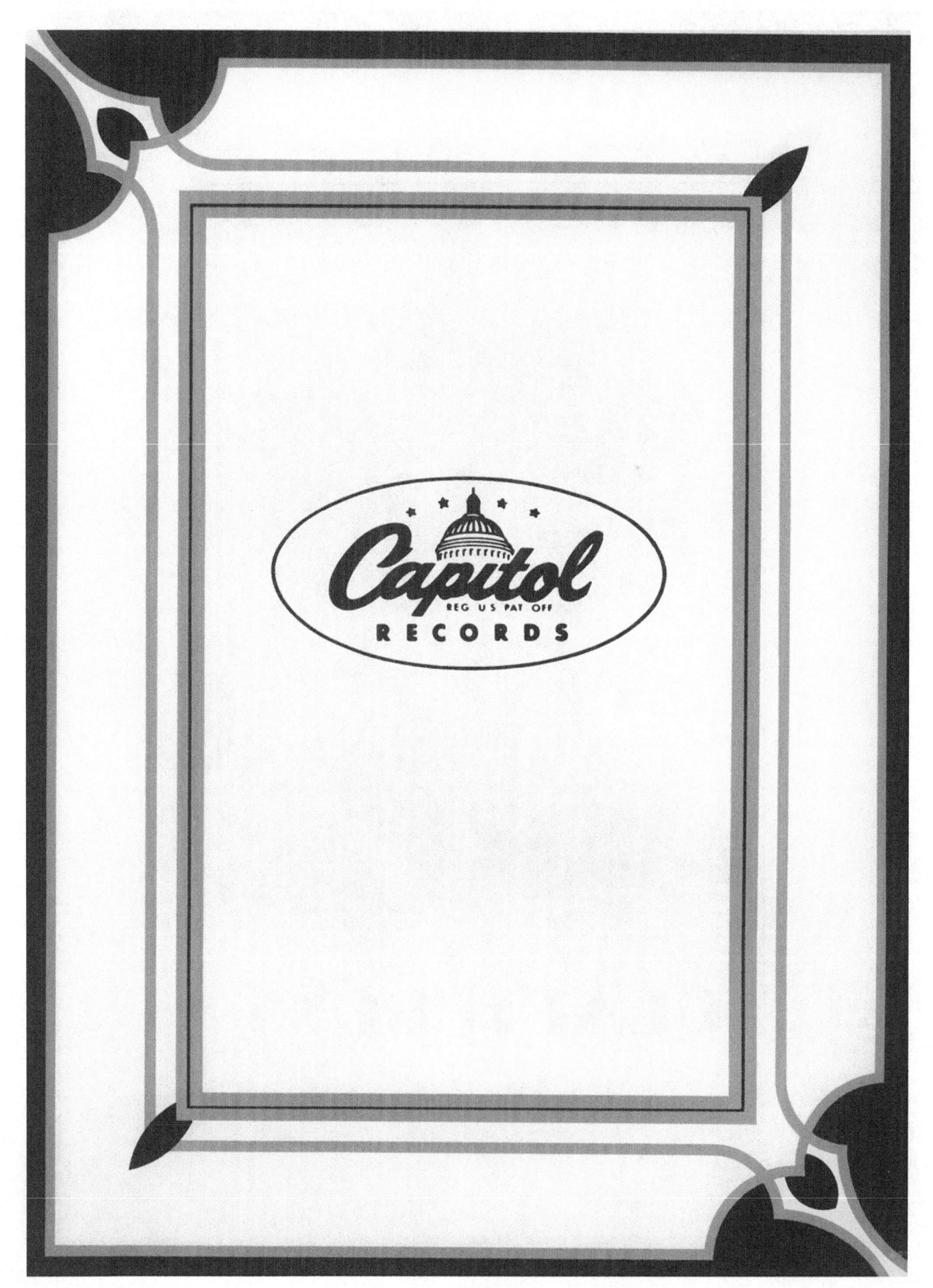

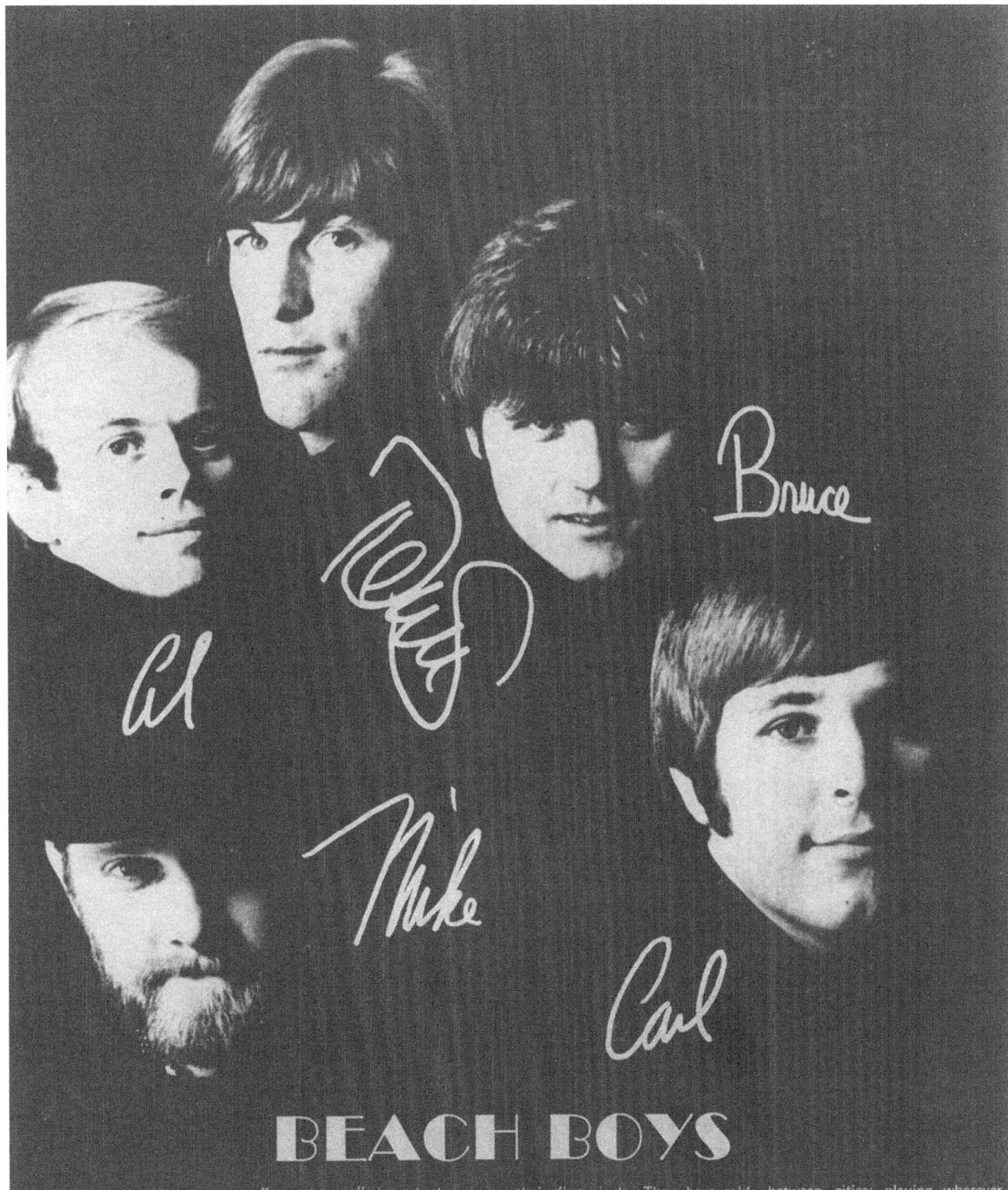

BEACH BOYS TOUR BOOK

BEACH BOYS

The Beach Boys are a phenomenon in today's music whirl where many talented people enjoy a brief visit; a flirtation with stardom, but where only a few survive long after their first hit record. People have wondered just what it takes to make one group survive long after others have fallen by the wayside. Why does one group continue to grow in popularity; to mature musically, and to expand their appeal from "teeny-bopper" through the young adult and into the adult musical sphere? By what yardstick does one measure "success" in the fickle world of music?

The Beach Boys' popularity can be measured in many ways. The most apparent, of course, is in the area of record sales. The Boys have earned Gold Records eleven times since December of 1961 when they cut their first single. They have sold more than 30,000,000 records during that brief span; positive testimony to their success in this area, at least.

Still another method of measuring success is public appearances...concert touring. From the early days when the Boys worked concerts all over the country; driving all night to make the often lengthy jumps between cities; playing wherever and whenever there were people to listen, they have developed into a group who travel, more often than not, in their own plane; who hire other top recording groups as second and third acts for their own concerts; who utilize up to thirteen musicians as backing on the concert stage, and who command "top dollar" for their appearances.

113

BEACH BOYS TOUR BOOK

"...God Only Knows..."

BEACH BOYS TOUR BOOK

The Beach Boys have never broken faith with their fans by selling out to fadism or by jumping from musical gimmick to gimmick. The Beach Boys have always been trend-setters and never fad-followers. They have engendered more imitators than any other group. Everywhere you turn there are synthetic Beach Boys. The Boys conceive and perform music that races ahead of the crest...music that influences trends the world over. They are originals, creators, innovators, and yet their music never loses the flavor of their zest for living and love of life. In concert or on record they have the rare ability to reach out and touch their audiences. They communicate in a language that is not restricted solely to the younger set, but in the universal language of talent, understandable to people of any age.

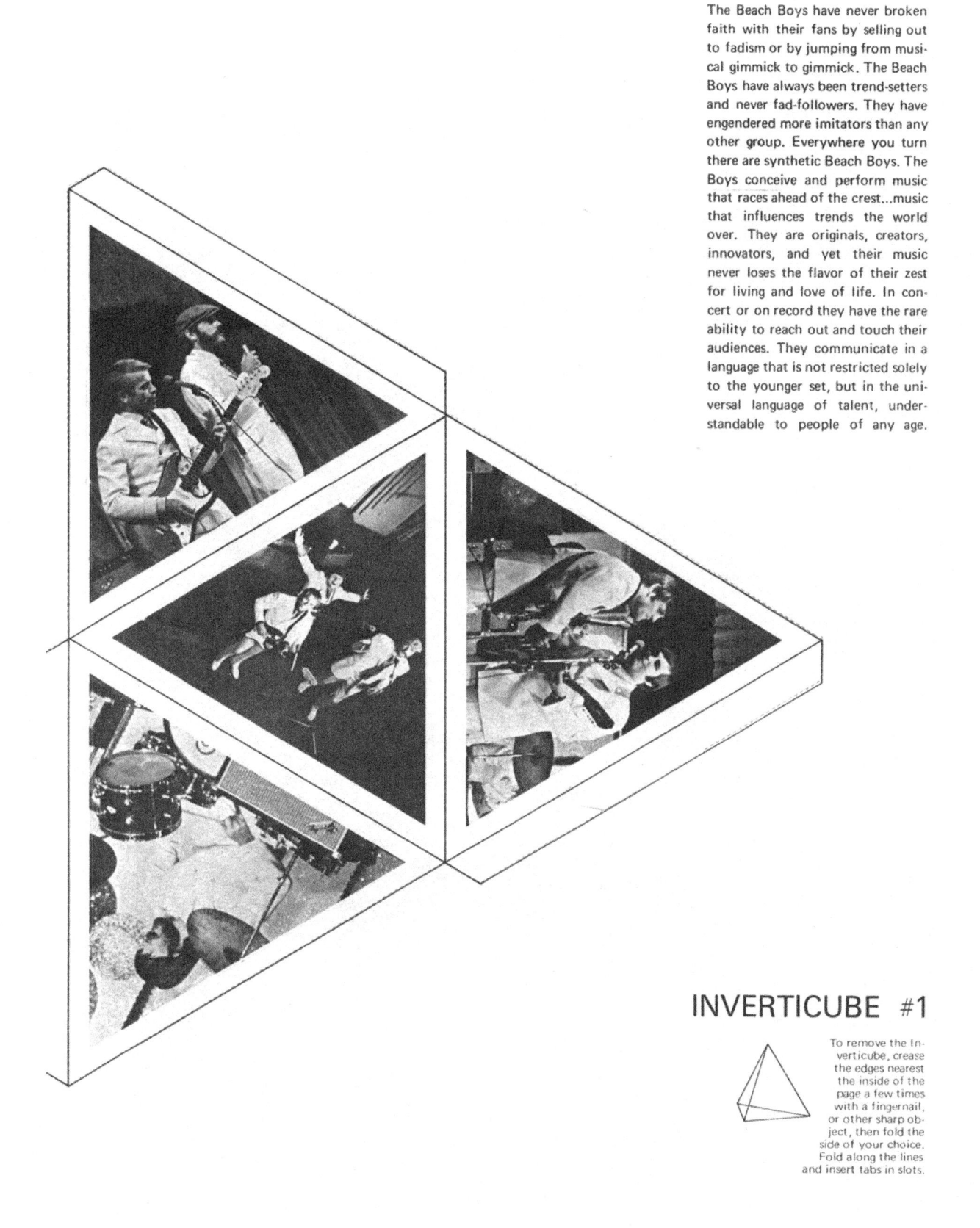

INVERTICUBE #1

To remove the Inverticube, crease the edges nearest the inside of the page a few times with a fingernail, or other sharp object, then fold the side of your choice. Fold along the lines and insert tabs in slots.

115

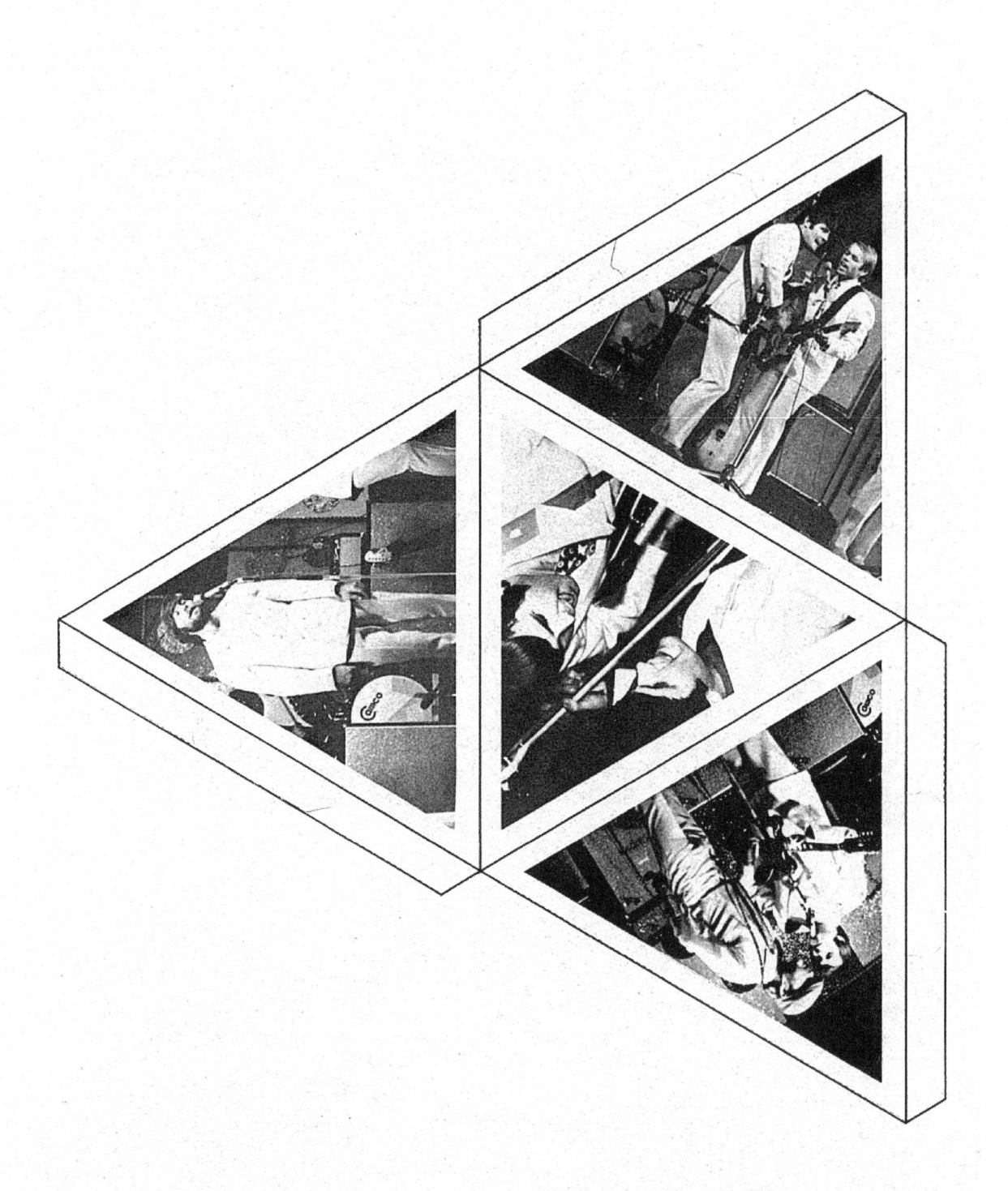

BEACH BOYS TOUR BOOK

BEACH BOYS TOUR BOOK

GOOD VIBRATIONS
GOOD VIBRATIONS
GOOD VIBRATIONS
GOOD VIBRATIONS
GOOD VIBRATIONS
GOOD VIBRATIONS
GOOD VIBRATIONS

The Beach Boys are a phenomenon in today's music whirl, and are continuing to grow in many ways, not the least of which is a deep awareness of the sound that is both today and tomorrow. They are firmly devoted to an understanding and love of life as well as people and things.

In concert or on record, the Beach Boys have the rare ability to reach out and touch their audiences. As a group or as individuals they constantly strive to grow and expand with positive dedication to their personal principles of freedom. Aside from concerts and recording sessions the Beach Boys have enthusiastically launched their own record label, Brother Records.

Friends

MUSIC MUSIC MUSIC...

PEACE

BEACH BOYS TOUR BOOK

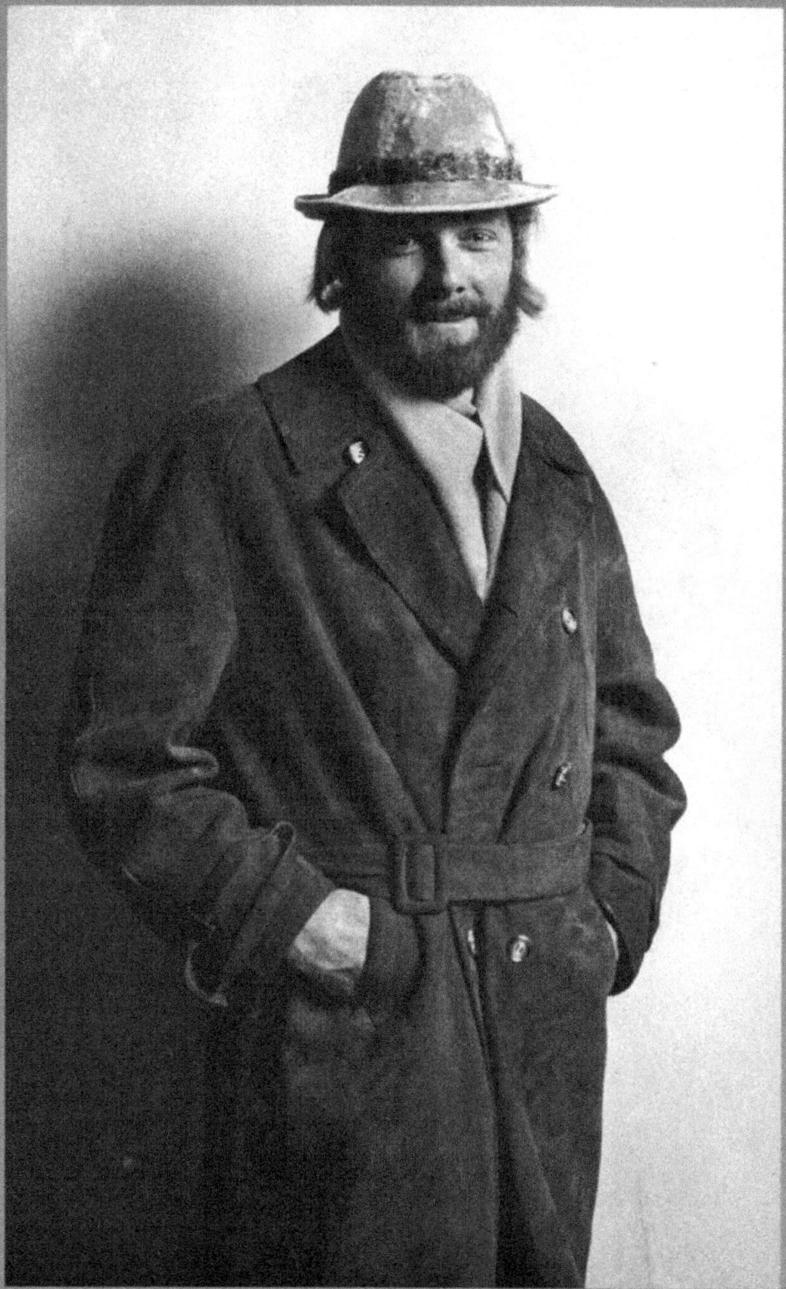

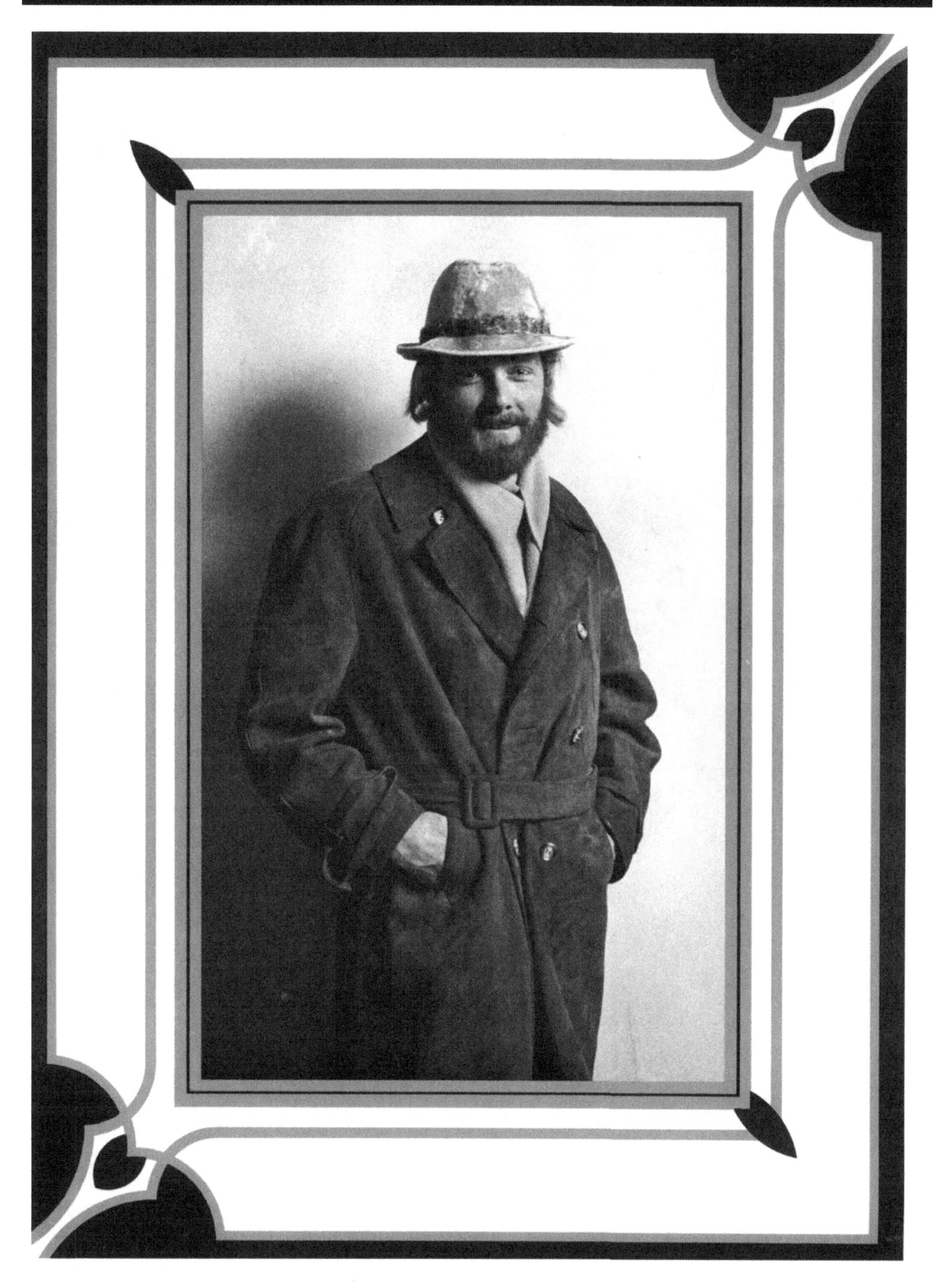

BEACH BOYS TOUR BOOK

BEACH BOYS TOUR BOOK

BEACH BOYS TOUR BOOK

BEACH BOYS TOUR BOOK

BEACH BOYS TOUR BOOK

BEACH BOYS TOUR BOOK

A great deal has been written about our group, but all those thousands of words have failed to mention one important point, the way we feel about you... our friends and audience.

Many of you have been with us since we kicked-out and made our first record in the early sixties, others are new faces and we welcome you. To each and all we extend our sincere appreciation for the opportunity of expressing ourselves musically. We like to think that every record, every opening night spotlights the best we have to offer. Your enthusiastic response has made it all worthwhile and we thank you.   The Beach Boys

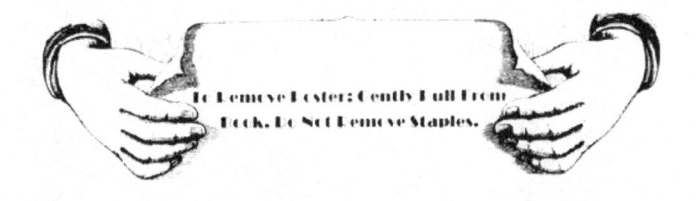

To Remove Poster: Gently Pull From Book. Do Not Remove Staples.

BEACH BOYS TOUR BOOK

BEACH BOYS TOUR BOOK

BEACH BOYS TOUR BOOK

BEACH BOYS TOUR BOOK

BEACH BOYS TOUR BOOK

NVERTICUBE #2

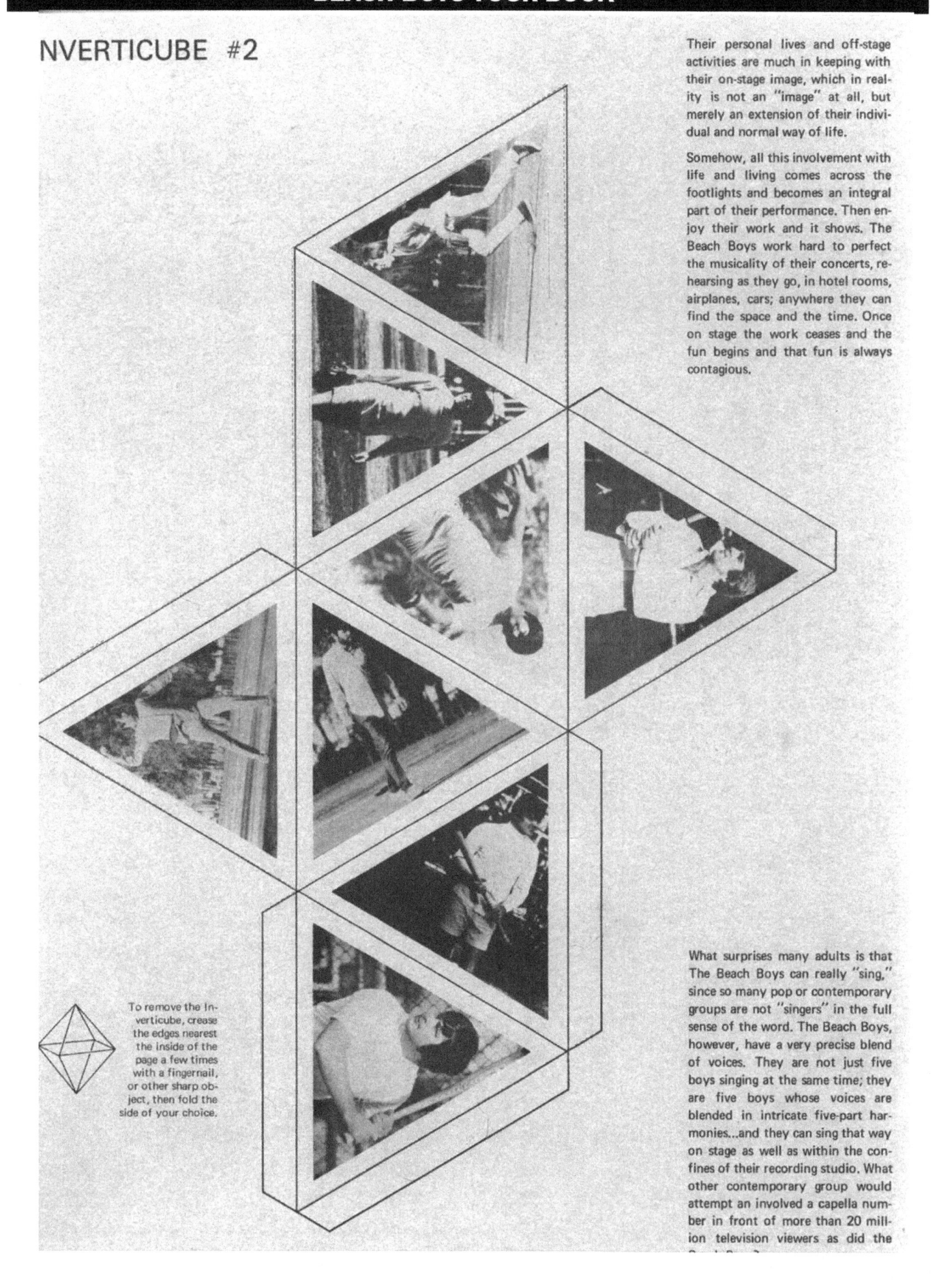

Their personal lives and off-stage activities are much in keeping with their on-stage image, which in reality is not an "image" at all, but merely an extension of their individual and normal way of life.

Somehow, all this involvement with life and living comes across the footlights and becomes an integral part of their performance. Then enjoy their work and it shows. The Beach Boys work hard to perfect the musicality of their concerts, rehearsing as they go, in hotel rooms, airplanes, cars; anywhere they can find the space and the time. Once on stage the work ceases and the fun begins and that fun is always contagious.

To remove the Inverticube, crease the edges nearest the inside of the page a few times with a fingernail, or other sharp object, then fold the side of your choice.

What surprises many adults is that The Beach Boys can really "sing," since so many pop or contemporary groups are not "singers" in the full sense of the word. The Beach Boys, however, have a very precise blend of voices. They are not just five boys singing at the same time; they are five boys whose voices are blended in intricate five-part harmonies...and they can sing that way on stage as well as within the confines of their recording studio. What other contemporary group would attempt an involved a capella number in front of more than 20 million television viewers as did the

BEACH BOYS TOUR BOOK

The Beach Boys are not only the country's number one contemporary music act, they are also the #1 consumers of automotive equipment among the entertainment set. While none of the Boys are actually "collectors", they seem to accumulate all manner of transportation.

132

BEACH BOYS TOUR BOOK

JAG XK-E

BRIAN   CARL   DENNIS   MIKE   AL   BRUCE

SEE IF YOU CAN MATCH THE BEACH BOYS WITH THEIR EXOTIC FORMS OF TRANSPORTATION...!!!

1. 1965 Aston—Martin _____
2. BSA Cycle _____
3. BSA Cycle _____
4. 1966 Ferrari _____
5. 1967 Jaguar _____
6. Jeep _____
7. 1947 MG Classic _____
8. 1968 Mercedes 200 SL _____
9. 1968 Mustang _____
10. 1968 Porsche _____
11. 1938 Rolls Cabriolet _____
12. 1967 Rolls Phantom Limo _____
13. 1966 Rolls Limo _____
14. 1967 T—Bird _____
15. Triumph Cycle _____
16. Yamaha Cycle _____
17. 1967 XKE _____

1. _____
2. _____
3. _____
4. _____
5. _____
6. _____
7. _____
8. _____
9. _____
10. _____
11. _____
12. _____
13. _____
14. _____
15. _____
16. _____
17. _____

Answers To Game On Bottom of Next Page. Motoring Accessories Courtesy of Vilém B. Haan, Inc., Los Angeles, California

BEACH BOYS TOUR BOOK

The Boys are insatiable experimenters. They are devotees of change; they are perfectionists. Mike Love began as a saxaphonist, changing to a lead-singer when the group felt the direction they were headed. He now plays a complicated electronic device called a Theramin. Dennis was originally a singer, playing no instrument, but he demonstrated a facility with the drums and so moved from the front to the back of the stage. Along the way he has "picked-up" piano, guitar and flute. Brian started out as the group's drummer, later changing to the 12-string guitar until the pressures of management and writing forced him to drop out of the concert activities. He still sings and plays on all their records, however. On the road, he is ably replaced by Bruce Johnston who is an accomplished musician, playing piano, organ, and bass. His fine singing voice is a welcome addition to their record sounds. Both Carl and Al have remained true to their guitars, but have become increasingly involved in the writing of the original Beach Boys music.

Mike Love, who sings lead, is a sports car buff, and more recently a collector of cars, having restored a 1938 Rolls Royce Cabriolet to go along with his 1947 MG. In addition to an occasional dip into the surf near his beach home, Mike has taken a fancy to boating in his spare hours.

Dennis Wilson, the handsome, muscular drummer, is active in many outdoor sports. He is a fisherman and a hunter and trapper. He is a skin and scuba-diver; he plays tennis almost every morning and then races to the ocean where he heads for the open sea in his 40-foot cabin cruiser.

Carl Wilson, whose activities once involved motor sports, has moved "inside" since becoming more deeply involved in the production and writing of Beach Boys songs. Carl, however, still finds time for motoring, but has given up the competition in favor of pleasure driving in his Aston-Martin, his fire-engine red jeep or his BSA Motorcycle. For relaxation he finds enough time to enjoy tennis and swimming.

Alan Jardine, the "Quiet Man" of the group, has tenaciously stuck to his favorite sports of surfing and swimming. On the road, he likes to manage a line or two on the nearest bowling lanes, or weather permitting and location allowing, to take off for the nearest water and a few hours of swimming.

Bruce Johnston is involved in just about every sport from surfing, water and snow skiing and scuba-diving, to flying about in his brother's plane. He is also an avid cyclist, running around Los Angeles on his Yamaha. He is a fine tennis player and a more than passable golfer.

Brian Wilson, the oldest of the Wilson brothers, and the force behind the formation and growth of the Beach Boys, has given up traveling because of the heavy pressures of writing, directing and producing their records; of running his publishing company and the newly formed Brother Records. Brian, recently selected as "Record Producer of the Year," by a national teen publication, has received seven song-writing awards from B.M.I.; the most ever awarded an American composer. With all this, he still finds time for tennis and swimming in his back-yard pool.

When each of these factors is fitted into place, the result is considerably more than "just another group." The Beach Boys have consistently demonstrated that they are something special, both on-stage and off. Behind the obvious talents that constitute the public Beach Boys, lies the most important factor of all: They are real human beings; really nice people to know. They will remain at the top just as long as there are audiences who can recognize the difference between music and noise; between talent and mediocrity; between originators and imitators and between the "real" people and the false.

BRIAN: 8, 10, 12. CARL: 1, 2, 6. DENNIS: 3, 4, 13. MIKE: 7, 11, 15, 17. AL: 5, 9. BRUCE: 14, 16.

BEACH BOYS TOUR BOOK

For Further Information Concerning Additional Books or Posters Write to Beach Boys International Fan Club, P.O. Box 110, Hollywood, California..

MEMBERSHIP IN THE BEACH BOYS INTERNATIONAL FAN CLUB $2.00

NAME
ADDRESS
CITY
STATE
ZIP CODE
AGE

BOOK DESIGN BY:
GELLER & BUTLER ADVERTISING

ART PRODUCED BY:
TOTAL IMAGE COMMUNICATION

LITHOGRAPHY BY:
QUANTUM PRESS

COVER & POSTER PHOTOGRAPHS:
COURTESY OF BERNARD LE LOUP

BEACH BOYS TOUR BOOK

BEACH BOYS TOUR BOOK

INSIDE POP

chapter 12
SUNKISSED POP IDOLS
the beach boys

Standing, left to right: Bruce Johnston, Carl Wilson, Dennis Wilson, Al Jardine; front: Mike Love.

IT'S "CALIFORNIA, HERE I COME" for America's pop music and record business.

Increasingly, California, the biggest state in the U.S. in population (20,000,000), is challenging the supremacy of New York and Nashville, the traditional pop music citadels. More and more hit recordings and more and more music crazes are conceived there. These days there are seemingly as many record companies in the Golden State as drive-ins. California is presently headquarters of such major record companies as Warner Brothers-Reprise, A & M Records, Dot, Capitol, Liberty, and such minor companies as White Whale. Every other top disc firm, such as Columbia, RCA Victor, and Decca, maintains an A & R department sensitive to the musical moods of the West Coast.

And, simultaneously, more new personalities in the

137

INSIDE POP

world of recordings begin on the West Coast. In this they are following the sandy, sunflecked path of the Beach Boys, who are as Californian as oranges.

The Beach Boys are, of course, five handsome guys: Brian Wilson (twenty-six, hazel-blue eyes, 6'2"), Dennis Wilson (twenty-four, blond, blue-eyed, 5'9"), Carl Wilson (twenty-two, dark brown hair, blue eyes, 5'10"), Mike Love (twenty-seven, blond, blue-eyed, 6'1"), and Alan Jardine (twenty-six, blue-eyed, 5'5"). Their record sales are spectacular: as of mid-1967 they had sold fifteen million singles in four years. Eight out of thirteen albums have earned gold records for sales equivalent of one million dollars per album.

"We're only part of a worldwide pop movement in which millions of people have a part to play," says Carl Wilson. "Fans who come to see us, spending precious dollars, record buyers who properly expect value for their support and expense, and all the thousands of people behind the scenes in the industry. We are simply the frontmen for what's happening. Without each other, we'd all be dead. And going way back, without our parents' support we'd never have gotten off the beach."

In a way, the beach and the sun, help explain the Beach Boys—for they have portrayed in song, name, and image the youthful California scene.

It all started in Hawthorne, a dot of a town, five miles from the Southern California beaches where the breakers roar, and the surfers ride their gleaming, lacquered boards. Until 1961, there was nothing special to distinguish the small five-room Wilson home in Hawthorne. It looked like all the other bungalows where families lived their typical suburban lives and clustered around their TV sets.

THE BEACH BOYS

Here lived the three Wilson boys, Brian, Dennis, and Carl. They seemed just average guys—going to school, surfing, playing football, drag-racing, and taking local girls to dances, parties, and drive-in movies. They and their future partners, Mike Love, a cousin, and Al Jardine, a school chum, shared little in common and usually went their separate ways. Even Brian, Dennis, and Carl, living under the same roof, saw little of each other.

Brian entered college, studied music, and in his spare time staged jam sessions with Mike, Al, and some of his other friends. The enthusiasm generated at sessions infected Carl (guitar), Dennis (drums), and Al (guitar).

By 1961, the Wilson home had turned into a den of do-it-yourself din and clamor. In time the noises became identifiable as vocal and instrumental harmonies with a rock beat. The Hawthorne hopefuls were now dreaming of becoming a professional pop music group.

One day Dennis, Hawthorne's champion surfer, raced in from the beach with an idea that Brian should write a song about the fab new surfing craze. Brian's imagination caught fire. He and Mike began to sweat out the music and lyrics. But before they had time to write the number, a music publisher invited Al Jardine to come to his office to discuss a folk song recording. Al brought the others with him. Instead of talking folk music, the five boys bent the publisher's ear with a glowing description of the new surf fad and their song about it. He showed interest—not knowing it hadn't been written yet.

Brian and Mike rushed home and wrote "Surfin'." Later, during a driving rainstorm, the Wilson brothers (Brian, Dennis, and Carl) along with cousin Mike and Jardine, drove to a small recording studio in Hollywood. There

THE BEACH BOYS

they cut a record at their own expense. Carl, the only one who could pick out a tune on a guitar, provided the instrumental backing. The completed record was sold to the Candix label, and they were dubbed the Beach Boys to fit the title of the song, "Surfin'."

The disc sold forty thousand copies and the Beach Boys collected nine hundred dollars. "This early chapter of Beach Boy history has been forgotten," says Brian, "but in truth it was the simplest and most uncomplicated rise to popular stardom I've known or heard about. Consequently, there is little we can say about our long, hard bitter struggle for success."

The Beach Boys' sound fascinated Capitol's A & R vice-president, Voyle Gilmore, who signed them to an exclusive contract. Their first Capitol single, "Surfin' U.S.A.," was a smash hit of 1963, and their surfing album was one of the top-selling albums of the year.

The Beach Boys are pleasing, all-American types. They stick to an outdoor image. Their dress is California-casual —usually slacks and striped short-sleeved shirts on stage. They favor mocassins, loafers, and leisure-wear.

This California-casual-sportswear look can be seen on most of the Beach Boys' album covers. And, of course, inside, on the record grooves, you find characteristic themes. After the initial success with "Surfin'," Brian continued to follow the surfing curl with such variations as "Surfer Girl." An excerpt goes:

Little surfer, Little one
Made my heart come all undone
Do you love?
Do you? Surfer Girl?

The music for the lyrics resembles a straightaway pop tune. There's nothing in the music, or the arrangement, to suggest the sea. Later on, Brian moved to become the lyrical historian of the hot-rods with "Shut Down." Later he gave the motor-scooter industry a fabulous twin-carburetor burst of publicity with "Little Honda." A sample goes:

It's not a big motorcycle
It's just a groovy little motorbike.

The steady, unwavering focus by the Beach Boys on the California scene even includes hymns to the sun ("The Warmth of the Sun") and girls. There's nothing like "California Girls," sing the foursome. As Brian Wilson put it:

Well, East Coast girls are hip
I really dig those styles they wear
And the Southern girls with the way they talk
They knock me out when I'm down there.

The Midwest farmer's daughter
Really makes you feel all right
And the Northern girls with the way they kiss
They keep their boyfriends warm at night.

I wish they all were California,
Wish they all were California,
Wish they all were California girls!

Brian has been described as intellectually inquisitive, hip, restless, and a painstaking craftsman. Although he's leader of the group, the others can outvote him on any decision that must be made. Usually the group goes along with his ideas, plans, projects.

He represents the newest trend: a writer, performer, singer, arranger, engineer, and producer with complete control, even over packaging and design of albums.

139

"I'm very aware of the value of speaking through a song, I'm not talking of messages—just about saying what you have to say through music. This is why I get such a kick out of bending electricity and recording techniques to make them work for us. They're there to be used—maximum," he says.

In 1966, Brian gave up the grueling road tours both at home and abroad to focus on songwriting and record-producing. When on the road, a young guitarist, Bruce Johnson, takes Brian's place.

Carl Wilson plays lead guitar, the sonic anchor of today's highly amplified music. He sings, too, of course. Some say he has the biggest appetite since Charles Laughton played Henry VIII. Brian asserts that Carl has such exquisite musical taste that he'll "change any arrangement Carl doesn't like."

Recently Carl ran into trouble with his Los Angeles draft board, but was cleared of a draft-evasion charge. He said he would gladly accept a noncombatant military job. "We were put here to live," he insisted. "Killing is very evil and destructive and results in human suffering. I won't take part in the destruction of people."

Dennis Wilson plays drums and is an all-around sportsman. He enjoys fishing, racing boats, cars, horseback riding, swimming. Extremely handsome, he is considered the romantic symbol of the group. It was he who prodded Brian to write the first surfing song.

Live concerts are an important ingredient in the Beach Boys' success story. And one who figures prominently in these tours is Mike Love. With or without his red beard, his rangy figure prowls the stage, hugging a microphone and whipping the group and the audience into mutual excitement. He has a gift for clowning. He also sings bass as lead vocalist and on occasion plays guitar. He's married, and has a baby daughter, Hayleigh.

A true, typical Californian is Alan Jardine. He's typical because like many of the millions who live there, he was born elsewhere—in Lima, Ohio. He's the rhythm guitarist. Once he thought of becoming a dentist. He's neat, and smiles a lot. He is married (wife's name is Linda) and has a new baby boy, Mathew. Bruce Johnson, who subs for Brian on road tours and personal appearances (born June 27, 1944), is 5'8", weighs around 150 pounds. He wants to be a songwriter. Besides his activities with the Beach Boys, he has an income from a family trust fund derived from drug stores and canning.

The Beach Boys' songbook contains easy-going pop tunes, up-tempo melodies, and funky, foot-stomping rock. Their vocal arrangements often display an imaginative sense of design. Their sense of harmony has won them many admirers in the music business, including the Beatles and the Rolling Stones. One example of their tasty lyricism is the soft, cool, swinging sound they achieve in the arrangement of a pop tune called "Oh Caroline."

In a recent album, *Pet Sounds*, they have experimentally moved into a new area–sound effects. In the title song, "Pet Sounds," the Beach Boys do not sing at all. What you hear is strictly an instrumental, punctuated by sounds of the California landscape presumably: bells clanging, ships' horns, railroad sounds, dogs barking.

The Beach Boys are a West Coast pop music success story. And they reflect, as noted earlier, a growing native pop music and record business. Once there was hardly any pop music activity in California, in terms of an industry.

Later, silent movies prodded the beginning buds of an industry as it developed music accompaniment to its films. When sound movies came in, the West Coast became increasingly involved in the music business. Gifted composers and lyricists (such as George Gershwin and Rodgers) were hired by music departments set up in the leading studios.

Today California, with its large number of young people who buy records, and a built-in youth culture, has evolved into a leading pop music center. There are enormous outlays of capital, merchandising forces, writing talent, and recording studios. The proximity of Hollywood and TV production factories assists the California record business. California-bred recording stars sing and create for movies and TV, and that provides a lot of exposure. The surfing craze built up by the Beach Boys, for example, led to a tidal wave of beach boy and girl musical movies.

Sitting in the midst of this pulsating West Coast pop music world are the Beach Boys. They remain hyperactive. They tour, they appear at concerts and on TV, and, of course, continue to record. Some interesting notes about their recordings not found on liner notes are added by Capitol Records executive Karl Engemann. "The Beach Boys record themselves and, relatively speaking, they get along very well at sessions. As to sales, it's quite interesting that according to sales figures, the Beach Boys sell 65 per cent to the college and over-twenty market, and 35 per cent to teen-agers. Another thing, Beach Boys LP's remain in the catalog, and have consistent sales patterns for years."

Besides the regular members of the Beach Boys, one other man has figured prominently in their esthetic and corporate activities. He is Murray Wilson, father of three of the Beach Boys. He is manager and coowner of their Sea of Tunes music publishing company. He also aided in getting the group organized, and gave them the concept of their image as fresh, wholesome teenagers.

Brian, the leader-creator, is no longer a teenager, nor are the other members of the combo. The simple pop songs celebrating California-living no longer seem enough. Lately, 250-pound Brian, a compulsive eater of sweets (from whipped synthetic toppings to milk shakes and candy bars) has been writing more ambitious and probing commentary-type songs. These resemble the songs in the Beatles album, *Sgt. Pepper's Lonelyhearts Club Band* in terms of experimentalism. Recently, he even composed several semimystical hymns. Some of his recent works which display his experimenting are two singles, "Good Vibrations" and "Heroes and Villains."

Brian, a stormy and complex man, often works at the piano right into the dawn. He also does a lot of creating in recording studios—not so much of the original raw material but in the conjuring up of fresh sounds. He works hard and spends an extraordinary amount of time approving the final tapes. "Good Vibrations," for example, consumed more than six months of production and ninety hours of taping.

Though they started professionally in California, the group's way with a song has gone over big throughout the world since 1961. Today the Beach Boys, under the guiding eye of Brian Wilson, seem to be edging into more stormed-tossed waters as they try to maintain their popularity while trying "*avant-garde* pop."

BEACH BPYS PUBLICITY PHOTO

The Beach Boys

TWO LANE BLACKTOP MOVIE PROMO MATERIAL

ADVERTISING PUBLICITY PROMOTION

When in Southern California visit Universal Studios

JAMES TAYLOR IS THE DRIVER
WARREN OATES IS GTO
LAURIE BIRD IS THE GIRL
DENNIS WILSON IS THE MECHANIC

TWO-LANE BLACKTOP IS THE PICTURE

TWO-LANE BLACKTOP

STARRING
JAMES TAYLOR · WARREN OATES · LAURIE BIRD · DENNIS WILSON
Screenplay by RUDOLPH WURLITZER and WILL CORRY • Story by WILL CORRY • Directed by MONTE HELLMAN
Produced by MICHAEL S. LAUGHLIN • A MICHAEL S. LAUGHLIN PRODUCTION • A UNIVERSAL PICTURE • TECHNICOLOR®

R — RESTRICTED, Under 17 requires accompanying Parent or Adult Guardian

Ad Mat No. 401 — 4 Col x 9¾" — 550 Lines

MAT NO. 401

TWO LANE BLACKTOP MOVIE PROMO MATERIAL

PUBLICITY
TWO-LANE BLACKTOP

the cast

The Driver	JAMES TAYLOR
GTO	WARREN OATES
The Girl	LAURIE BIRD
The Mechanic	DENNIS WILSON
Needles Station Attendant	DAVID DRAKE
Needles Station Mechanic	RICHARD RUTH
Hot Rod Driver	RUDOLPH WURLITZER
Driver's Girl	JACLYN HELLMAN
Texas Hitchhiker	BILL KELLER
Oklahoma Hitchhiker	H.D. STANTON

production credits

Produced by MICHAEL S. LAUGHLIN; Directed by MONTE HELLMAN; Screenplay by RUDOLPH WURLITZER and WILL CORRY; Story by WILL CORRY; Associate Producer, GARY KURTZ; Photographic Advisor, GREGORY SANDOR; Color by TECHNICOLOR; Director of Photography, JACK DEERSON; Film Editor, MONTE HELLMAN; Unit Production Manager, WALTER COBLENZ; Assistant Director, KEN SWOR; Costumes, RICHARD BRUNO; Production Sound, CHARLES KNIGHT; Music Supervisor, BILLY JAMES; A UNIVERSAL/MICHAEL S. LAUGHLIN PICTURE.

RUNNING TIME: 102 Minutes
FILM RATIO: 2.35 x 1
MPAA RATING: R

THE STORY

(Not for Publication)

The Driver (JAMES TAYLOR) spins out of Los Angeles with the Mechanic (DENNIS WILSON) after winning a late-night drag race. The two young men head southeast on the freeway, stopping only for food, gas or a delicate adjustment on their primer grey '55 Chevrolet.

Outside of Flagstaff, they take time out for lunch at a diner. When they return to their car, there is a new passenger in the back — a girl (LAURIE BIRD) with a tear-stained face. No questions are asked; no explanation is offered. They move off.

When they hit Santa Fe, they cruise up and down the streets, looking for an unsuspecting country boy to challenge their beat-up sedan. They find him sooner than expected in a '32 Ford roadster, follow him to the outskirts of town, race him and beat him. That night the girl shares a motel room with the Mechanic, while the Driver prowls the bars.

Next day, as the roads stretch out before them with monotonous precision, they take note of a bright orange Pontiac G.T.O. The driver of the car, known only as G.T.O. (WARREN OATES), is an aging playboy with a slight maniacal smile. Each time they see him, a new hitchhiker is seated to his right.

Finally there is a confrontation between the two cars and the ultimate bet is made: a cross-country race for the pink slip title to the loser's car. The destination is Washington, D.C.

Driving is no longer a sport as the two cars speed along the two-lane blacktops, sometimes helping each other, but always maneuvering for the advantage. On they go, through New Mexico, Oklahoma, Arkansas and Tennessee, making bets and winning races along the way. They even switch cars occasionally to relieve the boredom.

As the Driver and the Mechanic await their turn at the Memphis race track, G.T.O. triumphantly moves ahead, the girl now his traveling companion. They enter the Green Mountains of North Carolina and stop at a diner for breakfast.

The momentary triumph of winning the race is dimmed when the Driver learns that the girl has left with G.T.O. A furious pursuit begins. With the Mechanic's half-hearted assistance, they find them at the diner. By this time the girl wants no more of this strange trio. She gets up without a word and leaves with a cyclist who caught her eye.

G.T.O. picks up two more hitchhikers, alters his destination, and keeps moving eastward. The Driver and Mechanic go on to another race, in another town..........

\# \# \#

All advertising in this press book, as well as all other advertising and publicity materials referred to herein, has been approved under the Standards for Advertising of the Code of Self-Regulation of the Motion Picture Association of America. All inquiries on this procedure may be addressed to:

Director of Code for Advertising
Motion Picture Association of America
522 Fifth Avenue
New York, New York 10036

711/7 (8.7) ©1971 UNIVERSAL PICTURES AND MICHAEL LAUGHLIN ENTERPRISES, INC. PRINTED IN U.S.A.

TWO LANE BLACKTOP MOVIE PROMO MATERIAL

ADVERTISING SUPPLEMENT
TWO-LANE BLACKTOP
UNIVERSAL CITY STUDIOS

When in Southern California visit Universal Studios

She's gone farther than you think! Hitchhiking her way from driver to driver... thrill to thrill!

"TWO-LANE BLACKTOP"
STARRING
JAMES TAYLOR · WARREN OATES
LAURIE BIRD · DENNIS WILSON

Screenplay by RUDOLPH WURLITZER and WILL CORRY · Story by WILL CORRY · Directed by MONTE HELLMAN · Produced by MICHAEL S. LAUGHLIN
A MICHAEL S. LAUGHLIN PRODUCTION · A UNIVERSAL PICTURE · TECHNICOLOR® R — RESTRICTED Under 17 requires accompanying Parent or Adult Guardian

TWO LANE BLACKTOP MOVIE PROMO MATERIAL

When in Southern California visit Universal Studios

You can never go fast enough...

TWO-LANE BLACK TOP

STARRING **JAMES TAYLOR · WARREN OATES · LAURIE BIRD · DENNIS WILSON**

Screenplay by RUDOLPH WURLITZER and WILL CORRY • Story by WILL CORRY • Directed by MONTE HELLMAN • Produced by MICHAEL S. LAUGHLIN
A MICHAEL S. LAUGHLIN PRODUCTION • A UNIVERSAL PICTURE • TECHNICOLOR® [R] RESTRICTED Under 17 requires accompanying Parent or Adult Guardian

MAT NO. 402

Ad Mat No. 402 — 4 Col x 9-3/4" — 550 Lines

SIMILAR AD 303
Ad Mat No. 303 — 3 Col x 9½" — 400 Lines

TWO LANE BLACKTOP MOVIE PROMO MATERIAL

When in Southern California visit Universal Studios

JAMES TAYLOR IS THE DRIVER
WARREN OATES IS GTO
LAURIE BIRD IS THE GIRL
DENNIS WILSON IS THE MECHANIC

TWO-LANE BLACKTOP IS THE PICTURE

TWO-LANE BLACK TOP

STARRING
JAMES TAYLOR · WARREN OATES · LAURIE BIRD · DENNIS WILSON

Screenplay by RUDOLPH WURLITZER and WILL CORRY • Story by WILL CORRY
Directed by MONTE HELLMAN • Produced by MICHAEL S. LAUGHLIN
A MICHAEL S LAUGHLIN PRODUCTION • A UNIVERSAL PICTURE • TECHNICOLOR®

R — RESTRICTED
Under 17 requires accompanying Parent or Adult Guardian

MAT NO. 101
Ad Mat No. 101
1 Col x 1" — 14 Lines

MAT NO. 205
Ad Mat No. 205 — 2 Col x 5" — 140 Lines

SIMILAR AD 204
Ad Mat No. 204 — 2 Col x 3½" — 100 Lines

JAMES TAYLOR IS THE DRIVER
WARREN OATES IS GTO
LAURIE BIRD IS THE GIRL
DENNIS WILSON IS THE MECHANIC

TWO-LANE BLACKTOP IS THE PICTURE

A UNIVERSAL PICTURE • TECHNICOLOR® R

MAT NO. 203
Ad Mat No. 203 — 2 Col x 2½" — 70 Lines

TWO-LANE BLACK-TOP

STARRING
JAMES TAYLOR · WARREN OATES
LAURIE BIRD · DENNIS WILSON

A UNIVERSAL PICTURE R
TECHNICOLOR®

MAT NO. 102
Ad Mat No. 102
1 Col x 2" — 28 Lines

TWO LANE BLACKTOP MOVIE PROMO MATERIAL

STREET RACING IN "TWO-LANE BLACKTOP"

Packed with all the excitement of automobile drag racing and the clandestine street speed gambling on hopped-up cars by hopped up men, the Michael S. Laughlin production in Technicolor for Universal, "Two-Lane Blacktop" comes . . . to the . . . Theatre. It stars James Taylor, Warren Oates, Laurie Bird and Dennis Wilson, and three of that foursome make auspicious screen debuts in the vehicle.

While Oates is the only one seen before on film -- he's a veteran of more than 20 years of professional acting -- Taylor and Wilson are not unknown to the public. A gifted composer and singer, Taylor rose swiftly to superstardom in the folk-rock music field with his record albums, notably "Sweet Baby James" and "Mud Slide Slim and the Blue Horizon." As the Driver of the finely-tuned 55 Chevy -- one of the two automobile protagonists of the story -- in "Two-Lane Blacktop" he gives a straight dramatic performance without any reliance on music.

Wilson, a drummer, singer and composer for The Beach Boys, and a millionaire at the age of 25, makes an impressive dramatic debut as the Mechanic. Constantly, in the film, he adjusts the motor to keep it purring at its peak of efficiency and maximum speed, and it is he who rolls on the racing slicks, replacing the regular tires, whenever a competitor is found. As with the others in the story he is known by no other name than the Mechanic.

Oates is the flashy playboy in a fairly new GTO who makes the sport worthwhile by wagering his car against that of the Driver and the Mechanic in a cross-country race with time out en route for many drag runs and the many street challenges. GTO, as Oates is known in the film, acts as his own mechanic in the thrilling undertaking.

Miss Bird -- "the Girl" - joins the Driver and the Mechanic when the latter two stop at a roadside diner for lunch. She becomes part of the action as it develops, riding part of the time also with GTO and finally, when the cars near their destination, she gets up and leaves with a motorcyclist, as simply as she had joined the others in the beginning. A New Yorker, interviewed there originally, the teen-ager was signed in Hollywood by director Monte Hellman after studying scores of applicants.

Rudolph Wurlitzer (of the musical family) and Will Corry wrote the screenplay of the latter's story. Laughlin, at the age of 32, is one of Hollywood's youngest producers. His most recent release is the critically acclaimed "Dusty and Sweets McGee."

Laughlin signed Hellman to direct after seeing two unusual westerns the director made five years earlier which were released only in France. They garnered high critical acclaim and enjoyed a unique cult following. Other of his credits include "The Shooting" and "Ride the Whirlwind."

"Two-Lane Blacktop" is rated "R — Restricted. Under 17 requires accompanying Parent or Adult Guardian."

TWO LANE BLACKTOP MOVIE PROMO MATERIAL

ROCK MUSIC SUPERSTAR JAMES TAYLOR MAKES FILM ACTING DEBUT IN "TWO-LANE BLACKTOP"

"A songwriter writes a song so he doesn't have to talk about it."

That's James Taylor's explanation for his reluctance to analyze the folk rock songs that have catapulted him to superstardom as a composer-singer.

The tall, bony-faced troubadour who makes his acting debut in the Michael S. Laughlin production in Technicolor for Universal, "Two-Lane Blacktop," coming . . . to the . . . Theatre, doesn't sing a note in the thrilling drama about street drag racers who travel the country's highways between midnight and dawn.

But music is nevertheless where it's at for the "Fire and Rain" man whose albums achieve sales in the millions and whose concerts are instant sellouts.

The Boston-born star entered the music world in the summer of 1966 as a member of a group called The Flying Machine, which disbanded a year later.

In 1968 he arrived in London and was signed to a contract, later dissolved, as a recording star for the Beatles' Apple label. Paul McCartney played bass background for the "Carolina In My Mind" cut in his first album.

Since then, Taylor's "Sweet Baby James" and "Mud Slide Slim and the Blue Horizon" albums have established him as a phenomenon in pop music.

Producer Laughlin persuaded him to try acting in "Two-Lane Blacktop" in the conviction that he was not only physically right for the role of The Driver, but that he was a natural actor. The film also stars Warren Oates, Laurie Bird and Dennis Wilson, another musician making his motion picture debut.

# # #

3 PLAYERS FROM WORLD OF MUSIC MAKE ACTING DEBUTS IN "TWO-LANE BLACKTOP"

Director Monte Hellman thought he had commandeered only two names from the world of music when he began filming the Michael S. Laughlin production in Technicolor for Universal, "Two-Lane Blacktop," which comes. . . to the . . . Theatre.

James Taylor, who plays the Driver in the tense drama of night street and drag racers, was making his acting debut after achieving superstar status as a composer-singer in the folk rock music field.

Dennis Wilson, also facing cameras for the first time, was the drummer for The Beach Boys, as well as a composer and singer who is a millionaire in his own right at the age of 25.

Then Hellman was advised that Rudolph Wurlitzer, the noted novelist who co-authored the screenplay of "Two-Lane Blacktop" with Will Corry from a story by Corry, was a member of the famous Wurlitzer musical instrument family. The director pressed the writer into service in a small part to make it a trio from the music world.

Other stars in "Two-Lane Blacktop" are Warren Oates and Laurie Bird.

# # #

TWO LANE BLACKTOP MOVIE PROMO MATERIAL

SHORTS

"Two-Lane Blacktop", a Michael S. Laughlin production in Technicolor for Universal, starring James Taylor, Warren Oates, Laurie Bird and Dennis Wilson, opens . . . at the . . . Theatre.

Monte Hellman directed the drama of night street racers from the screenplay by Rudolph Wurlitzer and Will Corry based on a story by Corry.

The new film marks the screen bows of rock music stars Taylor and Wilson, drummer for The Beach Boys, in straight dramatic roles.

# # #

There's a new way of discovering acting talent!

Singer-composer James Taylor was cast in the starring role of the Michael S. Laughlin production in Technicolor for Universal, "Two Lane Blacktop," which comes . . . to the . . . Theatre, after the producer saw his photo on the cover of his "Sweet Baby James" record album. The suggestion of rural America in the singer's face and the haunting look in his eyes prompted Laughlin to seek him out.

Although Taylor had never acted before, he agreed to do a screen test for the picture. The results confirmed the producer's hunch that the young folk rock star was the character come-to-life from the screenplay written by Rudolph Wurlitzer and Will Corry.

# # #

Warren Oates, for whom major stardom is predicted, found himself surrounded with non-actors when he began his stellar role in the Michael S. Laughlin production in Technicolor for Universal, "Two-Lane Blacktop," which comes . . . to the . . . Theatre.

His fellow stars on the male side, James Taylor and Dennis Wilson, were rock music idols, but had never delivered a line of dialogue until they started to work in the drama about night street racers.

And Laurie Bird, who plays the feminine lead, had graduated from high school only a few months earlier and had never dreamed of an acting career.

"It didn't bother me at all," says Oates, who has been a professional actor for 20 years. "As a matter of fact, the experience was refreshing. They all give fine performances."

# # #

"Two-Lane Blacktop," the Michael S. Laughlin production in Technicolor for Universal nominated as the Movie of the Year by Esquire, comes . . . to the . . . Theatre.

James Taylor, Warren Oates, Laurie Bird and Dennis Wilson star in the exciting drama of night street racers directed by Monte Hellman.

Rudolph Wurlitzer and Will Corry wrote the screenplay, published in its entirety in Esquire Magazine, from a story by Corry.

# # #

Talent comes in triplicate in the family of singing idol James Taylor, who stars with Warren Oates, Laurie Bird and Dennis Wilson, in the Michael S. Laughlin production in Technicolor for Universal, "Two-Lane Blacktop," which comes . . . to the . . . Theatre.

Taylor's sister, Kate, recently recorded her first album.

His brother, Livingston, is also an up-and-coming recording star.

The source of the Taylors' talent?

Their mother was an acclaimed opera singer who enjoyed singing for her family after she retired.

# # #

Director Monte Hellman interviewed scores of young New York and Hollywood actresses trying to find the girl who would fit the "on the go" heroine in the Michael S. Laughlin production in Technicolor for Universal, "Two-Lane Blacktop," which opens . . . at the . . . Theatre.

Not until two weeks before the principal photography began did Hellman recall a tape session in New York some months before with a 16-year-old girl named Laurie Bird. She was asked to fly to Hollywood for a screen test and a few days later she was signed to star in the film which also stars James Taylor, Warren Oates and Dennis Wilson.

# # #

TWO LANE BLACKTOP MOVIE PROMO MATERIAL

"TWO-LANE BLACKTOP" — (1—A)

Restless hitchhiker Laurie Bird waits for a car to slow up and for the Driver to invite her to ride in the Michael S. Laughlin production in Technicolor for Universal, "Two-Lane Blacktop."

(Still No. 5099-25)

"TWO-LANE BLACKTOP" — (2-B)

GTO driver Warren Oates confronts (from left) Mechanic Dennis Wilson, hitchhiker Laurie Bird and Chevy Driver James Taylor in the Michael S. Laughlin production in Technicolor for Universal, "Two-Lane Blacktop." The action-packed drama is the story of the itinerant drag race-drivers and the hopped-up automobiles they handle.

(Still No. 5099-1)

"TWO-LANE BLACKTOP" — (2—A)

Mechanic Dennis Wilson, left, hitchhiker Laurie Bird and Driver James Taylor smile as they watch a rival they passed on the road in the Michael S. Laughlin production in Technicolor for Universal, "Two-Lane Blacktop." Story is the exciting drama of hopped-up cars and itinerant drag racers.

(Still No. 5099-4)

"TWO-LANE BLACKTOP" — (1-B)

James Taylor, the gifted folk-rock composer and singer, makes his dramatic acting debut in the Michael S. Laughlin production in Technicolor for Universal, "Two-Lane Blacktop."

(Still No. 5099-12)

151

THE ROCK MARKETPLACE

Let's go surfin' with... Bruce Johnston

As we noted in our Phil Spector story last issue, Bruce Johnston was loosely alligned with a group of California hitsters like Sandy Nelson, Jan Berry, Phil Spector, Terry Melcher, and Dean Torrence. Spector had his first hit on Dore (with the Teddy Bears) in late '58, and Jan and Arnie (Dean's predecessor) had topped the charts on Arwin at about the same time. Bruce was closely associated with these performers, both as a friend and fellow musician. Johnston would often jam with various aggregations, mainly on piano, and it was in this capacity that he played on Sandy Nelson's big hit "Teenbeat" issued on Original Sound in Jul '59. Unfortunately for Bruce, he sold his writing royalty for a paltry sum, and his name was forever erased from label credit. This was just the first in a long series of events that would keep Bruce in a "behind the scenes" capacity, granting him almost total anonymity.

Being small local labels, Arwin, Dore, and Original Sound are not the easiest establishments to keep track of. Surely Bruce participated in numerous sessions, especially when Kim Fowley became involved, as Kim recorded under dozens of names for as many labels. But that story comes later...

Bruce's first known release was issued on Arwin late in the summer of '59. "Take This Pearl" b/w "I Saw Her First", was issued under the name Bruce & Jerry---probably one Jerry Cooper. Johnston's "Take this Pearl" is a ballad ripped off from the Jan & Dean early school of wimp-rock....Lots of doo-wops and heart throb lyrics. "I Saw Her First" is again a Jan & Dean cop, this time a rather lame uptempo bopper with interspersed vocals between Bruce (high voice), and Jerry (deep voice). A novelty for sure, but little more... Arwin was owned by Terry Melcher's father, and the respective publishing company, Daywin, was also controlled by the Melcher family, alias Doris Day. So here is probably where Bruce came into working contact with Terry Melcher.

The Bruce and Jerry 45 was not a hit, so Bruce reverted back to his strong points, playing piano and writing songs. His first success came in late '59 when he became involved with Ron Holden's hit, "Love You So". It was a simple, catchy song with an R'n B flair to it. The flip, "My Babe", was an uptempo rocker with a pounding boogie-woogie piano riff. The followup single, "Gee But I'm Lonesome", was written by Bruce, and boasted a more professional production. Unfortunately, this took away from the appeal of its predecessor, and it achieved only minor success. Holden issued an album on the strength of "Love You So", and then followed a string of singles. They usually followed a prescribed pattern- a ballad on one side, and a rocker on the other. As on the album, Bruce wrote (or co-wrote) many of these songs, played piano, and was heavily involved in the production. As Holden's commercial appeal faded out, so did Bruce's affiliation, but he had gained valuable writing and studio experience.

His stint at Donna led him to record a solo single entitled, "Do The Surfer Stomp", which despite (or perhaps because of) its banality, caught on and was picked up for wider distribution by Donna's parent company, Del-Fi. All in all, the record sold about 150,000 copies, and was clearly a strong regional hit. Under Del-Fi's guidance, the record was issued several times, under names Bruce Johnston, or The Surf Stompers. Instrumental versions were also released, so throughout '62 & '63 the record, in one form or another, was getting some plugs. It even traveled across the Atlantic to be issued under the group name, The Bruce Johnston Combo!

The success of "Surfer Stomp" called for an album, so Del-Fi came to the rescue with Surfers Pajama Party by the "Bruce Johnston Surfing Band", in mid-'63. Alledgedly recorded "live on the UCLA campus at the Sigma Pi Fraternity House", Surfers Pajama Party is a rather slipshod effort of instrumentals like "Green Onions" and "Pajama Party". On the vocal end "Kansas City" isn't too bad, and side one's standout is Bruce's version of "Gee But I'm Lonesome"---the song Ron Holden had done a few years earlier. It's a nice simple ballad with Bruce's lead vocals backed up by piano and drums. Side two features yet another version of "Surfer Stomp" and a good bluesy version of "Something on Your Mind". Some of these Bruce Johnston Pajama Party LP's include instead a lame instrumental album by the Centurians, so Caveat Emptor. The Bruce Johnston Surfing Band LP was re-issued a short time later with a different cover under the name The Surf Stompers. Those guys at Del-Fi would do anything to make a buck!

Musically, the Surfer Stomp LP didn't turn any heads around, but it did get Bruce's name known a bit. By late 1963 Terry Melcher was working at Columbia as a producer, so he got Bruce on the label to record a solo album. Produced by Terry, the Surfin Round the World LP almost spawned a hit with 'Surfin's Here to Stay". It is clearly the best track on the album, boasting a fine melody, Spectorish production, and pounding drums. The album is a lot more together than the Del-Fi one, but about half the album still consists of instrumentals. The vocal tracks are almost all uniformly good, beginning with the opening "Surfin Round the World" which features the Honeys on backup vocals. This move to Columbia was an important step in Bruce's career. He began to associate and co-author material with Terry Melcher, worked with the Honeys (therby bringing him closer to the Beach Boys family), and was introduced to California session musicians like Hal Blaine. In fact, the one track co-authored by Blaine here is tremendously commercial,("Down Under")---sort of like Freddie Cannon singing about Australia, instead of Palisades Park.

Midway in 1963 an album by Tom & Jerry was released on Mercury. Titled Surfin' Hootenanny, there is a strong chance that Bruce produced and played on it. Any definitive information would be welcomed.

THE ROCK MARKETPLACE

With all his solo and studio work gaining Bruce some measure of fame and fortune, he began to do work for other labels. Early in 1964, Arwin, with Kim Fowley in the producers chair issued a version of Melcher-Johnston's "Gone" under the name The Rituals. It is possible that Bruce helped out here, tho no concrete evidence is available...

Midway thru '64 Bruce did some work for Smash, who were looking for a quick album to cash in on the surf/hot rod craze. Bruce wrote and sang "In My 40 Ford", a rather lame song in a Bobby Vee Style. The "B" side and most of the rest of the subsequent album contained hack instrumental work by Steve Douglas. Then it was over to Dot where Bruce and Terry worked with Pat Boone on a great two-sided platter. Pat was perhaps the lamest singer to attempt to handle "Little Honda" but the production and backround vocals were enthralling---courtesy of course, of Bruce and Terry. "Beach Girl", a song taken from the Rip Chords 2nd lp was total Beach Boys, and quite brilliant.

Then it was time for some more hack work so Bruce joined a session band which included Steve Douglas, Ray Pohlman, Hal Blaine, Tom Tedesco, Billy Strange, Jay Migliori, Bill Pitman, Jerry Kole, and Leon Russell. Voila! A new "surf-hot rod group" was born---The Catalinas. The album, recorded in two dates, included typical cover versions of "Surfin USA", and "I Get Around", as well as some saxophone instrumentals. Then there were some Darin-Melcher compositions, and an updated rendition of Melcher-Johnston's "The Queen",(titled here, "Queen of the Hot Rods"). Overall, the musicianship is pretty good, but the putrid vocals stick out like a sore thumb. No credits are given for the voices, but they are uniformly deep-voiced and plain. Occasionally some good background vocals emerge, like on "The Queen", which is one of the strongest cuts. The album was rushed togather, which is too bad, because with a little more care (and better lead vocals), the LP could have turned out nicely. Probably the best cut is "Summer Means Fun" with its high background falsetto sounding suspiciously like Bruce Johnston.

Terry Melcher was the most consistent independent producer around in the surf/hot rod genre, and was hired to produce a Wayne Newton single. "Coming on Too Strong" (written by Gary Usher & Raul Abeyto), emerges as an excellent record, covering up Wayne's wimpiness with a full vibrant backing, and strong background vocals. This was issued late in 1964, and then early the next year Bruce released what was really the closest thing to a solo record since <u>Surfin Round the World</u> in 1963. It was issued on Jubilee by a group dubbed the Sidewalk Surfers, but was all Bruce. He wrote both sides, and undoubtedly sang lead and backup on both tracks. "Skate Board" was tight and enticing, with a strong melody accented by the highest pitched vocals since David Seville and the Chipmunks; "It started on the coast where the surfers rule/ They did it every day 'fore and after school/ Even surfer girls were allowed to try it/ Once you walk the nose you want to go out and buy it.../ Skater boys and girls are everywhere/ From California now to Delaware/ There they Go/ Watch 'em Go..." The flip, "Fun Last Summer" was a shuffling ballad, nice but not outstanding.

These releases did little to get Bruce's name up on the charts, and the Rip Chords and Rogues were both dissolving, so "Bruce & Terry" returned again with a Spectorized-Four Seasons type track, "Carmen". Wimpy, but not too distasteful. "I Love You Model T" sounded amazingly similar to Melchers previous work with Frankie Laine. Hopefully tongue-in-cheek Bruce and Terry synthesized all the banal cliches available at the moment. The spoken section sounds like Cheech and Chong vs. The Mothers circa 1966; "My father wanted me to get a Stingray or XKE like all the other kids in the neighborhood./ They didn't want me to get an old rusty car and have it sitting in our driveway./ But I didn't want <u>anybody</u> to give me my first car/ I wanted to earn it myself/ All my own/ So it would be all mine/ Mine alone/ You know, I LOve You Model T, I Do..."

Signed to Columbia as a producer, Bruce handled singer Mandi Martin for one single which made little impression to anyone. "Don't let Him Get Away From You" was a throwback to the Carol King-Ellie Greenwich style prevelant in the early sixties---this one copping much of its flavor from "Don't Say Nuthin' Bad About My Baby". "This is Goodbye Forever" was a rather limp ballad mashing the Paris Sisters, and Lesley Gore into a single unit.

"Bruce & Terry" came back with a good version of Ian Tyson's "Four Strong Winds", and a schmaltzy rendition of "Rainin' in My Heart", much inferior to Melcher's version cut with Eddie Hodges 4 years earlier. Johnston was losing interest in the Bruce and Terry act, and Terry handled most of the work on the last three singles--- usually doing simplistic covers of non-original material. Save for an overproduced ballad "Come Love" (which made Top 10 in Hong Kong!), Bruce and Terry's records made little impact by any standards. Their final opus, Mann-Weils "Girl It's Alright Now" was an attempt to modernize their sound copping riffs from the Byrds and Sonny & Cher's "I Got You Babe". Johnston's flip, "Don't Run Away" was a modest MOR ballad, which only served to certify that Bruce wouldn't have to worry about losing his high-pitched voice.

Bruce's main problem was that he could never get his own thing together, preferring one-shots to any dedicated push for himself. Perhaps this was because he came out of a highly affluent background, and the drive for success and money was not necessary. Numerous projects like solo albums, or Bruce and Terry albums never materialized, and even after declaring publicly some future activity, it often never appeared. Such was the case when Bruce visited England in May of 1966. He took an interest in Tony Rivers and the Castaways, actually jamming with them one night, and promised to produce them. Nothing ever came of that. Later that year he did produce Graham Bonney in London, cutting "Thank You Baby", a single side for Bruce and Terry some months earlier. Reviewed glowingly in the British press, the record is little more than an interesting novelty. A few nice touches are present, but on the whole it's rather undistinguished. In December '67, Bruce went to France to produce Eddie Carter for Polydor. (Eddie was the fellow Bruce had reccomended to the Beach Boys when they needed a replacemnt for Brian---a position ultimately filled by Bruce.) Eddie was in the process of forming a trio for these sessions, and I don't know if any Carter-Johnston material was ever recorded or issued. On numerous other tours, Bruce announced plans to move to England and Australia---neither of which reached fruition.

In early 1966 Bruce became a member of the Beach Boys, replacing Brian Wilson who retired from touring. Noted surf historian Gene Sculatti evaluates Bruce's contribution to the Beach Boys for TRM; "Bruce Johnston's entry into the Beach Boys came in 1966, and it found him- like Glen Campbell before him- stepping into Brian's stage shoes. A formidable task to be sure, but one he handled admirably, if we're to judge him on the basis of his contribution (bass, vocals) to the <u>Live in London</u> (import) set.

153

THE ROCK MARKETPLACE

His recorded side doesn't surface until 20/20, in the weepy instrumental, "The Nearest Faraway Place", which is notable only in that it left but one direction for him to follow is subsequent attempts up. By Sunflower, aided my Michel Colombier's fancy arrangements, BJ shapes up. "Deidre" (co-penned with Brian) seems to have inspired all the Boys; its airy expanse and wistful lyrics compliment each other in a way that is distinctly Johnstonian. Both "Deidre" and its companion piece, "Tears in the Morning" are pulled from the same strain of classic pop sentimentality; "Tears" veers toward pro soap lyrically, with the musical arrangement somewhere between Percy Faith and Van Dyke Parks. Interludes aplenty.

"Disney Girls 1957" from Surf's Up is his last official Beach Boys act, and it's lyrically the most evocative of his three similarly themed tunes. It's semi-static, faraway and irretrievable, very much a receding summer tan, full of as many irretrievable essences as you care to imagine. And it sports real Four Freshman harmonies".

It took a while for Bruce to really be considered a Beach Boy, and he could never be on equal emotional footing with the other "originals". During his first year or two with the group, he continued his outside projects like Bruce and Terry and Graham Bonney records, and often split with the group on subjects open to public scrutiny. One such subject was Transcendental Meditation which Bruce, tho initiated, never really followed, preferring "something more physical". His position as a group member became more fixed and stabilized over the years, as his work on 20/20, Sunflower, and Surf's Up gave him an outlet for his musical ambitions. He also toured with the group during the period which brought them back into the public eye again---spreading the Beach Boys magic to a whole new generation of fans.

But by the early 70's, Bruce's penchant for wandering began to take over. There was talk of a solo album, then that was scrapped. When Brother Records was getting off the ground, he was enthused about producing a "female Mary Hopkin singer called Amy". That too was shelved. Bruce also was the liason with the press throughout these years---especially in Britain---which may have seperated him from the rest of the group a bit. By early '72, personality differences, and some business hassles, forced Bruce into an uncomfortable position; Should he remain in a group where he thought he wasn't particularly wanted, or should he go his own route? He chose to leave, but the question as to whether he did so by force or by choice was never answered too clearly.

Musically, his work with the Beach Boys usually centered on ballads, which by design were made for a solo spotlight. The group felt that Bruce's writing lent itself more towards a solo attitude, so Bruce was encouraged to pursue that avenue. Towards the end of his Beach Boys days, Bruce's spotlight was his solo rendition of Elton John's "Your Song"--perhaps that's why Elton asked him to sing backup on his forthcoming album...

It's been almost two years since Bruce left the Beach Boys, and he's done little publicly to make a name for himself. During the late sixties and early seventies, Bruce made guest appearances on numerous records by Sagitarius, Spring, Cyrus, Shaun Harris, and Roger McGuinn. On the Shaun Harris LP, he helped make "Love Has Gone Away" standout, with his trademark high pitched vocals. On the McGuinn LP, his piano graced a few tracks, but again it was his vocal aid which made "Draggin" the standout track on the album.

Last year Dean Torrence's Legendary Masked Surfers utilized Bruce on some updatings of Jan & Dean cuts like "Summer Means Fun", which eventually led to an announcement of the formation of a new group, "California". It was supposed to consist of Terry Melcher, Bruce Johnston, and Dean Torrence, and the result could only have been fabulous. But after numerous rumors as to signing (Columbia, Warner Brothers, and Rocket Records) were printed and retracted, little has been heard. It seems the "California" idea has been shelved until Terry Melcher's 'solo' album is released...

An incident which has come to light bears noting here. Seems the first song Bruce ever wrote (mid 50's) was about surfing. He was watching some guy surf from the Beach, he composed the song, and later sought out the guy and told him of the song. The guy alledgedly beat him up for his artistic vision!!! Maybe that's why he's stayed in the background ever since, but now (almost 20 years later!), it's about time Bruce got his career into high gear. His relationship with the Beach Boys seems amicable---he recently joined them onstage in Madison Square Garden and ran thru a slew of "oldies" to the seeming delight of all---so that could be a starting point. A solo album that veers away from maudlin pretentiousness would be a good idea, and the debut of "California" would probable be even better! Bruce has had a hand in making a lot of great music in that past, and right now we need some new fresh 1974 music. Hopefully Bruce Johnston will rise to the occasion and give it to us.

DISCOGRAPHY

Bruce & Jerry: Take this Pearl (Johnston)/I Saw Her First (Johnston-Cooper)		Arwin 1003	7/59
Ron Holden: Love You So/My Babe		Donna 1315	10/59
Gee But I'm Lonesome/Susie Jane		Donna 1324	7/60
Everythings Gonna be Allright/True Love Can Be		Donna 1328	10/60
Who Says There Aint No Santa Claus/You Line is Busy		Donna 1331	11/60
The Big Shoe/Let No One Tell You		Donna 1335	3/61

Love You So: Donna 2111: Here I Come; Everythings Gonna Be Allright; Gee But I'm Lonesome; Susie Jane; Let No One tell You; Love You So; My Babe; True Love Can Be; Seeing Double; Do I Have the Right; You Line is Busy.8/60.

Bruce Johnston: Do the Surfer Stomp Part 1/Do the Surfer Stomp pt 2(Instrumental)		Donna 1354	2/62
The Surf Stompers: The Original Surfer Stomp/Pajama Party (E)London HL 9780		Del-Fi 4202	3/63

The Bruce Johnston Surfing Band: Surfer's Pajama Party: Del-Fi 1228: Surfers Delight (same song as Pajama Party); Kansas City; Mashin The Popeye; Gee But I'm Lonesome; Green Onion; Ramrod; Last Night; Surfer Stomp; What'd I Say; Something on Your Mind. 6/63.
The Surf Stompers: The Original Surfer Stomp: Del-Fi 1236: Same as Above, but different cover. 9/63.
"Surf Party" (also known as "Pajama Party" & "Surfers Delight") appears on Battle of the Surfing Bands; a regional album marketed by DEL-FI during 1963. Del-Fi 1235.

CONTINUED ON PAGE 22.

THE ROCK MARKETPLACE

Meanwhile, Columbia had picked up the Rip Chords, another local California act which consisted of Bernie (sometimes Ernie) Bringas, Phil Stewart, Arnie Marcus, and Rich Rotkin. Their first Columbia release was produced by Terry Melcher, and arranged and conducted by Jack Nitzsche. "Here I Stand" wasn't "surfy", but rather a well produced pop song with high California vocals. The flip, "Karen" was a simple rocker somewhat in a Buddy Holly vein. The followup, "She Thinks I Still Care" was another tightly conceived pop-rock record with some tasty lead guitar work. The flip was co-written and arranged by Bruce Johnston and Terry Melcher, and apparently featured Bruce on lead vocals. By the time the next Rip Chords single rolled around, Bruce and Terry really took over. They produced both sides, as well as writing the "B" side. On the vocal end, their harmonies and arrangements were becoming quite overpowering and distinctive. "Three Window Coupe" was the resulting smash, and an album was called for. Unfortunately it seemed that the real "Ripchords" couldn't get the album done with much speed or skill so Johnston and Melcher took over everything---from writing, to arranging, to producing, and singing.

By now the surf craze had graduated from similar sounding instrumentals into a realm of similar vocal records by the Beach Boys and Jan & Dean. The Rip Chords fit in perfectly, boasting tight musicianship, fine original songs, and excellent vocals. The Rip Chords debut LP did have some earlier recorded cuts, rather plain, but did feature strong tracks like "Hey Little Cobra" and "Trophy Machine". Nice cover versions included "Little Deuce Coupe" and "Drag City". A good, though perhaps just a bit too non-original first album.

The next single, "Three Window Coupe" b/w "Hot Rod USA" was perhaps their best effort yet, exhibiting fine vocals and dynamics. It too was a hit, and another LP was rushed out. While the first album was fairly derivative, Three Window Coupe showed a distinct talent and style emerging, and remains today one of the finest albums of the period. Lyrically, the tunes all dealt with cars, surfing, and hard times---not to mention girls. The trio of songs on side one that run: from "Gas Money" to "This Little Woodie", to "Hot Rod USA" are all performed perfectly, and all could have been hits in their own right. "This Little Woodie" is especially outstanding with the high falsetto soaring throughout. "Woodie" is but the first of three Sloan-Barri compositions contained on the LP, all of which are standouts. In short, a brilliant LP, and one which certainly stands the perverbial test of time.

The Rip Chords success gave the Johnston-Melcher team room for expansion, so they created the team of Bruce and Terry. For their debut effort, released early in '64, they chose a Brian Wilson composition, "Custom Machine". Here is the entire essence of the vocal surf genre compacted into 2:00 of brilliant sound. They were so sure of success that they didn't even bother to hack out a "B" side---instead they took an instrumental track off the few-years-old Bruce Johnston Columbia solo LP! But chart success was not easily won, although the record did reach #85 nationally. Determined, Bruce and Terry bounced back with a Sloan-Barri composition, "Summer Means Fun". Amazingly enough, the song was the equal of the tremendous "Custom Machine", and did get some strong airplay. After some two months of push 'n play, the record topped at #72. Unfortunately, it didn't break nationally, and the Bruce and Terry team (probably surprised and depressed at their lack of success) retired for a while.

Meanwhile things were moving fast at Columbia, and a new Rip Chords 45 was issued. Once again, the Johnston-Melcher team chose two Sloan-Barri songs, "One Piece Topless Bathing Suit" and "Wah Wahini". Both were strong tracks, but neither could do better than the lower reaches of the Hot 100. In early '65, what was to become the final Rip Chords single, was issued. "Don't be Scared" was good, although a blatant cop of "Little Honda", and the flip was non-descript instrumental.

Although given label credit as arranger, writer, or producer on most of these tracks, one gets the feeling that Terry Melcher was the instigator, and Bruce was more of an all-around session-man. It's also hard to understand why after only two non-hit singles, the Rip Chords were folding up. Perhaps the English Invasion was really wiping the surf sound off the charts, but the Beach Boys (and even Jan and Dean to some extent) moved with the times, and continued to have hits thoughout 1965.

Anyway, with the Rip Chords folding, Bruce and Terry created yet another studio name, this time the Rogues. The first release was an updated version of Buddy Holly's hit, "Everyday". Lively and energetic, the song was quite possibly recorded for a Rip Chords track, then shelved. The followup was Richie Valens' "Come On, Let's Go", which simply oozed vitality and punch. Unfortunately the Rogues' attempt to spearhead a rock 'n roll revival dissolved after these two releases.

Terry Melcher was tremendously successful as a producer, gaining million sellers with the Byrds and Paul Revere and the Raiders, during those groups most artistically fruitful periods. (Bruce was rumored to have helped out on the Raiders LP's, as the group was often changing personnel.) Terry also undertook numerous single production jobs at Columbia, including: Emil 'O Connor, Frankie Laine, Eddie Hodges and Doris Day. Most of these sessions utilized Jack Nitzsche as arranger or conductor, and conceivably used Bruce as a session musician. In fact, the final Columbia Eddie Hodges 45 was a version of "Rainin' in My Heart", later done by Bruce and Terry. On most of these records, Bruce's participation, if any, was minimal---altho he might be responsible for the fine backup vocals on Doris Day's "Move Over Darling".

THE ROCK MARKETPLACE

Bruce Johnston Discography, con't from previous page.

Bruce Johnston: *Surfin Round the World*; Columbia 2057/8857; Surfin Round the World; Makaha At Midnight; Down Under; Cape-town; Biarritz; Jersey Channel Islands-part 7; The Hamptons; Virginia Beach; Surf-A-Nova; Hot Pastrami, Mashed Potatoes, Come on to Rincon-Yeah!!!; Malibu; Surfin's Here To Stay.   8/63.

Rip Chords:
Here I stand/Karen	(71062/70935)	(#51)	Columbia 42687	2/63
Gone/She Think I Still Care	(71367/71322)	(#88)	42812	8/63
Hey Little Cobra/The Queen	(71578/71577)	(#4)	42921	11/63
Three Window Coupe/Hot Rod U.S.A.	(71670/71673)	(#28)	43035	5/64
One Piece Topless Bathing Suit/Wah-Wahini	(71936/71914)	(#96)	43093	8/64
Don't Be Scared/Bunny Hill	(72177/72178)		43221	3/65

Hey Little Cobra & Other Hot Rod Hits: Columbia 2151/8951; Hey Little Cobra; Here I Stand; The Queen; 409; Trophy Machine; Gone; Little Deuce Coup; 40 Ford Time; She Still Thinks I Care; Shut Down; Drag City; Ding Dong.   2/64
Three Window Coupe: Columbia 2216/9016; Three Window Coupe; Bonneville Bonnie; Gas Money; This Little Woodie; Hot Rod USA; Old Car made in '52; Surfin Craze; Beach Girl; My Big Gun Board; Surf City; Summer USA; Big Wednesday. 7/64
"Here I Stand" & "She Thinks I Still Care" appear on Columbia Sampler: The Swingers: CSP 176.
"Red Hot Roadster" (a fine middle period cut) appears on A Swingin Summer; HBR 8500.

Bruce & Terry:
Custom Machine/Makaha at Midnight	(71618/71356)	(#85)	Columbia 42956	1/64
Summer Means Fun/Yeah	(71809/71659)	(#72)	43055	6/64
Carmen/I Love You Model T	(72009/71641)		43238	3/65
Four Strong Winds/Raining in My Heart	(72623/72616)		43378	9/65
Come Love/Thank You Baby	(112317/112318)		43479	1/66
Girl, It's Allright Now/Don't Run Away	(113532/113533)		43582	4/66

Rogues:
Everyday/Rogers Reef	(71798/72162)	Columbia 43190	12/64
Come On, Let's Go!/Roger's Reef Part 2	(72248/72249)	Columbia 43253	4/65

The Rituals: This is Paradise/Gone   Arwin 127   11/64
             Gone/Surfers Rule   Arwin 128   4/65
Kustom Kings: In My 40 Ford/Clutch Rider   Smash 1883   5/64
    Kustom City USA: Smash 27051/67051   6/64
Catalinas: Fun Fun; Ric 1006   8/64
           Boss Barracuda/Surfer Boy   Ric 164   7/65
Pat Boone: Little Honda/Beach Girl   Dot 16658   8/64
Wayne Newton: Coming On Too Strong/non BJ/TM Cap. 5338 11/64
Sidewalk Surfers: Skateboard/Fun Last Summer Jub. 5496 2/65

Also: Beach Boys from 1966-1972.

Mandi Martin: Don't Let Him Get Away From You (72164)/ 4/65
              This is Goodbye Forever (72163) Col.43254
Graham Bonney: Thank You Baby/(non BJ) UK Col. DB 8111 1/67

Misc. Appearances on:
Cyrus: Elektra 74105   Sagittarius: Col. 9644
Spring: UA 5571   Shaun Harris: Cap. 11168
Roger Mc Guinn: Col. 31946

Mike Clifford: Bruce wrote the "B" side of the following:
    Barbara's Theme/Don't Make Her Cry   UA 794   11/64
"Don't Make Her Cry" also appeared on Mike Clifford's LP:
For the Love of Mike: UAL/UAS 3409/6409   2/65

-22-

FUSION 1972

THE BEACH BOYS
BILL REED/RANDAL HIGH

...wonderful things for the human spirit.

Whatever happened to The Desi-Rays? Ruby and the Romilars, Urban Sprawl, The Triffids and Axe-Meat? It's assumed most of the groups have broken down into their component parts? But if you're wondering about Carl and the Passions, who played for your Ritchie Valens Memorial sock hop, New Year's Eve, 1961, in Long Beach, California—they're still around. Intact. As the world's longest-lived rock group. The Beach Boys!

And from that auspicious beginning, followed hit single after hit single, until they reached the crest of the surfin' wave around 1966. But with the incursions of psychedelia, The Beach Boys' celebrity began to wane. Increasingly, since then, their records have gone begging. And yet, perversely (and inversely) enough, their music has gotten better. Much better!

1970 found them perhaps a little long in the tooth; it's hard to recall when last they actually had a hit record. And seeing as how hip capitalism is still capitalism, their former label, Capitol, has "prudently" deemed it necessary to lop off its list many of their once lucrative albums. Still, rumor has it Reprise had to ransom Trendy Lopez and Nancy (she hasn't had a hit in years) Sinatra's father for the cash outlay to lure the group to their label. Could it be that Warner/Reprise (a division of Kinney Leisure Systems) knows something that EMI-Capitol doesn't?

Sunflower, their first album for Reprise (Brother/Reprise), may have sold slightly fewer copies than their friend Van Dyke Parks' *succes d'estime*, *Song Cycle*. But critical response in the right places ran from respectful to reverent.

Better still, a recent coast-to-coast tour (which climaxed at New York's Carnegie Hall) found them, at long last, as successful a performing group as they've long been a recording unit. It's not necessarily that they now sound "gee, just like they do on records," but rather that The Beach Boys have translated their recording arrangements into a different, but equally exciting "live" sound. The group now tours with a dozen or so auxiliary musicians in order to approximate the fullness of their recording arrangements. Reed instruments now take on vocal parts to compensate for effects that, on record, are achieved by complicated over-dubbing processes.

One would have expected their opening number at Carnegie to be something "easy." But bravely, they began with the seemingly impossible-to-perform "Heroes and Villians" (from *Smiley Smile*). It almost worked, and, as it stood, was a minor musical miracle. The wild applause that followed the performance of this V. D. Parks/Brian Wilson composition appeared to catch the "Boys" by surprise. Counter to expectations, the audience that night wasn't a half-full house of New York's aging oldies-but-goodies crowd. Instead, Carnegie was SRO with a youthful gathering fully initiated into the musical world of The Beach Boys. Not even a titter during the salute to The Four Freshman number, "Their Hearts Were Full of Spring."

The concert was a capsule history of their recording career, which generally can be divided into two sections: before *Pet Sounds* (bPS), when the group was hot, sale-able, relatively limited, but musically quite bright; and after *Pet Sounds* (aPS) which in turn marks diminished record sales, a flummoxed, puzzled Capitol Records and increasing "experimentation" which has reached a high-water mark with the release of the group's brand new *Surf's Up*, their second album on Reprise.

So, at the Carnegie concert, the performance moved backward in time, from their recent material (aPS), to, toward the end of the show, the great goldies from the group's surfin' and striped pants period: "I Get Around." And the Carnegie contingent seemed equally satisfied with the old and the new: "Heroes and Villians" (a berserk "Good Vibrations," the lyric an urgent mind-blown story lost in the telling); "Cool Water" (Moog droplets *everywhere*); "Vegetables" (an organic goof); "Good Vibrations" (in its context—1967—a prelude and fugue for Sunset Strip, and a blessing on the summer of love from its voice from the Past); "Aren't You Glad" ("I'd love just once to see you in the nude."); "California Girls" (which at least in part motivated the migration to the summer of love);

FUSION 1972

BEACH BOYS

"Surfer Girl"; and "It's About Time." In addition, Mike Love led the group through a shitkickin' rendition of Merle Haggard's "Okie from Muskogee." The concert ended on such a high note of commotion and enthusiasm you'd have thought The Beatles were back together again.

Has there ever been another instance of a group packing so much authority after such a long streak of foundering record sales? In a field where usually you're only as hot as your last hit record, The Beach Boys are anomalously and blissfully oblivious to petty commercial considerations.

Advanced as it is, *Sunflower* is still readily identifiable as a Beach Boys album. A careful listener will find himself tracing a road backward to the group's earliest culture-bound surfin' and hot-rod sides. *Little Deuce Coupe*, the fourth in their sixteen album catalogue, gave clear evidence the "Boys" were intent on breaking away (*vide*, "Break Away," Capitol single No. 2530) from endless variations on their one good trick: providing a background music suitable for Southern California teeners living out their idea of the good life. On "Coupe" the rhythm section was suddenly much more flexible, and even though the lyrics still concerned themselves with topics endemic to Southern California, they also began to hint at good-natured self-parody. Many of the stylistic devices The Beach Boys first explored on that fourth album still sound daring eight years after the fact. A tone poem to a car that looks so very much better than it actually performs, "No Go Showboat" ends on a note of voices spiraling wildly heavenward, an angelic white noise dissolving into the ether of Plato's Heaven. This three-octave leap, effected by a variable speed tape recorder, sounds today just as audacious, puckish, and musically adventurous as it did in 1964.

Brian's fascination with the once-popular vocal group, The Four Freshman, is legend. That pioneer of overdub, Les Paul, also was an influence. For even in The Beach Boys earliest recordings they were reaching for that Sistine Chapel Choir effect that still characterizes their most recent recordings. (The Four Freshman produced by Les Paul, with Mary Ford on joints?)

Multiple-tracking has long been a standard practice in the production of rock recordings. The Beach Boys, though, are the only group that has thoroughly explored the potentialities of richly multi-layered vocal tracks. Actually, many of their sides come quite close to being purely *a cappella* productions, with a heavy underlay of percussion added to sustain the illusion of denser orchestration. You think you're hearing instruments, but it's actually voices. For example, in the title tune on *Friends*, the instrumentation is bass and drums, and little else. But it comes on like a full band. What you hear is an organic unity, but it's actually made up of interweaving musical lines of vocals: voices as voice, voices as non-sense-syllable background, voices as counterpoint and augmentation, even voices as percussion, interweaving unobtrusively and angelically throughout the whole treble range.

The Beach Boys are a testament to the wonders of recording technology, but this strong emphasis on the human voice gives them the chance to move out from under the overproduction pall that hangs over much cybernetic recording studio wizardry.

Ironically, considering the emphasis on vocal pyrotechnics, lyrics have never been The Beach Boys' strong suit. So when Bob Dylan came along to rearrange the priorities of lyric content, they began to lose public favor. But there was no honest way for them to re-trench. How sing of a social problem when you've never seen one in the relative vacuum of Southern California? How effect a turn to Byronically introspective lyrics after a life of painless, ocean-sprayed hedonism? And how evoke the milieu of blacks after having grown up in the environs of Waspy Hawthorne, California?

Eight years ago when they were singing:

> When some loud bragger tries to
> put me down,
> And says his school is great,
> I tell him right away,

> 'Now whatsamatter buddy,
> Ain't you heard of our school?
> It's number one in the state.'

they were trafficking in direct experience. School loyalty loomed large in their ethical code, so what could be more natural then to write a song about it? In their direct musical retelling of life experience, they avoided the temptation of turning the banal into the metaphysical.

Things in 1971 aren't much different. It's obvious most of the songs on *Sunflower* were triggered by personal incidents. Of course, school loyalty has been superceded by a concern for universal love. But Brian doesn't insist that it must rule the world; he simply tells the listener to his song, "This Whole World," that "Late at night I think about the love in this whole world/ Lots of different people everywhere."

Since their artistic breakthrough, *Pet Sounds*, all the members of the six-man group have penned some remarkably good lyrics, but the songs always reflect the sphere of their personal activity. None of their songs are "relevant" in the same sense that Bob Dylan's earlier lyrics were. Curiously enough, Dylan's lyrics are now beginning to sound a lot like those of The Beach Boys.

Pet Sounds also marked the beginning of five years of recording activity that contain a number of mysteries within enigmas that continue unsolved by even some close associates. No one, for example, has ever been able to explain adequately the year-and-a-half wait between the successful *Pet Sounds*, and the release of their next album, *Smiley Smile*. Their giant single, "Good Vibrations," hit the top of the charts, then disappeared. No album followed to capitalize on the success of "Vibrations," and a follow-up single, "Heroes and Villians," was almost three-quarters of a year in arriving. When *Smiley Smile* (an evisceration of the long-awaited *Smile* album) did at last arrive, it was hoped that the album would help the group regain some of its former power. In its own oblique way *Smiley Smile* was even more experimental that the music of The Rolling Stones or The

Beatles, the prime usurpers of The Beach Boys' following. The album bombed, however. It was too long in arriving. By the time the so-called summer of love (and *Smiley Smile*) hit, the group had long been given up on. To the body of the record-buying public they were "irrelevant," and five years later they are still not deemed "serious."

During the span between *Pet Sounds* and *Smiley*, they were not only on the verge of splitting with an uncomprehending Capitol Records, but, rumor had it, were almost ready to disband the group itself. Viewing the on-stage compatability of the group in 1971, it seems unlikely that there ever really was much danger of the group splitting up. After all, how do you go about dissolving a group consisting of three brothers, a cousin, and a next-door neighbor? Nevertheless, albums which once bore the legend "Produced by Brian Wilson" now read "Produced by The Beach Boys," so some internal power struggle of sorts must have been occuring. Apparently everybody won!

The four albums that followed in the wake of *Smiley Smile* are the works of a musical collective that provides an expressive outlet for each of its members. This is especially true of their preceding two albums, *20/20* and *Sunflower*, and of *Surf's Up*. The Beach Boys are moving into their classical period; a phase of their career where the musical direction is clearly established. And while this may seem a rather pretentious overview of "mere" rock, I fully believe Brian and his brothers are about to usher "lowly" pop music into an unprecedented realm of respect and achievement.

While it is true that their more up-tempo material on *Sunflower* and *Surf's Up* is as eminently danceable as the very best of rock, there is something about this same music that almost forces the listener to regard it as something more than serviceable dance music. There is a depth-involving and, at the same time, elusive shifting center in the compositions on their three latest albums that beckons the listener in a manner much more typical of classical modes.

I've played *Sunflower* for a diverse group of people; the response is invariably the same: first, there is a marked relaxation, and secondly, a giving up of the body to the vibrations of the music. It's almost as if The Beach Boys have discovered a physics of musics and

DISCOGRAPHY (all are Capitol albums except where noted): *Surfin' Safari* (1808); *Surfin' U.S.A.* (1890); *Shut Down* (1918); *Surfer Girl* (1981); *Little Deuce Coupe* (1998); *Shut Down Vol. II* (2027); *All Summer Long* (2110); *Christmas Album* (2164); *In Concert* (2198); *Beach Boys Today!* (2269); *Summer Days and Summer Nights* (2354); *Beach Boys Party!* (2398); *Pet Sounds* (2458); *Best of* (2545); *Best of Vol. II* (2706); *Smiley Smile* (Brother 9001); *Deluxe Set* (2813); *Wild Honey* (2859); *Friends* (2895); *Best of Vol. III* (2945); *Stack O'Tracks* (2893); *20/20* (133); *Sunflower* (Brother/Reprise 6382); *Surf's Up* (Brother/Reprise 6453).

sound. The liner notes for *Sunflower* finds the writer refering to "*total* stereo capturing the ambiance of the room and the sound in perspective as heard naturally by the ear. Although more difficult to perfect, this type of recording is far more satisfying to hear, as will be demonstrated upon playing this album." Sounds more like an ad for Chinese tea than for a recording; it is still true that when I play *Sunflower* not only the glasses in the kitchen, but also a few chakras and my inner ear are resonanted.

Their on-again, off-again association with Van Dyke Parks is especially apparent on the last three Beach Boys albums. There is much about them that recalls Parks' *Song Cycle*. But the music made by The Beach Boys today still accurately reflects their earliest recordings, and it is much more buoyant, and so much less forboding than *Cycle*.

In turn, both Parks and The Beach Boys bring to mind the compositional methods of American composer Charles Ives, who drew widely upon a variety of sources—hymnody, folk music, ragtime, and light opera (among other referents)—for his eclectic, but always personal and disciplined works. Similarly, The Beach Boys frame their quotations paralleling Ivesian techniques.

The history of American pop music abounds with instances of attempts to lend to the music a respectability long-associated with the music of the European concert hall. The most famous example of this is George Gershwin's *Rhapsody in Blue*. And Gershwin's "jazz symphony" more or less established the guidelines within which countless other pop/classic fusions would be conducted. The one constant was that there had to be a cumbersome symphony orchestra sawing away, whilst in front the pop or jazz group would continue to do its "thing." This was the *modus operandi* behind all those Modern Jazz Quartet Third Stream recordings of a decade ago, and one can still hear the same philosophy in operation on a number of ludicrous Moody Blues albums. The Beach Boys, with their self-confident "grass roots" approach to formalism, have evolved a form of pop music classicism that is much more successful than any of the above-noted two-way bastardizations. "Successful" if for no other reason than that you can still boogie to it!

If beauty, skill and care have gone into the creation of the previous sixteen albums, that is even more evident on their recently released second Reprise album. The apparent premise of this latest work is the creation of a permanent musical statement, an increasingly rare commodity in rock music. "Surf's Up," Brian's fabled but long-unreleased masterpiece, is simply all that it's been cracked up to be. Throughout the album, the Moog is used artfully and sparingly. "Long Promised Road," "Until I Die" and a quasi-commercial for clean water, "Don't Go Near the Water," contain all the dedication and craftsmanship of a lunar launch.

The Beach Boys have less politico-sociological significance than any other act in the rock pantheon. If there is an extra-musical consideration hidden in there somewhere, it must simply be that a little bit of Transcendental Meditation and (at one time?) a lot of acid—all catalyzed by the California sun—can do wonderful things for the human spirit.
END

THE ROCK MARKETPLACE

The Rock Marketplace $1-

THE BEACH BOYS

Where are they going?
(and where have they been?)

Beach Boys 'come back'? Darling, they never left!!

A Selective History of **British r'n'b**

✲**Flower Power's** final hours✲

Red-Bird Goldies!

THE ROCK MARKETPLACE

THE BEACH BOYS

INTRODUCTION:

A musical career as lengthy and varied as that of the Beach Boys is a tough one to examine within the space of a few pages. So contrary to last issue's detailed examination of Jan & Dean, our editorial comments on the Beach Boys career will be decidedly less verbose, and divided into four distinct sections. First comes some random observations via this introductory section. Then comes Gene Sculatti's "Appreciation of the Beach Boys", which consists of impressions and images called to mind during a few days in July 1974. A detailed discussion of Brian's non-Beach Boys work follows, and the whole package culminates in a collector's orientated annotated Beach Boys discography.

Perhaps the reason we have chosen four sections is because the Beach Boys career can be divided into four distinct musical eras: the early 1963-'65 hit-surfing-hot rod period; the more serious, artistically acclaimed Pet Sounds-Smile '66-'68 era; the transitional, Capitol-fighting 1968-'70 years; and the modern, searching-for-inspiration 1970-'74 span.

One constant remains fixed throughout all these years: the influence of Brian Wilson upon the group. In no other modern pop-unit of note does one member play such an important and all-encompassing role. Musically, spiritually, economically, and emotionally, Brian Wilson has shouldered the responsibilities and received both the praise and criticism. I do not pretend to know Brian personally, (nor do I wish to downgrade the contributions of the rest of the group or family), so I state outfront that the opinions and ideas discussed here are conceptions (not facts, for sure) formed by reading other people's words, and more importantly by listening to, and following the development of Beach Boys music over the years.

Realistically, Brian's musical creations (and hence those of the Beach Boys), have always had to compromise. The group, especially during the mind and soul expanding 1966-'68 years wanted to break down all barriers, yet had to work within the given record-company marketing structure. Brian once stated that he would never record material specifically because he knew it would make money or be a hit. ("I've never written one note or word of music simply because I think it will make money.") Yet without commercial success, he wouldn't be able to pursue his goals. Perhaps that's what once made him say: "I don't like to plan our future more than a couple of months ahead. Meanwhile we'll do more beat ballads like 'I Get Around' and 'When I Grow Up (To be a Man)'. But when a new fad comes along, we'll be the first to ride it." (Both quotes attributed to Brian from Teen Set #1, 12/64.) Of course I'm not holding Brian to something attributed to him a decade ago, but it is obvious that Brian has been a person with heavy and serious pressures bearing down on him from many different directions--- and this has to make it incredibly hard for someone to decide upon a direct course and follow it through.

In deciding which direction to go, one's life (and accompanying musical creations) has to deal with the always-present compromises and contradictions of external realities. Some have said that if Brian could live in a protected environment, and create without external pressures, his work would astound us all. Yet Brian seems to have thrived on "competition" (and the fine line between competition and pressure is indeed thin). For instance, there is no doubt in my mind that some of the most adventurous and successful pop music was created during the '65-'68 years. My guess is that Brian and the Beach Boys were all caught up in the groundswell of great leaps forwards. Without the new recordings by the Beatles, Procol Harum, Jimi Hendrix, whatever...,Brian may never have been spurred on to creating Pet Sounds and Smile: "When I hear really fabulous material by other groups, I feel really small... Then I just have to create a new song to bring me on top. ...I do my best work when I am trying to top other songwriters and music-makers." (Teen Set 12/64.) Isolation or confrontation??? More contradictions. Maybe that's why Brian has been so idle the last few years---no competition---no musical inspiration to spur him on.

It's a sad commentary when "Surfin' USA" is bullet-ing up the charts and the Endless Summer LP re-package is Top 10. Not that all that stuff isn't great and fun and exciting to listen to on its own terms, but where does that put Brian and the group? If that stuff is what success is based on, then why not junk all the rest?? Why was all the pain and toil and anguish and money and emotional turmoil necessary??? For "Surfin' USA"???? No way.

It's a rare gift when a musical creator can move millions with his work, and "Surfin' USA" is just a minute example of his talents. To have Brian and the group once again typed or pressured into this era would be a sad and dismal direction to pursue. But yet, in the long run, it just may spark Brian to get up and create some new masterpieces. Shit, if there's no one else to compete with, or outdo, he'll compete with himself. He'll show those assholes what it's all about!

"My ideas for the group are to combine music that strikes a deep emotional response among listeners, and still maintains a somewhat untrained and teen-age sound. I depend upon harmonics more than before, and fuse it with a rhythm and a modern approach in production." Write on Brian, and welcome home...

by Alan Betrock

"THE MEN AND MACHINE HAD GIVEN FAIR WARN/THEY'D SET A NEW RECORD THAT WARM AUGUST MORN..."*

An Appreciation of The Beach Boys
by gene sculatti

One of the great things about discussing the Beach Boys is that nobody's got it all covered. As fans, none of us have the whole story down to ever last detail, which means there's room for infinite conjecture about why they did what they did at such and such point. Despite the acknowledged facts (that they maybe wrote the "all time greatest song" in "Don't Worry Baby", "I Get Around" or a dozen others), everybody has their own favorite reasons for liking the affable "brawny, suntanned fivesome". It all boils down to individual nuances and conceits that, added up, make their music something just a little bit different.

NOW THAT EVERYTHING'S BEEN SAID

Like, the triumph of Beach Boys Party! Back in '65 they loosened up more than most groups of 1974, cavorting with oldies like "Alley Oop" and "Mountain of Love", goofing on themselves ("I Get Around", "Little Deuce Coup") and, in an age when everybody else was paying homage to the Poet of Our Times in silk-spun folkrock, they tackled "The Times They Are A-Changin'" and destroyed Dylan. Byran Ferry's got nothing on the brawny sun-tanned fivesome; when Little Al sings "and Accept it that soon you'll be drenched to the bone..." somebody splashes him with beer. What a move!

* "Spirit of America".

-3-

There's always the humor, from Surfin' Safari through the first Concert set (somebody stealing an off-key note at the close of "Graduation Day"), from the silliness of Smiley Smile to the occasional antics of the current stage-show. But most of all there's this self-cognizance, this recognition of what they are (at the start, five talented kids equal parts polite performer/wise-ass teens) that kept them from ever taking themselves too seriously. It took the Beatles half a career and a series of embarrassing adventures like the Maharishi, acid testimonials and Jesus baiting, to get to the point ('67) in "All You Need is Love", where they actually could parody their former selves.

Hell, the brawny suntanned fivesome got down to it early on (1964) on the epic "Cassius Love vs. Sonny Wilson" on Shut Down Vol. 2. Mike mimics Brian's mousesqueak, Brian belts Mike's nasalteen approach in the nose while Carl, Denny, and Al sit around in the background, making fun of how lame the whole bit is in the first place. The laughs are priceless and the end effect was devastating on fans who'd never in the history of rock 'n' roll heard their big beat idols regard themselves so lightly. Love's final "You really think you're some kind of an opera star, doncha?" sounds exactly like Eddie Haskell talking to Wally Cleaver.

> Dear Miss Stavers,
> Please print this picture of me with CARL WILSON of the BEACH BOYS. I think he's the fabbest. I would also like a pen-pal from *England*.
> Rodney Bingeenheimer
> 230 Velarde St.
> Mtn. View, Calif.

"YOU GUYS READY? LET"S MAKE ONE"

And it keeps up. Today's "Bull Session with the 'Big Daddy'" (Carl, what did you find most interesting about France?" "...The bread, I guess") serves only as filler, but All Summer Long's "Our Favorite Recording Sessions" would have to be regarded as a magnum opus; Bri-fi again attacks Love's surliness and Love, defined as George Washington by his hat, threatens to throw cuz "across the Pontiac" (Potomac or what?). More extraneous farting around follows until somebody breaks someone else's tie clasp. When the victim bawls that "I Bought it for 99¢", the offender mock sympathizes with a guileful "ya did?" that's as teen-facetious as any study hall putdown. See also the back cover pix on Little Deuce Coup; all decked out in three button suits at a SoCal auto show (palms swaying gently behind the fivesome standing by a sharp Stingray), Brian is fingering Carl's lapel as much to chide him for being such a foppy dude. Moon-equipped indeed.

Covers, of course, are a whole 'nother thing. All those critics who explained away Brian's surf paens as a result of his being too tubby to hang ten should give a look; he ain't fat, he's tall, that's all. There's five boats on the offshore smog horizon on the cover of Surfer Girl, and Love and Brian are out of step. Brian is the spittin' image of the big El himself, cuddling Marilyn in the upper left corner (inside) of Party!, but the primo graphics are reserved for Shut Down, Vol. 2, which shares the paradox of showcasing their sharpest songs and being an obvious filler set. The front pose is hard and heavy but w/ marshmallow; Mike grins a gritty smile while his hairline recedes, Carl and Al squint into the smaze, Dennis hards it up, doing the gangster lean against the door of his Ray and Brian is bemused by the whole mess. On the back, they're all tough as nails (Dennis looks like Fonzie from Happy Days), except for Carl (beatific as always) and Brian is disgusted, showing just how bored he is by the whole session and affecting an appropriately casual and apathetic casual slouch.

THE WARMTH OF THE FUN

Vol. 2. is kinda interesting in that you get the collison of two tuff strains head on, doowop and Spector, in "Why Do Fools Fall in Love"; George Goldner never heard it like this (incredible drums, can't be the same guy who wails in anguish 5 tracks later; ok, though, as Carl blows his big chance on the next album). Everybody's who's heard the Era (Candix) stuff knows Brian's roots were as thoroughly grounded in dumb Rosie & The Originals piano stuff as in the Four Freshmen (Ballad of Ole Betsy", "A Young Man is Gone", "Summer Means NewLove" etc.), but there is dumpy doowop too- "I'm So Young" obviously, a "Hushabye" that annihilates the Mystics' NYC pipes, "We'll run away" (stunning), "Barbara Ann" and "Spirit of America".

The Spector swipes begin way back (according to one-time collaborator Gary Usher, "Be True to Your School" was Brian's first foray into noisewall action); "Car Crazy Cutie" is obvious and incredible, and not the least of the beauty of "California Girls" derives from its eloquent matching of Spector space and Dion buoyancy. And there's Today, maybe the supreme Phil tribute (Eric Carmen got half of his inspiration and maybe 10% of his songs off "She Knows Me Too Well")..

Plus there's "There's No Other Like My Baby", "Then I KIssed her", and "I Can Hear Music."

There's so much to like about Beach Boys music- from the opening Okie notes of Love's vocal on "Surfin' Safari" through the disarming directness (naivete) of the conception and delivery of "California Saga" ("Country Joe will do his show and sing about li-ber-ty"). Who can forget the immortal Christmas Album or the leakage on Stack O' Tracks, or the frontspiece to the Adventurous Period, "She's Not The Little Girl I Once Knew", or whoever it is who jumps in a few bars early with "stereophonic speaker" on "Custom Machine", a move as off-handed and rockessential as that guy doing the same thing in the Kingsmen's "Louie Louie", etc. What a Gig. This friday night we'll be jacked up on the football field... (GS).

What's next for the "brawny sun-tanned fivesome" (sevensome???) is not known. Most long time BB followers are disheartened by much of the recent recordings and live shows. They surely do have talent (lots of it) of their own, but Brian seems to have the magic formula for making it all work together. We can only hope that they all get together on the right track in the (very) near future. (AB/TRM.)

Beach Boys: Annotated Discography

Surfin'/Luau	"X" 301		12/61
Surfin'/Luau	Candix 301 (also 331)		2/62

CAPITOL

Surfin' Safari/409	4777	PS	5/62
Ten Little Indians/County Fair	4880	PS	11/62
Shut Down/Surfin' U.S.A.	4932		3/63
Little Deuce Coup/Surfer Girl	5009		7/63
In My Room/Be True to Your School	5069		10/63
Little Saint Nick/Lord's Prayer	5096		12/63
Fun Fun Fun/Who Do Fools Fall...	5118	PS	2/64
I Get Around/Don't Worry Baby	5174	PS	5/64
When I Grow Up/She Knows Me Too Well	5245	PS	8/64
EP: 4 By the Beach Boys: Wendy; Little Honda; Hushabye;			
Don't Back Down	5267	PS	10/64
Dance Dance Dance/Warmth of the Sun	5306	PS	11/64
Blue Christmas/Man With All the...	5312		12/64
Do You Wanna Dance/Please Let Me...	5372	PS	3/65
Help Me Rhonda/Kiss Me Baby	5395	PS	5/65
California Girls/Let Him Run Wild	5464	PS	8/65
Little Girl I Once Knew/No Other...	5540	PS	11/65
Barbara Ann/Girl Don't Tell Me	5561	PS	1/66
Sloop John B/You're So Good To Me	5602	PS	3/66
Caroline No/Summer Means New Love	5610	PS	4/66
(Released under the name Brian Wilson)			
Good Vibrations/Let's Go Away...	5676	PS	6/66
Wouldn't It Be Nice/God Only Knows	5706		9/66
Wild Honey/Wind Chimes	2028	PS	3/67
Darlin'/Here Today	2068	PS	12/67
Friends/Little Bird	2160		4/68
Do It Again/Wake The World	2239		7/68
Bluebirds Over The Mountain/Never Learn Not To Live	2360		10/68
I Can Hear Music/All Iwant To Do	2432		2/69
Breakaway/Celebrate the News	2530		5/69
Cottonfields/Nearest Faraway Place	2765		4/70

BROTHER

Heroes & Villains/You're Welcome	1001	PS	7/67
Gettin' Hungry/Devoted to You	1002		9/67
(Released as Brian Wilson & Mike Love)			

REPRISE

Add Some Music/Susie Cincinatti	894		2/70
This Whole World/Slip On Thru	929		8/70
It's About Time/Tears in the Morning	957		11/70
Cool Cool Water/Forever	998		2/71
Long Promised Road/Deidre	1015		5/71
Til I Die/Long Promised Road	1047		9/71
Don't Go Near the Water/Surf's Up	1058		12/71
You Need A Mess of Help/Cuddle Up	1091		3/72
Marcella/Hold on Dear Brother	1101		6/72
Sail On Sailor/Only With You	1138		1/73
California Saga/Funky Pretty	1156		4/73

NOTES, RUMORS, EXPLANATIONS ET AL:

"Surfin'" was originally on the "X" label, but it may have been issued as the Pendeltones (or Pendeltons). Shortly thereafter, "Surfin'" appeared on Candix. There is also the possibility that the first record the group recorded was earlier in 1961 under the name Kenny and the Cadets. There is also a 1962 single (see second page of discog.) purported to be the Beach Boys on Dot. Until recently, this was thought to be a different group, but since Brian's earliest production effort was on Dot (Rachel & The Revolvers), the possibility now seems more concrete. These "X" and Candix cuts were later issued on numerous budget-line albums (see discog.), as well as on Capitol.

Most of the singles were the same as the album versions, but their were frequently different mixes. On many of the later singles, their were often edited down album versions, as on "Cool Cool Water". "Cottonfields" on the 45 is different than the album version, containing an extra pedal steel section. "Be True To Your School" has some very prominent Honeys vocals on the 45, and a much more powerful feel to the whole record.

Brother records only released one non-Beach Boys record, the Flame (see Discog.). However, Bruce Johnston was supposed to produce a folk-singer called Amy, and other records were almost released. These included singles by the Honeys, and the Redwoods (who later became Three Dog Night). It's quite interesting to note the almost-release of the Redwoods on Brother, because as the story goes, both "Good Vibrations" and "Darlin'" were written for Danny Hutton.

"Cuddle Up" is different on the single than album version, and "Add Some Music to Your Day" was originally scheduled to be released on Capitol. In fact there are some promo pressings of "Add Some Music" on Capitol in existence, but they never passed that stage.

Capitol has issued numerous back-to-back hits 45's and we have not attempted to list them at all. The Beach Boys have also appeared on numerous Capitol samplers, and we have listed some of those. However, as with re-issues and Greatest Hits packages, and Samplers, we have only tried to list the more interesting offers, or the ones that offer something new to the collector or fan. The same goes for material released in foreign countries. Most of the world had picture sleeves for dozens of Beach Boys singles, and each country issued their own singles, album packages, and re-issues. We have only attempted to list the records that are different, and leave it to the avid collector to follow picture sleeves and compilations from other countries. And of course if you really want to get down to the nitty gritty, almost all Beach Boys singles in the U.S. had different pressing, often with different label lettering; so if you want to collect variations on label lettering, go right ahead.

Finally I would like to thank everybody who helped put this discography together.

ALBUMS: Capitol:

Surfin' Safari: T & ST 1808: Surfin Safari; County Fair; Ten Little Indians; Chug-a-Lug; Little Girl (You're My Miss America); 409; Surfin'; Heads You Win-Tails I Lose; Summertime Blues; Cuckoo Clock; Moon Dawg; The Shift. (12/62)

Surfin' USA: T & ST 1890: Surfin' Usa; Farmer's Daughter; Misirlou; Stoked; Lonely Sea; Shut Down; Noble Surfer; Honky Tonk; Lana; Surf Jam; Let's Go Trippin'; Finders Keepers. (4/63)

Surfer Girl: T & ST 1981: Surfer Girl; Catch a Wave; The Surfer Moon; South Bay Surfer; The Rocking Surfer; Little Deuce Coup; In My Room; Hawaii; Surfers Rule; Our Car Club; Your Summer Dream; Boogie Woogie. (7/63)

Little Deuce Coup: T & ST 1998: Little Deuce Coup; Ballad of Ole' Betsy; Be True to Your School; Car Crazy Cutie; 409; Shut Down; Spirit of America; Our Car Club; No Go Show Boat; A Young Man is Gone; Custom Machine. (10/63)

Shut Down, Vol. 2: T & ST 2027: Fun Fun Fun; Don't Worry Baby; Warmth of the Sun; This Car of Mine; Why Do Falls Fall in Love; Pom Pom Play Girl; Keep an Eye On Summer; Shut Down Part II; Louie Louie; Denny's Drums; In the Parking Lot; Cassius Love vs. Sonny Wilson; (2/64)

All Summer Long: T & ST 2110: I Get Around; All Summer Long; Hushabye; Little Honda; We'll Run Away; Carl's Big Chance; Wendy; Do You Remeber; Girls on the Beach; Drive-in; Our Faveorite Recording Sessions; Don't Back Down. (7/64)

Christmas Album: T & ST 2164: Little Saint Nick; Man With all the Toys; Santas Beard; Merry Christmas, Baby; Christmas Day; Frosty the Snowman; We Three Kings of Orient Are; Blue Christmas; Santa Claus is Coming To Town; White Christmas; I'll Be Home for Christmas; Auld Lang Syne. (10/64)

Concert: T & ST 2198: Fun Fun Fun; Little old Lady From Pasadena; Little Deuce Coup; Long Tall Texan; In My Room; The Monster Mash; Let's Go Trippin'; Papa-oom-mow-mow; The Wanderer; Hawaii; Graduation Day; I Get Around; Johnny B Goode. (12/64)

Today!: T & ST 2269: Do You Wanna Dance; Good to My Baby; Dont Hurt My Little Sister; When I Grow Up; Help Me Rhonda; Dance Dance Dance; Please Let Me Wonder; I'm So Young; Kiss Me Baby; She Knows me Too Well; In the Back of My Mind; Bull Session with the "Big Daddy". (2/65)

Summer Days & Summer Nights: T & ST 2354: Girl From NYC; Amusement Parks USA; Then I Kissed Her; Salt Lake City; Girl Dont Tell Me; Help Me Rhonda; California Girls; Let Him Run Wild; You're So Good to me; Summer Means New Love; I'm Bugged at My Old Man; And Your Dreams Come True. (7/65)

Party!: T & ST 2398: Hully Gully; I Should Have Known Better; Tell Me Why; Papa-oom-mow-mow; Mountain of Love; You've Got To Hide Your Love Away; Devoted to You; Alley Ooop; There's No Other(Like My Baby); I Get Around/Little Deuce Coup; The Times They Are A-Changin; Barbara Ann. (11/65)

Pet Sounds: T & ST 2458: Wouldn't it Be Nice; You Still Believe in Me; That's Not Me; Don't Talk; I'm Waiting for The Day; Let's Go Away for Awhile; Sloop John B; God Only Knows; I Know There's An Answer; Here Today; I Just wasn't Made for These Times; Pet Sounds; Caroline No. (5/66)

(Con't on p. 8.)

THE ROCK MARKETPLACE

Brian Wilson's Greatest FLOPS

There is no person in the music business of any note who has a worse track record as an independent producer than Brian Wilson. Of the dozen or so non-Beach Boys records that Brian has directly had a hand in producing, not one of them has been a hit. In fact, I don't think that any one of them has even made the Top 100! This is quite amazing when one realizes the power and influence the Brian Wilson name had in the 1960's, and the tie-ups with major labels that each of the releases had. I'm not basing merit upon chart success (and besides Brian sold 60 million records with the Beach Boys), but it is worth noting this lack of chart success upfront for reasons that will become apparent later.

Brian's first effort is also his most obscure, hence the lack of details. What is known is that it was issued on Dot in late 1962, by a group called Rachel and the Revolvers. Both sides (see discography) were supposedly written and produced by Brian, but who else (if anyone) was involved is a mystery. It is possible that it involved members of the Beach Boys or Honeys, but those guesses are pure conjecture.

Regardless, after the first three Capitol Beach Boys releases had been smash hits, the brass decided that maybe 'this kid's got something', so they gave him the chance to prove himself. The first efforts revolved around a group called the Honeys, who consisted of sisters Marilyn and Diane Rovell, and their cousin Ginger Blake. (Being girlfriends of the Beach Boys didn't hurt either...) The first release was produced by Nick Venet (who also produced the first bunch of Beach Boys Capitol tracks), and was issued with a now-classic picture sleeve full of teased hair and smiling faces. Musically it was rather thin, and although novel lyrically, was rather wimpy. By the time the second Honeys record came out, Brian was listed as arranger and conductor, and the sound was decidedly more Spectorish. Saxophones blared, and drums pounded out a strong rhythm---the vocals on the flip even tried to portray a tough city-sound. But by now Brian was getting a bit pissed off by the lack of success, so he decided to take matters into his own hands. For the third Capitol Honeys release, he stuck an old throwaway track on the "B" side, and concentrated on the "A" side. He wrote, arranged, and produced this one, and it was by far the best one yet. It was pure Spector-inspired, especially the melody line and musical backing. Brian didn't go for the wall-of-sound Spector effect, but rather chose a more direct and simple synthesis Despite the rather weak vocals, the record holds together well, and it's lack of success must have bothered Brian considerably. Hmmmm.....

If the Honeys couldn't get a hit after releasing three singles in under six months, Brian decided he would try it again with some new names. First thing he did was to record four tracks at one session. The musicians were most probably the Beach Boys, and the instrumentation was basic and minimal--drums; saxophone; and occasional bass. Two of the four tracks didn't even bother to use guitar, which gave Brian the opportunity to use vocals in their place. Two of these tracks were issued under the name Sharon Marie (possibly one of the Honeys?), and combines Brian's two loves---Spector and Standards. The "A" side was another in his string of Spector cops and the flip was a decent updating of Gershwin's "Summertime". The other two tracks were issued under the name The Survivors, but it was undoubtedly The Beach Boys. "Pamela Jean" was a reworking of "Car Crazy Cutie", which appears on the Little Deuce Coup LP. It was Brian's closest approximation of the 1950's NYC white-group sound, with the touches of Dion and Spector quite obvious. The flips of both these releases are notable for the interesting percussion sounds, which later turned up, (and were acclaimed as "genius") a few years later on Pet Sounds. "After the Game" is an especially beautiful instrumental.

After these records flopped, Brian turned his attention to long-time friend and writing partner Gary Usher, for Usher's solo single. This was probably Brian's worst so far. Usher's lead vocals were terrible, and even the numerous male and female backup vocals couldn't help. The tunes themselves weren't so hot, and the production and arrangements were quite plain. The "A" side did have a simple string section, which probably ranks as Brian's first recorded use of strings. Brian closed out his early Capitol producing career with one final Sharon Marie record. He again went all out by writing, producing, and arranging both sides. He used the Beach Boys on instrumental and vocal backing to provide a good, solid, and full sound. But alas, no action...

This was probably just too much for Brian to accept. Here he had released seven records on Capitol in just over six months (when he was leading the hottest group in the country) and nothing was happening. None of the records were tremendous, but they were at least as good as lots of other stuff in the Top 100. Perhaps Capitol was satisfied with the Beach Boys success and didn't want their leader to have hits producing other records---i.e. "He just may run off and become his own boss..." (a la P. Spector). Or perhaps the charts were already feeling the influence on the English sound, and didn't want to make way for new American sounds. (This seems to be the flimsiest of rationalizations, for the charts throughout '63 & '64 were still overwhelmigly dominated by USA product).

The Honeys: (above); circa 1963: Ginger, Diane & Marilyn. (Left): The same trio in 1969, from a Capitol press photo.

Well, if Capitol's reasoning was to have Brian flop so he would just be content to produce the Beach Boys, then their plan back-fired. Brian went off on his own, and as an independent producer he issued three records within two months! Paul Peterson was given a Wilson-Christian song, "She Rides With Me", which Brian produced for Colpix. The record was pretty good, quite lively, especially the Spectorish drums and bending guitar notes. Unfortunately, all pressings of the single (both regular and DJ) seem to have been defective and are quite noisy and scratchy sounding. (An album pressing is rumored to be more formidable). After hearing what Colpix did to his work, Brian said Au Revoir, and went over to Warner Brothers.

165

THE ROCK MARKETPLACE

At Warners, there could be no doubts as to Wilson's influence or goals---he was running after Spector and was trying hard to catch him. This time, he made a smart move by not trying to copy Spector's vocal stars, but ratherto combine fresh California vocals and harmonies with a full, powerful Spector-type backing. He transformed "County Fair" into "I Do" for the Castells and the resulting mixture was brilliant. As a Beach Boys track it probably would have sold a million, but as The Castells, it sold perhaps 287 copies. The melody line was strong, and a high falsetto soared in and out. The backing was solid and together with intricate drumming, hand clapping, and bells featured throughout. Brian did the same for The Honeys nine-Warner Brothers-numbers-later, but it was all to no avail. He was jinxed, dejected, frustrated, and/or adamant. No more of this crappy reception for my work. So he went back to Capitol and all the executives beamed and nodded their heads as if to say "we knew it all along" or "see, we told you so".

Despite writing or helping to write numerous hits for Jan and Dean, The Hondells, Bruce and Terry, Dino Desi & Billy, and others, Brian Wilson's post-'64 production work was sparse and sporadic. (Who knows what course popular music would have taken if he had some hits...) In mid-'65 he produced his own replacement in the Beach Boys, Glen Campbell. "Guess I'm Dumb" was the result and it was quite listenable and professional. Strings, horns, falsetto, and backing vocals all meshed together nicely, but the record didn't exude any real life or spirit. It was a long layoff until late 1968 when he helped out ex-Surfari lead singer Ron Wilson and produced "I'll keep on Loving You". (In the interim, he had masterminded the Beach Boys golden era.) Brian's heart and head must not have been into this one as it must rank as one of his worst productions ever. There's a countyish flair to this boring ballad, and the vocals are just as bad. A half year later, he brought the Honeys back to life on Capitol by re-doing two old standards. The sound and feel was closest to that of early 1960's Paris Sisters, and this simplistic-naieviete set the stage for the full return of the Honeys via Spring on U.A.

By now they were down to just two, Diane and Marilyn, but when blessed with beautiful songs, tremendous production, perfect musical backing, and intricate arrangements, the results could only have been stupendous. Of course they were, as has been recounted in these pages many times. It is significant to note that when Brian's participation in the Beach Boys was on the wane, he was busy doing great work with Spring. (So any mention of a "loss of creativity" is therby rendered invalid.)

Towards 1972, Brian co-wrote a nice, moving song with Billy Hinsche which was recorded by Dino, Desi & Billy. The last non-Beach Boys work we have gotten from Brian has been a Spring single on Columbia, reviewed glowingly in TRM #3. These most recent exploits of Brian and Spring have been widely covered by TRM and other musical publications; most of the records are still available, so if you don't have them yet, be sure to pick them up.

The future of the Beach Boys, and the role Brian will play is unclear at the moment. A new studio album is being worked on at Jim Guercio's ranch, and a business tieup with Guercio seems likely as well. Brian has supposedly provided new material for the group, but the amount and quality of the material still remains unknown. It is clear that Brian, when he puts his mind and energies into something, comes out with a brilliant and extraordinary product. With so many of the sixties prime-movers returning to active chart smashes (Phil Spector, Lou Adler, Carole King, Kim Fowley, Neil Sedaka, Terry Melcher etc), it's only fitting that Brian Wilson re-join them and return to creating great music again. Whether it be with Spring, the Beach Boys, or some other entity,(jeez, how about Wilson and Spector together for a start?), nobody should really care. It's gonna be hot, hot, hot,hot---that's for sure---and that's all that anybody could possibly ask for.

THE BRIAN WILSON DISCOGRAPHY

Artist	Song	Matrix	Label	Date
Rachel & The Revolvers	The Revolution/Number One		Dot 16392	10/62
The Honeys	Shoot the Curl(Glantz/Rovell)/Surfin Down the Swanee River(BW)	(39313/39314)	Cap. 4952	5/63
	Pray for Surf(Glantz/Rovell)/Hide Go Seek(BW)	(50200/50201)	Cap. 5034	8/63
	The One You Can't Have(BW)/From Jimmy With Tears	(50832/39824)	Cap. 5093	12/63
Sharon Marie	Run-Around Lover(BW-Mike Love)/Summertime	(50609/50611)	Cap. 5064	11/63
The Survivors	Pamela Jean(BW)/After the Game(BW)	(50610/50612)	Cap. 5102	1/64
Gary Usher	Sacremento(BW-G.Usher)/Just the Way I Feel(GU)	(51666/51667)	Cap. 5193	6/64
Sharon Marie	Thinkin Bout You Baby(BW-ML)/Stroy of My Life(BW-ML)	(51905/51906)	Cap. 5195	6/64
Paul Peterson	Poorest Boy In Town/She Rides with Me ("B" side only BW)		Colpix 720	3/64
The Castells	I Do(BW-R.Christian)/Teardrops ("A" side only BW)		W.B. 5421	3/64
The Honeys	He's a Doll(BW)/Love of a Boy & a Girl(Glantz-Rovell)		W.B. 5430	4/64
Glen Campbell	Guess I'm Dumb(BW-Russ Teitelman)/That's All Right ("A" side only BW)		Cap. 5441	5/65
Ron Wilson	I'll Keep on Loving You/As Tears Go By (A side only BW)		Col. 44636	10/68
The Honeys	Tonight You Belong to Me/Goodnight My Love (Both sides BW)		Cap. 2454	2/69

Spring: UAS 5571: LP; plus singles UA 50848 & UA 50947. All from LP (Allow for singles mixes and edited versions).
Spring: (Issued as American Spring): Shyin' Away/Fallin in Love   Col. 45834   9/73

Note: This discography lists only those non-Beach Boys records produced by Brian Wilson. For his non-Beach Boys writing credits, see the Beach Boys discography elsewhere in this issue.

THE ROCK MARKETPLACE

The Beach Boys Annotated Discography, page 2.

Smiley Smile: Brother S-9001; Heroes & Villians; Vegetables; Fall Breaks & Back to Winter; She's Goin Bald; Little Pad; Good Vibrations; With me Tonight; Wind Chimes; Gettin' Hungry; Wonderful; Whistle In. (7/67).
(This album was originally scheduled as Smile; Capitol 2580; 1966, but was never released. After the album, in a totally different form was issued on Brother, it was scheduled to be released again on Capitol as T & ST 2891 with the same cuts as the Brother release. It was pressed in demo form, but never released.)

The original never-released Smile cuts were as follows: Old Master Painter; You Are My Sunshine; Our Prayer; Bycicle Rider; Cabinessance; Heroes & Villains; Do You Dig Worms; Child is Father to the Man; Barnyard; Holidays; Indian Wisdom; I Love to Say Dada (from The Water); Mrs. O' Leary's Cow (From the Fire); Vega-tables (From The Earth); Good Vibrations (From The Air); Can't Wait too Long; Surf's Up; Wind Chimes; Winderful. (A reprint of the original Smile cover appears in the TRM Book of Ads.)
Note: The first two minutes of "Cool Cool Water" contain the original vocals from "I Love to say Dada"; many other cuts released piecemeal on subsequent Beach Boys albums or singles.

The post Smiley Smile Beach Boys albums are all quite well-known and available so we have omitted track titles because of limited space.

Wild Honey:	Cap. T & ST 2859	1/68.
Friends:	Cap. T & ST 2895	5/68.
20/20:	Cap. SKAO 133	1/69.
Sunflower:	Brother/Reprise 6382	5/70.
Surf's Up:	Brother/Reprise 6453	6/71.
Carl & The Passions/So Tuff:	Reprise 2090/2083	3/72.
Holland:	Brother/Reprise 2118	2/73.
In Concert:	Brother/Reprise 6484	10/73.

(Notes: Pet Sounds was re-issued 5/74 as a single album on Brother/Reprise 2197. Wild Honey & 20/20 were re-issued 7/74 on Reprise 2166. The British version of Sunflower contains all the US cuts, plus an additional cut of "Cottonfields", which is the US single (pedal steel) version. Carl & The Passions was packaged with Pet Sounds, which was later re-issued as a single album. Holland was issued with a special EP extra. The original title for Surf's Up was "Land Locked", and the original title and label design for Sunflower was "Add Some Music".

SOME SAMPLERS & RE-ISSUES (CAPITOL):

Chartbusters '62; Cap. 1837; Surfin' Safari.
Shut Down ; Cap. 1918; Shut Down; 409.
Chartbusters Vol. 2; Cap. 1945; Shut Down & Surfin USA.
Surfing's Greatest Hits; Cap. 1995; Surfin USA; Surfin; Surfin Safari; Farmer's Daughter; Noble Surfer;
Chartbusters Vol. 3; Cap. 2006; Little Deuce Coup; Surfer Girl.
Big Hot Rod Hits; Cap. 2024; Custom Machine; No Go Showboat; Our Car Club.
Chartbusters Vol. 4; Cap. 2094; Be True to Your School; In My Room.
Big Hits From Eng. & USA; Cap. 2125; I Get Around; Don't Worry Baby.
Super Oldies; On various issues of multi-series.

Best of: Cap. 2545 1966: This is but Vol. 1; #'s 2 & 3 below.
Best of: Cap. 2706; 6/67; 12 cuts from previous LP's.
Deluxe Set: Cap. 2813; 11/67: 3-LP set consisting of Pet Sounds; Summer Days & Summer Nights; & Today!
Best of: Cap. 2945; 8/68: 11 cuts from Surfin' to Heroes & Villains.
Close-Up; Cap. 2LP 253; 8/69: Album cuts mainly from 2nd & 6th LP's.
Good Vibrations; Cap. ST 442; 2/70; LP cuts from '65-'67.
All Summer Long/California Girls;Cap. 2LP 500; More LP cuts. 8/70.
Dance Dance Dance/Fun Fun Fun; Cap. 2 LP 701; More LP cuts taken mainly from Today! & Shut Down Vol. 2.
Subsequent re-issues include the Surfer Girl LP & Concert LP on Pickwick.
And of course, the current Capitol rip-off job; Endless Summer; Cap. SVBB 11307.

BUDGET ALBUMS:

Beach Boys Biggest Beach Hits; ERA HTE 805; (1969); (Early Candix Cuts); Surfin' Safari; What is a Girl(Made of); Luau; Barbie; Surfin'; Judy; Beach Boy Stomp; Surfer Girl.
The above LP was later issued by Orbit(1971) OR 688 & Scepter-Citation(1972) CTN 18,004, with the omission of "Beach Boy Stomp". Some Era and Capitol cuts can also be found on numerous Trip re-issue LP's and 45's.

BOOTLEGS:

Two currently in circulation; Madison Square Garden; & California Surfin Music (from Princeton Univ.).

UNRELEASED CUTS:

Every group has recorded material that has not been released. Here are some of the more well known or circulating cuts; San Miquel; Good Times; I Just Got My Pay; Burlesque; (These four from late 1970 played on WNEW-FM NY when Beach Boys came by to talk---quite exquisite); "Flippety Flop" (Brian from 1969); Bobby Left Me; Bab Ba Black Sheep; Boys Will Be Boys; When Girls Get Together; Barbara; I've Got a Friend; The River Song; Holy Man and Pacfic H'way Blues; This Could Be The Night; others.

WRITTEN BY BRIAN WILSON:

There have been cover versions of B. Wilson songs. Here are some not recorded by the Beach Boys and not covered in our Brian Wilson Production article:
"My Buddy Seat"   Hondells 45 & LP Merc. 72366 Merc. SR 60982   11/64 & 2/65.
"Holly" & "Tell Someone You Love Her"   Dino Desi & Billy Reprise 698.   5/68.
"Lady Love" by Brian Wilson & Billy Hinsche   Dino Desi & Billy   Reprise 0965   11/70.
"Muscle Beach Party"   Wilson-Christian-Usher   by Anette on Muscle Beach Party Vista 433 & Super Stocks on Cap ST 2113.
"Surf City"   Berry-Wilson; "Drag City" Berry-Christian-Wilson; "Dead Man's Curve" by Berry-Christian+Wilson-Kornfeld; "Sidewalk Surfin" by Wilson-Christian (orig. Beach Boys "Catch a Wave); "New Girl in School" by Berry-Christian-Wilson-Norman (orig. Beach Boys 'Gonna Hustle You'); "Ride the Wild Surf" by Berry-Christian-Wilson; "She's My Summer Girl" by Berry-Wilson-Altfield; "Surfin Wild" by Berry-Christian-Wilson; & "Move Out Little Mustang" by Berry-Christian-Wilson; all recorded by Jan & Dean as well as covered by numerous other surf & hot-rod groups.
"The Day You Left Me" by Ray Sharpe Garex 203 1962 written by "B. Wilson"; probably Brian Wilson.
Many Sunrays songs credited to Murray Wilson may be Brian Wilson compositions or co-compositions.

MISCELLANEOUS: The Beach Boys Live In London (British Release only). The Beach Boys appeared in the films: TAMI Show & Girls on the Beach, altho most versions of TAMI Show have them edited out. They sing with Annette on "The Monkey's Uncle" which also appears in the film. They did a TV theme for "Karen", as well as commercials for TWA (in which they are shown on screen for a few seconds), and Barney's Boys Town. There was a special "Music City KFWB Promotional Copy" record pressed of "Boogie Woogie" b/w "Spirit of America" for a free giveaway. The group appears on the Ode Celebration LP and a single off the album as well; "Wouldn't It Be Nice" (Ode 66016). Carl Wilson produced the Flame LP & 45 (LP 2500 & 3500 respectively); and Dennis issued a 69/70 single in England "Sound of Free/Lady" (Stateside, and great by the way), as Dennis Wilson and Rumbo. "Lady" later was recorded by American Spring on Columbia, where the title became "Falling in Love". Dennis & Gary Usher also recorded 2 singles on Challenge as the Four Speeds; "RPM/My Sting Ray" (Challenge 9187) & "Cheater Slicks/Four on the Floor (Challenge 9202) (both 1963). They did a special Voting Spot ad which Warners put out as a promo item. Stack-O-Tracks, of course, Capitol's mid-'68 instrumental album, where you were supposed to sing & play along with the Beach Boys (Cap. 2893). The Dot 45 we spoke of was "Samoa/Lone Survivor" Dot 16354; (8/62). Murray Wilson put out an instrumental album on Capitol for which Mike Love wrote a song (Capitol 2819 LP & 2063 45). This covers the basic collector's stock; some additions next ish.

-8-

THE ROCK MARKETPLACE

THE ROCK MARKETPLACE

BRUCE JOHNSTON
Born Bruce Johnston; Chicago; June 24, 1944; 5ft 8in, 10st, brown eyes, blue hair, plays guitar; entered show business at 19; influenced by Four Freshmen; likes girls and travelling; dislikes phoneys.

DENNIS WILSON
Born Dennis Carl Wilson; Los Angeles; December 4, 1944; 5ft 10in, 10st 5lb, blue eyes, blond hair, plays drums; entered show business at 15; influenced by surfing; likes girls and money; dislikes loud people and crummy groups.

CARL WILSON
Born Carl Dean Wilson; Los Angeles; December 21, 1946; 5ft 10in, blue eyes, light brown hair, plays guitar, bass, drums; entered show business at 14; influenced by Chuck Berry; likes girls; dislikes conceited people and phoneys.

AL JARDINE
Born Alan Jardine; Lima, Ohio; March 3, 1942; 5ft 4in, 10st, blue eyes, light brown hair; plays clarinet, bass, guitar; entered show business at 19; influenced by Four Freshmen; likes Hawaii and walking at night along the beach; no specific dislikes.

MIKE LOVE
Born Michael Edward Love; Los Angeles; March 15, 1941; 6ft, 12st 2lb, blue eyes, blond hair; plays saxophone; entered show business at 20; influenced by Four Freshmen; likes movies, night clubs, parties and dancing; dislikes inarticulate girls.

SPECIAL WELCOME TO THE TRM's BEACH BOYS

With a new single tipped for the charts, a hit LP, TV dates and a nationwide concert tour — the Beach Boys have arrived — today!

4 extra pages of BB news, features and pictures ➤

FACTS COMMON TO ALL

First public appearance: Long Beach, California.
Biggest break in career: Getting a contract with Capitol records.
TV debut: Local Los Angeles station.
Radio debut: Radio KFWB in Hollywood.
First important public appearance: Ed Sullivan show and our English promotional visit.
Million selling discs: "I Get Around" and "Surfin' USA."
British hits and highest positions in NME chart: "Surfin' USA," (28); "I Get Around" (9); "When I Grow Up" (28); "Dance Dance Dance" (23); "California Girls" (28); "Barbara Ann" (4); "Sloop John B" (2); "God Only Knows" (2); "Good Vibrations" (1); "Then I Kissed Her" (5); "Heroes and Villains" (10); "Wild Honey" (29); "Darlin" (11); "Do It Again" (2).
Albums: "Surfin'," "Surfin' USA," "Little Deuce Coupé," "Surfer Girl," "Shut Down (Vol 2)," "All Summer Long," "The Beach Boys," "Christmas Album," "Beach Boys Concert," "The Beach Boys Today," "Summer Days (And Summer Nights!!)," "Beach Boys Party," "Pet Sounds," "Best Of The Beach Boys," "Best Of The Beach Boys (Vol 2 and 3)," "Friends," "Wild Honey," "Smiley Smile." EPs: "Beach Boys Concert," "4 By The Beach Boys," "Surfin' USA," "Fun Fun Fun," "Hits," "God Only Knows."
Origin of stage name: Capitol's Voyle Gilmore thought of it.
Present disc label: Capitol.
Recording manager and musical director: Brian Wilson.
Major awards: Key to the City of Sacramento, and group of the year and record of the year awards in the US.

CIRCUS RAVES 1972

beach boys

MIKE LOVE • CARL WILSON HANG TEN ON SURFIN', CRUISIN' AND HARMONIES

by Scott Cohen

THE CIRCUS RAVES INTERVIEW

Since 1961, when three brothers, a cousin and a neighbor from Hawthorne, California, got together and recorded "Surfin'," the Beach Boys have been knocking us out with ditties that reflect American culture in the past decade and a half better than any other rock 'n roll band's. Songs like "Surfin' Safari," "Surfin' USA" and "Surfer Girl" gave the Midwest farmer's daughter the most accurate picture of the Southern California beach scene imaginable, and songs like "Little Deuce Coup," "Shut Down" and "409" conveyed more information about cars than *Motor Trend Magazine*. The Beach Boys have the American scene covered: high school graduation, student demonstration, drag strips and hamburger stands; first dates and breaking up, ecology, hygiene and the right foods to eat.

It comes, therefore, as a great disappointment that Beach Boys records have not been pushed for the last few years. Often shined on, at best, as camp, and at the very best, as high camp, Beach Boys lovers have had to go on safaris of their own, hunting the cheap bins of record stores in search of Beach Boys records discontinued by the record companies.

Thankfully, however, through company maneuvers, Warner Brothers acquired from the Beach Boys' former label, Capitol, the master tapes of five

Mike Love: "Anyone who knows where there's a real cherry Woodie they'd like to sell to a Beach Boy, let me know."

CIRCUS RAVES 1972

old goodies, *Pet Sounds*, *20-20*, *Wild Honey*, and the latest two record package, *Friends* (a rare album even in its day) and *Smiley Smiles*, which contains "Heroes and Villains," "Vegetables" and "Good Vibrations," a song so pure and dazzlingly brilliant, it is like the coronation of Huey, Dewey and Louie Duck in heaven.

Circus: Is it true you've never surfed?
Carl: Not exactly. I tried it a couple of times, a long time ago, but I never was a good surfer. I could never, you know, do it very well.
Circus: Did Brian?
Carl: I don't recall. I suppose not. I think everybody tried it out, but Dennis was the one who was the good surfer.
Circus: How do you know so much about surfing and beach culture?
Carl: I think it has probably changed a lot since then. I'm not really into it now. It was just life, you know. It was just what was happening. Just like we know about other things, from friends and from being at the beach.
Circus: Like if you live in New York you don't have to be mugged to know what's it like to be mugged?
Mike: Yeah. We grew up in that Southern California environment. It was a very specialized jargon and way of not only talking but of looking and dressing and acting and there were different groups and one was the surfers and the other was the hoods or greasers or whatever you call them. We identified more with the athletic, you know, surfers, good time cruisers rather than the real heavy other kind of thing.
Circus: So your childhood was like your songs.
Carl: Definitely. It was a social thing at the time, a way of life at Hawthorne in what was that? 1961? It was something to do.
Circus: Were the people who were into surfing also into cars?
Mike: If you're landlocked you're into your car. That was about it, the whole culture set up and revolving around the A&W stand.
Circus: The A&W stand?
Mike: The hamburger stand or whatever you call them.
Circus: Which was your favorite A&W stand?
Mike There's one on Hawthorne Boulevard which the guys cruise in and out of. That and the Bob's Big Boy Drive-ins were the inspiration for "Fun Fun Fun," and the whole scene that took place there, the whole sociological interplay that went on there. It was like a real phenomenal kind of thing, definitely a whole unique condition to Southern California, or it was.
Circus: What kind of people go to Muscle Beach?

Dennis Wilson: He's the best surfer in the band.

Al Jardin: "'Shutdown' means when you win a drag race."

Carl Wilson: "There was a time when it wasn't cool to be in the Beach Boys."

MUSIC

Carl: We went to Muscle Beach. I recall a time going to Muscle Beach when there were a lot of people at the beach and we started going hysterical laughing, just standing there watching all the people go by. Every sort of person was there. God, that was a long time ago.

Circus: Which beach do Surfers prefer?

Carl: Then it was Dohini. It was really popular. That's pretty far south, near Newport. I'm not into the thing of THE BEACH anymore.

Mike: The problem with popularity is that if it gets too popular everyone leaves and goes somewhere else. It's kind of like a floating thing.

Circus: Do the best surfers get the best girls?

Carl: I wouldn't say so. The whole thing is set at the beach. Set in that outdoorsie setting.

Circus: Is it true that you found the words to "Surfer Girl" on a tablet in Hawthorne?

Carl: That's something Michael and Brian made up.

Circus: Was she more mythical than real?

Mike: No, she was definitely . . . the existing person. Her name is Judy and she lived out in Hawthorne, California, somewhat near Brian's house and he was kind of going out with her during his high school days; and later, he was a freshman in college, and he was driving down the street one day and he made up the song about surfer girl and we just started doing records then and it was one of the first songs that he wrote.

Circus: What about Rhonda, does she exist?

Mike: That was more or less a name, a covered up name, you know, a disguise rather than saying—like if you're with somebody and you're trying to get out of a bad bag with her (laughs), you're not going to, you know, use her name. It was kind of like a made-up name instead of using a real name.

Circus: What does "shutdown" mean?

Carl: "Shutdown" means when you win a race, you shut them down.

Circus: Did you once work in a gas station?

Carl: No, but Michael did.

Mike: Yep. I usually tell people I was in the oil business. Yeah, I was that for awhile and then I had a job as a sheet metal apprentice because my father and grandfather had a firm called Love Sheet Metal where they made boats and stuff.

Circus: What are some of the cars you've owned?

Mike: Oh, I've owned a whole lot of stuff, a 39 year old Rolls Royce, a '48 MG which I still have, a Volvo stationwagon I bought from Carl, I've had a Chrysler limousine (laughs), several Jaguars, one XKE and motorcycles, a Honda, Triumphs, Bonnevilles and GTO's.

Circus: What have you owned?

Carl: A '64 Pontiac, '65 Austin Martin, a jeep, can't remember the date, and a Bentley.

Circus: Is that what you're driving now?

Carl: Yeah.

Circus: Do you have a dream car?

Carl: No, I don't think I've used things like that since I was fifteen. Bentley's a neat car, but that's not it.

Mike: I like a Rolls Royce convertible. An old kind, and also a Woodie. I've never had a Woodie and I'm trying to find a cherry one right now. Anyone who knows where there's a real cherry Woodie they'd like to sell to one of the Beach Boys, let me know. I understand there's one outside covered with snow and no place to go . . . remember that one?

Circus: Do you remember the places you went cruising?

Carl: In high school we cruised, after a dance or after a football game. Oh, God, let's see, we cruised Frosty's and we cruised the A&W. That's where everybody was after school. It's the same thing as everything else. That happened to be the setting, you know, that happened to be the fascination, the beach and just sort of living in California and sort of hanging around things without it being difficult.

Circus: What do you think of the name the Beach Boys for the sort of image you're trying to project today?

Mike: I think it's great, I mean, it's a good name. It was just our beginnings. It's like changing your name.

Carl: I don't think it hurts. I think there was a time when it wasn't cool to be into the Beach Boys, you know, at a time when people thought the group was, I don't know, whatever. The thing about the group is that we come for music and that's where we're coming from and anything else isn't important next to the music.

Mike: It's only been a change for some people's heads who couldn't cut through the earlier lyrics and get into the essence of what's really going on. But once you get past that the Beach Boys just means we come from Southern California, we sing songs about surfing, we love the ocean and the outdoors and that was an appropriate name at the time and it's become a myth and a legend all of its own, blown all out of proportion, which is cool, and now it's just our name. It's become an institution.

Circus: You're the youngest Beach Boy, right Carl?

Carl: Yeah. I was just fifteen.

Circus: How old are you now?

Carl: 27.

Circus: Surfboards have changed a lot in the last twelve years.

Carl: Yeah, they're smaller and lighter.

Circus: And you and Carl are cousins?

Mike: Right.

Circus: Was Al Jardin a neighbor?

Carl: No, he went to high school with Brian. They played football together and sang, that's how that began.

Circus: Was Brian quarterback?

Mike: Yeah. Brian's a little bold, you know, throws a football 70 yards, hits home runs and pitches and all that.

Circus: Could he have been a pro athlete?

Mike: I think so, he's tremendous. He can really throw a ball. Football and baseball are his favorites. He was timid though, and because of his one ear being out he was always a little bit funny about balance, you know.

Circus: Was there much sibling rivalry when you grew up?

Carl: Yeah, I suppose, like with everybody else. I was the youngest one in the family so I guess I had it different, had a different viewpoint.

Circus: Are there any beach babies?

Carl: Yeah. I wouldn't say babies, but I have two boys; Brian has two girls; Dennis has two boys and a girl, and Alan has two boys, and Michael has a boy and a girl, and from another marriage he has two girls.

Circus: What do Beach Boys eat?

Carl: Beach Boys eat everything. Vegetables are great.

Circus: I've always wanted to know who sang lead on these songs:

"Surfin' " .... Mike
"Surfer Girl" .... Brian
"Little Deuce Coup" .... Mike
"I Get Around" .... Mike
"Don't Worry Baby" .... Brian
"California Girls" .... Mike
"Sloop John B" ..... Brian and Mike
"Good Vibrations" .... Carl
"God Only Knows" .... Carl
"Wouldn't It Be Nice" .... Brian
"Be True to Your School" ...... Mike
"In My Room" .... Brian
"Help Me Rhonda" .... Al
"Surfin' USA" .... Mike
"Shut Down" .... Mike
"Surfin' Safari" .... Mike
"409" .... Mike
"Fun Fun Fun" .... Mike
"Heroes and Villains" .... Brian
"Wild Honey" .... Carl
"Caroline No" .... Brian
"Darlin' " .... Carl
"Do It Again" .... Mike
"I Can Hear Music" .... Carl
"All I Want To Do" .... Mike
"Add Some Music To Your Day" Mike
"Slip On Through" .... Dennis

CIRCUS RAVES 1972

MUSIC

"Tears In The Morning"
.... Bruce Johnston
"Cool, Cool Water" .... Brian
"Deirdre" .... Bruce
"Marcella" .... Carl
"Sail On Sailor" .... Blondy Chaplin

Circus: Was "Surfin'" your first hit?

Carl: Yeah, that was sort of local.

Circus: When you do old material at a concert, who sings Brian's part?

Carl: Well, Alan does mostly, or something like that.

Circus: Who sings the high parts?

Carl: Alan, Billy and I do some of them.

Circus: Did Brian write most of the songs?

Carl: Yeah, in most cases. If there are two people, Brian would have done the music and someone else would have done the lyrics.

Mike: Brian would come up with some music and maybe an idea and I would come up with the concept and the lyrics like on "Fun Fun Fun," the whole story and how that relates, in "I Get Around," he had the music and I had the words.

Circus: What is your attitude towards the lyrics, such as "Fun Fun Fun." You're not exactly serious, but you're not goofing . . .

Mike: Not what?

Circus: You're not goofing on anyone . . .

Mike: We're not putting anybody on and yet it's a fun kind of thing alright.

Circus: In other words, you sing about it because it's there.

Mike: We always want to maintain a certain amount of humor. You see, I have a dry sense of humor and like, well
*she's got her daddy's car
and she cruises the hamburger stand
and seems she forgot about the library
like she told her old man . . .*
Well, it seems "she forgot all about the library" is delivered like, well, you know, like . . .

Circus: Like tongue in cheek.

Mike: Right. That kind of thing.

Circus: Do you listen to country music, because there's that simplicity in country music that everyone can relate to, they're easy to follow, and Beach Boy songs have it too. The words are very accessible.

Mike: Yeah, it's like we've never been over-intellectualized.

Circus: Except when Van Dyke Parks does the lyrics.

Mike: Oh yeah, he was over-acidized. I like some of his alliterations and some of the, what do you call it, allusions and delusions, allusions and all that stuff was good, but on the other hand I always thought if you're going to write something it ought to make some sense. To me a lot of it did, some of it did, and some of it didn't.

Circus: When Brian left the group it

Carl was only 15 when he joined the group. He was the youngest Beach Boy.

The Beach Boys' faces are covered with beards now, and their songs have become anthems to a generation.

173

Mike Love: "When we wrote 'Good Vibrations' we were being more sensitive to where people were coming from. It lead to a new phase in our career."

"The Beach Boys to me are all the people that make up the energy that makes up the music." Mike Love.

Circus: seems that you all collectively took over.

Carl: Well, when he stopped going on the road Glen Campbell came in, and then Bruce, to handle that part and we worked it out however it felt the best and sounded the best to us.

Circus: Which was the last album Brian produced?

Carl: The last album that he produced all by himself, him doing the whole thing would be, well, I don't know, the line is a little vague, because as we got more and more proficient we all started to help more. I guess around *Friends* or *Wild Honey*.

Circus: Is Brian still an influence?

Carl: Yeah, oh yeah, very much so. He helped me on everything I had done, he still sings on the albums.

Mike: Last night Brian and I stayed up really late in the morning or whatever, playing "Oldies But Goodies" and Four Freshmen records. We started out playing "Oldies But Goodies" and then we turned on the Four Freshmen. The Four Freshmen are the best vocal harmony group that ever was. When we came along we patterned them. Brian was like a disciple of theirs. He would come home from school and go right to the piano and play these Four Freshmen songs he had learned how to arrange. He would memorize them in his mind, which, of course, has an infinite capacity for music and he would deal out parts to us immediately. It never ceased to amaze me. It would be hard to grasp one part, yet he'd have all four in his head. He'd deal them out to us and we'd learn the parts and then sing them together. So we listened to this harmony by the Four Freshmen early this morning actually, and just got off tremendously. We were in the room with the lights off and I was like dancing in time to the music. A lot of people might think it's corny, but I don't think they've been exposed to them properly.

Circus: How much have the Beach Boys influenced commercial jingles?

Carl: A lot. I think Brian's influence is massive in all pop music. I think Brian had an influence I noticed in *Sergeant Pepper* and in Motown things.

Mike: He changed the whole thing around from big band jazz and corny lounge music to the falsetto trip. All the white commercials are patterned on the Beach Boys unless they're still hanging onto the big band trip to appeal to the 50 year olds or 40 and older, but then the other ones are black. So there's not much in between.

Circus: Would you say "Good Vibrations" was your most important song?

Carl: I guess so. It's just a record, you know. It's not that important, but I guess in the context of that particular concept, it is.

Mike: "Good Vibrations" epitomizes

kind of where we were at. Just before that was "I Get Around," "I'm getting bugged driving up and down the same ole strip, got to find . . ." What it meant was we had experienced a great deal of commercial success, a tremendous amount of success in terms of being creative, in terms of going around the world first class, tons of cars, nice houses, ladies, this and that, and yet there was something more to it than that. That's just the superficial material value of life and although it's beautiful and we're not knocking it, that wasn't it, you know.

*I'm getting bugged driving down
the same old strip
gotta find a new place where the
kids are hip.*

With "Good Vibrations" it got into a space of more like we're looking for the inner values in people, the inner values in life, not so subtle because really the inner is the basis of the outer, so we were picking up on the good vibrations, being more sensitive where people are coming from, you know, so that showed a change and growth, an awareness in the group that led into the next phase in our career, which in some ways was less dramatic in terms of overall popularity, but it was tremendously equally dramatic in terms of uniqueness and innovation, and, like the *Smiley Smiles* album and all that, they are tremendously unique albums and very avant garde and everything, so much so that we lost a lot of people on the way, but that's cool because they'll catch up.

Circus: Is it true that it took 96 studio hours to record "Good Vibrations?"

Carl: 96 studio hours? Ha, ha, yes. One complete version came out of it, but there are a lot of different things, different riffs and different directions, but Brian was going with it and just recording it as it came up and then chose what he wanted to do with it.

Circus: Would you say "Surf's Up" is your masterpiece?

Carl: That's a different piece, yeah, I enjoyed "Surf's Up."

Circus: Was that Brian's title?

Carl: Brian or Van Dyke thought of that title.

Circus: Leonard Bernstein says "Surf's Up" is the all time greatest album.

Carl: Oh, that's neat. It's a pretty even album. "Student Demonstration Time" is the only one that's a little rough.

Mike: The song "Surf's Up" is very unique and it has to be listed not in the context of what's number one this week, but a very unique piece of music, something which is a very highly individual thing. I appreciate it first of all for its musical form and content and then lyrically I kind of get off. It recalls to mind whatever it recalls to mind. It can call to mind a million different things to a million different people, but oh, I don't know what it means—"a diamond necklace plays the part and a handsome drummer drums along"—it's playing on words, double entendre and all that stuff and quite openly, I don't know what it means. But like, because I wrote the words I relate more to a song like, I mean musically more, to a song like "The Warmth Of The Sun," which we wrote the night or morning before we got up to the news that Kennedy was shot in Dallas. So it goes:

*What good is the dawn
that grows into today
the sunset at night
or living this way
for I have the warmth of the sun
within me at night
the love of my life
she left me one day
I cried when she said
I don't feel the same way
Still I have the warmth of the sun
within me at night . . .*

It's like the warmth of the sun, it means to me a memory and a feeling that you have from within no matter whether

"In an ocean, or in a glass, cool cool water is a gas"

they're there or not there, like Kennedy was gone too but still you have a good feeling towards some of the things he stood for. But instead of coming out and saying, "Oooh Kennedy was shot," we didn't do that, we knew all that was going on, but we were a little bit more subtle, we created more of a positive space rather than head-on negativity, because the choice is whether to confront negativity with negativity, or positively. I mean, things are bad enough, why sing about it.

Circus: That certainly is the Beach Boy vibe.

Mike: And that's why the atmosphere at our shows is so different than so many other shows, like "Surfer Girl," there's nothing intellectual at all about "Surfer Girl," and a lot of people have put us down over the years for lyrics not being heavy enough or whatever. They just don't understand or they're not into the real roots of what was happening. Anyway, what I was saying was "Surfer Girl" was straight from the heart. You can feel it too, like when we did Nassau Coliseum last time, like 19,000 kids were singing along, it was unbelievable. In fact, Elton was there and his producer said it was like an anthem, said he had never heard anything like that and Elton said it was the greatest audience response he ever heard, and that's a pretty big compliment coming from Elton.

Circus: Was *Pet Sounds* a major turning point in your career?

Carl: Yeah, definitely in our lives. In everybody's life at that point. Everybody's gone through and experienced incredible changes in the last five, six years.

Circus: Could you break your albums down into periods, like early, middle, late?

Carl: I would say the album *Summer Days Summer Nights* would be the transition, with *Pet Sounds* being the transition into the middle things, and I'd say the newer things would have to be *Sunflower* or *Surf's Up*.

Circus: There was supposedly a tape called "Fire Music." Was that destroyed by fire?

Carl: That's just part of "The Elements" that Brian did for *Smile*. It wasn't destroyed. We've all had intentions of finishing the album, but something persists that keeps that from happening, and I don't know what that is.

Circus: Who is the newest Beach Boy?

Carl: Ricky Fataar. He joined the group in February of '72.

Circus: Can you be a Beach Boy forever?

Mike: Well, I think I'll always have the philosophy of life that life is meant to be enjoyed and we always want to have a good time and sing positive and harmonious and uplifting songs and that's only been more and more refined in the past few years since we've been meditating and stuff.

Carl: The Beach Boys to me are all the people that make up the energy that makes up the music. I don't think of myself as a Beach Boy, or something like that, you know what I mean? It's the experience.

Circus: Have you ever kissed a Northern girl?

Carl: Yeah.

Circus: Think they keep you warm at night?

Carl: Yeah, but the point of that song is that we wish that they can all be California girls. It's not a judgment, it's a wish. We wish they could all be in California.

Circus: What's more beautiful than a twenty foot wave?

Carl: I don't know.

P.S. There is one thought that did occur to me, and that is we appreciate people allowing us to be part of their life.

P.P.S. Special thanks to Pete from all the Beach Boys. ♣

GREAT AMERICAN MUSIC FAIR CONCERT BOOK

JOHN SCHER PRESENTS

GREAT AMERICAN MUSIC FAIR

COLLECTOR'S EDITION STARRING

THE EVENING

BEACH BOYS ★ DOOBIE BROTHERS

very special guests

AMERICA

THE AFTERNOON

JEFFERSON STARSHIP

NEW RIDERS OF THE PURPLE SAGE

STANKY BROWN GROUP

SEPTEMBER 2

NEW YORK STATE FAIRGROUNDS
SYRACUSE NEW YORK

GREAT AMERICAN MUSIC FAIR CONCERT BOOK

"Light the heavens with a volley of joy!"

AMERICA

THE BEACH BOYS

DOOBIE BROTHERS

JEFFERSON STARSHIP

NEW RIDERS OF THE PURPLE SAGE

STANKY BROWN GROUP

GREAT AMERICAN MUSIC FAIR CONCERT BOOK

THE BEACH BOYS

THE BEACH BOYS

AN AMERICAN BAND

Because of their success, on many levels, throughout the previous twelve years, it may now be possible to speak of The Beach Boys in perspective—in terms of popular music in general, and in terms of their own growth.

Their success lies not in the fact that they have sold more records than any other American group; it is that their music has had inestimable influence on the very nature of the medium. No dinosaur, no "living legend"—The Beach Boys remain a vital force in the arena.

Beginning with their earliest efforts that certainly were responsible for the worldwide surfing phenomenon—they at one time made the Fender Telecaster a household word and everygroup necessity—"Carl and the Passions" from Hawthorne, California have been true innovators. Their influence in promugulating the "California Style" is obvious; their recording of "concept" albums set a precedent that has affected every album recorded since by anyone.

(The Beach Boys were, in fact, the first successful contemporary "concept" group—a "surf band"—which evolved naturally inland to The Beach Boys, neither boys nor of the beach.)

Through all of this, the primary motivation for the group has been the music itself. Brian Wilson, Dennis Wilson, Carl Wilson, Alan Jardine and Michael Love—the "original" Beach Boys and the nucleus around which The Beach Boys are structured today—are utilizing their energies to grow as musicians. As a musical endeavor, they are still evolving, changing, growing. These changes are noticeable in their onstage demeanor, their musicianship that has progressed with the technology of today, their willingness to experiment with form and content, and their expansion of the traveling band format that now includes such things as tympani, electronic instruments and whatever else is needed to present their music totally, not a slim copy or packaged self-parody. As always, what The Beach Boys derive in the studio, The Beach Boys play onstage—all over the world.

Naturally, as individuals The Beach Boys have pursued their separate interests ranging from a dedication to the principles of Transcendental Meditation, to acting, to the operation of a health foods store. And typically, the energies invested in such endeavors as these are of the same intensity with which The Beach Boys approach their music.

As in any evolving creative effort, there have been changes; and the personnel is an example. But The Beach Boys of today are the same Beach Boys that changed the sound and shape of American music. Brian Wilson now concentrates his energy in the recording studio and on his writing, while Carl, Dennis, Alan and Michael, along with Ricky Fataar and other carefully selected musicians, devote a large part of their time to playing music on the road.

They have brought politics and philosophy to concerts, and vice versa. The success of The Beach Boys—spanning much more than a decade—is full of special events and memories; but the success of The Beach Boys is today. Everybody has an ocean, and The Beach Boys are music from America.

BEACH BOYS ALBUM ADS

Beach Boys

There's more to The Beach Boys than just "Surfer Girl," "Fun, Fun, Fun," "Good Vibrations," "California Girls," "Help Me, Rhonda," "Surfin' U.S.A.," "Wouldn't It Be Nice," "Sloop John B.," "I Can Hear Music," "God Only Knows," "Don't Worry Baby," "Wild Honey," "Caroline, No," "Do It Again," "Darlin'," "Sail On Sailor" and "Heroes and Villains."

The Beach Boys Friends & Smiley Smile
Includes: Meant for You / Little Bird Heroes and Villains / Good Vibrations
TWO RECORD SET

The definitive Beach Boys collection—including all the songs mentioned—is on Brother / Reprise Records. The newest addition to the family is FRIENDS & SMILEY SMILE, a double-album reissue of two legendary, out-of-print LPs.

Friends & Smiley Smile
2MS 2167

20/20 & Wild Honey
2MS 2166

Pet Sounds
MS 2197

The Beach Boys in Concert 2RS 6484

Holland
MS 2118

Pet Sounds/So Tough
2MS 2083

Surf's Up
RS 6453

Sunflower
RS 6382

BEACH BOYS ALBUM ADS

...Spring Is Here and the Time Is Right for

The Beach Boys

It's that time of the year again. Each season is marked by its own annual rites. Summer brings festivals, fall heralds supergroup reunion rumors and winter means Phil Spector's Christmas album and the restaging of *Tommy*.

The swallows' return to Capistrano notwithstanding, in many cognizant quarters spring has come to signify the Return of *Pet Sounds*, a phonograph record of the first magnitude and the album frequently referred to as the apex of the Beach Boys' rich and varied musical career.

No one really knows why, but *Pet Sounds* and spring have been synonymous since 1966, when the redoubtable program was first released to accolades, hoopla and consumer acceptance (it was a Top Ten album first time out).

Twice Is Nice

Two years ago, Brother/Reprise brought it out again as the "something old" half of the *Carl And The Passions—So Tough* package (2 MS 2083).

Third and Gold to Go

This year, *Pet Sounds* is being released again. This time it's a single record set, put out with the intended goal of snagging those folks who might've been out to lunch or momentarily indisposed the previous springs.

Some Kinda Consummate Work

Pet Sounds was a single inspired performance by the group, fashioned from compositions (all Brian's), arrangements and a production approach of enduring excellence. Tracks like "Here Today," "That's Not Me," "God Only Knows," the exuberant "Wouldn't It Be Nice," "Sloop John B," "Caroline No" and "You Still Believe In Me" (the latter four still alive and well in concert) pointed the way toward an even more adventurous growth period. "Do It Again" is a handy byword when it comes to Beach Boys music. Some people just can't get enough of it. We're some. *Pet Sounds*, still something special, on Brother/Reprise records and tapes. Keep an eye on summer.

Pet Sounds

The Beach Boys

You couldn't count on fifty hands the number of times "genius" has been used in print in relation to Brian Wilson. Even Leonard Bernstein verified same in introducing number one Wilson son on one of his TV specials.

Accordingly, Brian has played the role, both publicly and privately (and consciously or unconsciously?) to the hilt. He is to rock as dramatist Alfred Jarry is to French arts and letters. Jarry's death-bed request for a toothpick (indeed his last pronouncement in this life) has met its outlandish match in Brian's "Fire Music" debacle. In what, in most respects, seems like a parody of mad genius, he destroyed all the tapes of a very expensive recording session of an extended piece entitled "Fire Music." Why? At the time of the session, a number of fires had unexplainedly flared up in L.A., and mere coincidence was not a suitable enough explanation for the composer. Consequently, he destroyed the tapes (burning them, of course), and "Fire Music" was lost to the ages.

There are a number of stories in circulation that go even farther in their depiction of Brian as Beethoven incarnate. Publicly, though, they're dismissed by his intimates as just "well, Brian's strange sense of humor."

Perhaps the "Seconds" episode is apocryphal, but it deserves another telling. In some of the middle period recordings, The Beach Boys showed the heavy influence of Phil Spector. Eventually, so it goes, Brian began to obsess on the possibility that Mr. Wall of Sound was out for revenge, angered by the fact that some of his highly original techniques had not only been copped but improved upon by Brian. This distraction absorbed his attention at a time when Spector was involved in a production deal with Paramount Pictures. That's the set-up.

Now picture Brian deciding to go to a movie, perhaps to get his mind off the Spector spectre. The film is, unfortunately for purposes of well-integrated Brian Wilson, the Paramount film "Seconds." Now, imagine Brian walking into the theater just as the screen is filled with a close-up of a character looking out and saying (in the context of the film) "Good afternoon, Mr. Wilson." The rumors vary as to the degree of Brian's upset, but significantly the whole affair was seen by our Brian as the upshot of a carefully timed, exquisitely wrought Goldfinger-like plot on Spector's part.

This was several years ago. Today Brian acknowledges the Spector-Ronettes

ROCK 1974

By Bill Reed

ROCK 1974

Mike Love (above left) Carl Wilson (above right) Al Jardine (below left) Bruce Johnston (below right).

Photos: Emerson-Loew

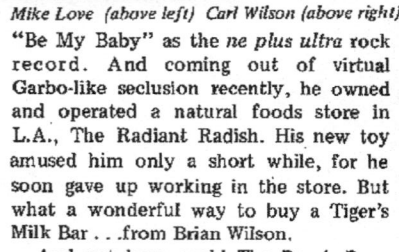

If only they'd called themselves the Band

"Be My Baby" as the *ne plus ultra* rock record. And coming out of virtual Garbo-like seclusion recently, he owned and operated a natural foods store in L.A., The Radiant Radish. His new toy amused him only a short while, for he soon gave up working in the store. But what a wonderful way to buy a Tiger's Milk Bar...from Brian Wilson.

And yet how could The Beach Boys possibly have known way back in balmier, pre-acid, surfin' days that their then-catchy name would ultimately be the cause of their undoing? If only they'd called themselves "The Band" back in '60.

With some of rock's most influential critics on their side, and after five years of movement away from their surfin' and striped-pants phase, Brian Wilson and company have yet to escape the stigma of their anachronistic agglomerate name.

Relatively few are aware that the group is still recording, and some of those who do know are laboring under the delusion that the group is still doing surf music.

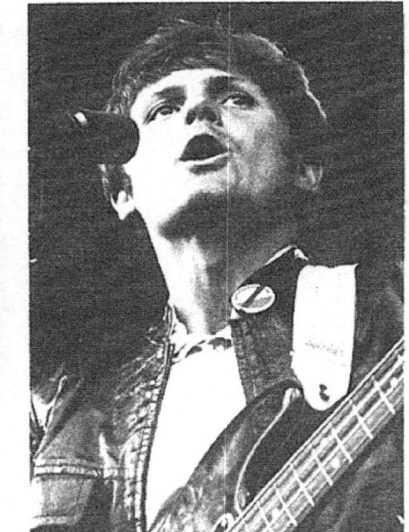

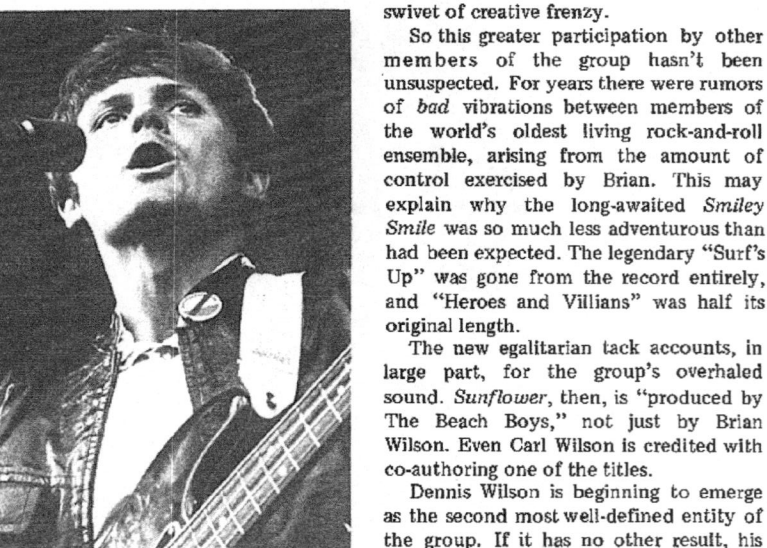

swivel of creative frenzy.

So this greater participation by other members of the group hasn't been unsuspected. For years there were rumors of *bad* vibrations between members of the world's oldest living rock-and-roll ensemble, arising from the amount of control exercised by Brian. This may explain why the long-awaited *Smiley Smile* was so much less adventurous than had been expected. The legendary "Surf's Up" was gone from the record entirely, and "Heroes and Villians" was half its original length.

The new egalitarian tack accounts, in large part, for the group's overhauled sound. *Sunflower*, then, is "produced by The Beach Boys," not just by Brian Wilson. Even Carl Wilson is credited with co-authoring one of the titles.

Dennis Wilson is beginning to emerge as the second most well-defined entity of the group. If it has no other result, his highly publicized friendship with Charles Manson should affect the stubborn all-American image that has been anathema to the group in their attempts to gain a share of the attention they deserve. (Apocalyptic that the two

ROCK 1974

"Good Vibrations," the group's number one single in 1966, marked the last time that The Beach Boys made much of an impression on the mass of record buyers. Since then their ability to capture the public's fancy has dwindled with mathematical regularity. Ironically, though, their only *really* interesting work has been produced during this period of waning popularity.

They've been very much boxed in. And, rather than fight fire with fire, they have refused to plunge indiscriminately into momentarily prevailing musical fashions. *Sunflower*, their very recent album, reveals only slight interest in what is being laid down outside rockdom. Several of the cuts fall outside even the broadest definition of "rock."

Paul Williams remarked on this quality in the group's music when he wrote of their 1967 album, *Wild Honey*. Williams then read this seemingly regressive tendency as a way of countering the post-*Pepper* hysteria evidenced by a lot of the music being performed and recorded during that acid summer. "Dylan," he wrote, "told them what to do, he's leading the way again with *John Wesley Harding*. He's told everyone to go back to simplicity and forget wild production albums and just put it where it's at. And then all of a sudden I realized Brian had been there first with *Wild Honey*." Williams came to appreciate the album, but only after he'd listened to it for a quite lengthy period. I had a very similar reaction to that same album. At the time I too was puzzled by the simple compositions and the sparse construction of most of *Wild Honey*. With its Webcor-in-the-garage sound and one-take texture there was nothing initially for me to latch on to. Even some very good groups were coming out with some very

bad Sgt. Pepper imitations—over-extended compositions based on dubious "concept" themes.

In the midst of all this, there was Brian, just screaming rock blues past the top of his range, backed by the funkiest bass lines this side of "Louie, Louie." Nothing on *Wild Honey* lasted longer than two minutes and forty seconds.

Next they presented us with *Friends*, as difficult to approach as the pre-*Honey Smiley Smile* album, but curiously even simpler compositionally than *Wild Honey*.

Each successive album has been not only as good as the last, but has also presented us with a radical departure from the one before. Perhaps only The Beatles have mastered the art of musical surprise quite as well. Unlike The Beatles, though, each new Beach Boys release meets with increasing public indifference. This blessed flux in their music is one other reason for the "Boys" shifting popularity. For one group that occupied such a fixed place in the public's mind, this constant change in musical approach proved just too confusing.

All of this is compounded by The Beach Boys' deportment during live appearances. A Fillmore East concert of a year and a half ago was a near disaster. They came onstage decked out in matching ice cream-colored suits. And since, generally, Fillmore habitues like their groups gunjey, raw and *au courant*, the Good Humor hallucination on the stage couldn't help but bring out the sadistic side of the audience. By the end of their set, the aging "Beach Boys" were like panicky circus ponies. Granted, they got it on approximately during the last

number. But the previous fifty minutes of self-deprecation had taken its toll. Too much goosing and horsing around betrayed the fact that they really were ashamed of being simply The Beach Boys.

At the time, and for several years prior to this, Brian hadn't been performing with the group in public. Instead, he opted to seclude himself in Belair, California, and act as producer and arranger-writer for the group.

Until very recently, then, the group has traveled without its nucleus. This lack of focus has obviously contributed to the overall shabbiness of a typical "live" Beach Boys show. It's not, as has been suggested, that they're "incapable of sounding good live," but rather like the "old" Byrds, they just don't know how to approach the problem of performing outside studio walls.

Until the release of 20/20, each Beach Boys album was of a whole cloth. *Pet Sounds* betrayed the heavy influence that Phil Spector had on the group. And til 20/20 all of the albums were almost exclusively the result of Brian Wilson research. But the latter album and the recent *Sunflower* even more so, are indicative of a much more democratic apportioning of responsibilities. Apparently Brian is no longer the sole instigator of the group's musical direction. *Pet Sounds* reportedly had Brian playing almost all of the instruments, composing all the material, and mixing the album in a months' long

figures mentioned most frequently in connection with Manson are (1) a member of The Beach Boys, and (2) Terry Melcher, son of the high priestess of the American cult of prolonged virginity, Doris Day.)

Sunflower amassed a set of almost unqualified raves, and generally Dennis' name is mentioned in reviews with almost as much frequency as Brian's.

During the last three or four lackluster years, these grand purveyors of post-scarcity, California, sun-baked hedonism have been helped, in large part, to get by because of a little help from their musical friends. Such strange bedfellows as James Morrison and Paul McCartney have repeatedly praised the excellence of the group's efforts. And, too, rock journalists and a small but staunch group of loyals have lent support. Because of this they've been able to maintain a sort of celebrity during the year and a half of musical silence brought about by the legal encumbrances of Capitol Records. Their recent contract with Reprise gives them the creative autonomy that was sought, but never achieved, during their eight year relationship with Capitol.

Incidentally, the disparity between the generally highly favorable reviews for *Sunflower* and the skimpy amount of airplay that the work has received on the hipper New York FM outlets goes a long way in reinforcing the contention of those who insist that rock journalism doesn't really have that suffocating control over the mind of the rock fan that it's often been accused of having. I log a lot of hours during the week listening to "underground" radio, and yet I've only heard one track from *Sunflower* played on the air during first month of

continued on page 31

185

But astonishingly, they've come through it and now are indicating, to what will be hopefully an ever-widening audience, just how "seriously" they should be taken. Their integrity and the certainty of their musical vision are in no way better underlined than by Brian's decision to tour with the group again.

Their performance at the October 3rd Big Sur Folk Festival marked their belated initiation into the ways of the music festival. Their success at Big Sur could come as a real surprise only to those unfamiliar with *Wild Honey*, the one album that really shows they're capable of something other than the brilliant recording-studio surgery typical of most of their other albums. And only *Wild Honey* displayed well the extent to which each member of The Beach Boys deserves being considered a first-class musician.

Those attending had a chance to experience this first-hand when The Beach Boys played at Big Sur. Perhaps the best indication, though, that The Beach Boys are out front and have a clearly-marked path staked-out for themselves is the simple one of Brian's submission to the tradition of interview, a tradition he has conspicuously ignored for quite a few years.

It was just three days after the group's performance at Big Sur that an extremely open Brian Wilson spoke with me on what is one of my favorite subjects, The Beach Boys. Also participating in the conversation were Beach Boy Carl Wilson and publicity aide Jack Riley. The interview was conducted via a long-distance phone call, (the brevity of many of Brian's remarks arises from the fact that he was having a hard time finding an extension in his home that worked properly. Carl came through loud and clear; it's obvious that he enjoys acting as a spokesman for the group. He appears to be very dedicated to The Beach Boys, and his enthusiasm for all facets of the group's activities is close to peak. Amazing, considering the ten-year association with one group.)

How was the response at Big Sur?

Carl: It went fine. I only wish we'd had a little more time. There were a lots of

things straight.

Carl: Well I've always been amused by it. I know what you're talking about, though; and I suppose we all feel a little bit differently about it. Like at Big Sur after the show you'd see one person turn to another and say, "Did you dig it?" And the other person would say, "Well, I don't know? Did you dig it?"

A little paranoid about comitting themselves.

Carl: Yeah.

How do you get together now on producing an album?

Carl: Well, *Sunflower*, I'd say, is the truest group effort we've ever had. Each of us was deeply involved in the creation of almost all the cuts. Say, someone would come to the studio early and put down a basic track, and then someone else would arrive and think of a good line to overdub....

So it really is accurate to say "produced by The Beach Boys." (At this point Brian interjects a question that still has me a little baffled. Who in his right mind wouldn't want to do the following?)

Brian: Bill?

Yes, Brian?

Brian: Have you ever talked to Mick Jagger?

No, I never have. Why?

Brian: Are you going to?

I'd like to, sure. But I don't foresee it in the near future. Why?

Brian: I think you should.

What do you mean?

Brian: I think he would be a really interesting rap. He's in this movie "Performance" where he's dressed like a girl, and I just think he'd make a good rap.

Okay. Are you tired of being asked about "Surf's Up"?

NO

Do you think it might make it onto a future album?

Brian: No.

Why?

Brian: We lost it.

No dubs or anything?

Brian: Nope, its gone.

Carl: I think we still have an eight track on it.

Brian: I don't think so.

And one of things noted was that you were going to do a soundtrack for an Andy Warhol movie about a spade gay surfer.

Brian: A what?

A spade gay surfer.

Brian: SPADE GAY SURFER? Uh-huh.

Brian: That's what I thought you said. Nope. Never even met Andy Warhol.

What individual projects are you guys involved with, right now?

Brian: Dennis is doing a film, acting. Carl is producing an album for a South African group, The Flame. And I'm working on an album with a country singer.

Who's that?

Brian: (Faintly, because of bad connection) Fred Veil.

I can barely hear you. Fred V A L E? Like Jerry Vale?

Brian: Jerry Vale? No, V E I L. We've just finished the instrumental tracks but still haven't had a chance to get down the vocals.

What sort of a singer is he?

Brian: He sounds sort of like Johnny Cash.

Carl: (laughing) A very far-out Johnny Cash.

Brian: (also laughing) Uh-Huh, a *very* far out Johnny Cash.

What kind of group is The Flame, Carl?

Carl: We were in London finishing up a tour when we heard them.

Are they black?

Carl: Well no, I don't think so. They're Malaysians who grew up in South Africa.

What kind of music?

Carl: (laughing) Rock!

Following the tradition of The Beach Boys, how will the next album differ markedly from Sunflower?

Brian: We actually went well out and bought a Moog synthesizer. All of the albums from now on will have more Moog. We used it on "Cool Water" on *Sunflower*. We're also working with quadraphonic sound. "Cool Water" is recorded quadraphonically.

Carl: The industry is trying to hype the public into believing that you have to buy a lot of new equipment to get

the album's release.

Apparently The Beach Boys will continue to prevail though. Several incidents indicate that the group is moving into a phase of their career that will prove more exciting and productive than anything that has occurred up to this point.

A recent tour of Britain met with at least half as much raw excitement and press coverage as would have been accorded to The Beatles if they were back on the touring circuit again. The trip coincided with the unexpected success of a single of "Cottonfields" that Capitol culled from 20/20. The Beach Boys topping the charts in several European countries had the makings of an exciting comeback story. By the time the British music press finished with them, The Beach Boys found themselves emanating a sort of charismatic urgency that had been missing from the British music scene for quite some time.

By the standards of the music world, The Beach Boys have been through some "perilous" territory these last few years. acts so even with two sets we didn't get a chance to play as much as we'd have liked to. I liked playing there, though.

Has your approach to live performing changed much? Are you still concerned with trying to duplicate the recorded sound in "live" performances?

Carl: We're not so much trying to re-do the records now, although we still travel with that big sound system. We're loosening up in our interpretations. It seems like a much more realistic thing to be doing.

What material are you using in public performances now?

Carl: Well, "Darlin'," "Aren't You Glad," "Vegetables." Like that.

Newer material, too?

Carl: Some stuff from Sunflower.

Brian, did you perform with the group at Big Sur, or during the recent English tour?

Brian: No, but I'm going along for the European tour in mid-November.

Was the group surprised with success of "Cottonfields" in England?

Carl: Well, its really Al's record. We weren't surprised because Capitol told us they were going to promote it in England, but not in the States. Since we've split with them, they're not expecting to make a lot of bread off 'The Beach Boys in this country. But because of the steam the group has built up in other countries, everyone was pretty sure it would be big in Europe.

With the people I talk to, I find a lot of ignorance about what the group is doing these days. When someone asks me my favorite group and I say "The Beach Boys," most often I get those hipper-than-thou raised eyebrows. Of course, it's easy to remedy the situation, all I have to do is put on "How She Boogalooed It" from Wild Honey to set *Brian, do you ever listen to any classical music?*

Brian: A little Beethoven, but that's about all.

What happened with Capitol that made the group split after such a long time?

Carl: They were against Pet Sounds and all the albums that came after. They wanted us to stick with surfin' and hot rod records, you know. But we said, Well you know, we don't want to do that. We're doing other music now. But they really weren't going for it. And so they had all these hundreds of people in their organization pushing another thing. People were bound to get the wrong impression about the group.

So the public was stuck with the ideas of The Beach Boys, circa '63.

Carl: Exactly.

Wasn't there also some dissension in the group about just how progressive your music should be.

Carl and Brian: No!

Brian: And I don't think The Beach Boys have ever really been that far out.

Come on, now. Smiley Smile?

Carl: Well, maybe that one.

Brian: There's a drug abuse clinic somewhere in Texas that uses Smiley Smile to help people out of their bad trips.

(Thinking that perhaps my leg is being pulled, long distance) Come on!

Carl: Jack, you know more about it.

Jack: This drug abuse clinic, when someone on a really bad acid trip comes in, helps them calm down and gets them back into a good head by playing Smiley Smile. They don't tell them what they're going to hear, but they play Smiley Smile on headphones. And in almost every case the people suddenly start smiling.

Brian, Rolling Stone ran a short piece about the group a couple of months ago. four-channel sound. But a system developed by a company in Philadelphia, Dynaco, has devised a recording process where all you have to do is have two extra speakers and a little bit of lamp cord.

And with "Cool Water" played with the system, you can actually get four distinct channels of sound?

Carl: Yes. It was on the front page of Billboard a few weeks ago. And you can hear "Cool Water" quadraphonically by wiring up the speakers according to a very simple circuit.

When does the European tour begin?

Carl: On November 18th. And we've got a couple of gigs before then. The Whisky a GO GO.

I guess you'll be pretty busy till then, so I'll let you get along. Just one more thing Brian, have you ever considered producing an album for the Chordettes?

Brian: (pause) "Sh-Boom," right?

Nope, "Lollipop".

Brian: You mean(proceeds with a few bars of same.) Yeah, I love that record. The Chordettes, huh?

Perhaps I planted a seed. The Chordettes Sing the Brian Wilson Songbook?

Chatting with The Beach Boys, even on the telephone, is a semi-celestial experience. Like rapping with angels. Deleted from the above transcript of our conversation is a period of about five minutes of blithering encomium from my end of the wire. About how their music helped me through the "bleech-est" periods of my life, etc. My "pleth" of praise seemed to be accepted as sincere, though; it really sounded as if they were as excited talking with me as I was with them.

Still, it's a shame they didn't call themselves The Band.

187

'Spirit Of America' — A Beach Boys Retrospective

Never have two monster groups been so united as the Beach Boys/Chicago tandem which is touring America like blood brothers.

by Michael Gross

Carl Wilson: In 1966, he was indicted for refusing induction into the U.S. Army. In 1969, he was cleared on the grounds that he was a Conscientious Objector.

Touring America is usually a matter of glorification. You go see one band, and maybe, if you're lucky, you get another thrown in. Sometimes on major tours there's a special guest. With luck that means Suzi Quatro with Alice Cooper. Without luck that means that some management firm or record company has forced promoters to take a second act in order to get the first—often at a distinct musical loss to the audience. But this summer's Beach Boys/Chicago tour is a different story. Two bands at peak popularity, both absolute sellout SRO headliners, are sharing bills across America as naturally as they put on their socks and tune their guitars in the morning. Everyone loves bands like the Beach Boys because, even in 1975, there's room for high spirits in the summertime. That's why albums of re-packaged hits like **Spirit Of America** (Capitol) and **Good Vibrations** (Reprise) do things like go gold a week after their release.

Good vibes and vigah: People were not too self-conscious about good vibes back in November, 1962, when a new group called the Beach Boys rose from the bleach blonde surfer dreamlands of Hawthorne, California, with a single called "Surfin'" and a debut album called **Surfin' Safari**. America had just lived through the Cuban Missile Crisis, and though the vibes were a bit threatened, America's spirit had emerged intact. The Beach Boys did nothing to disperse the clean-cut, 'go forth with vigah' determination of the Kennedy years. They sang all about matching sweaters and matching girls and toothy smiles and maybe, for fun, some riding of the waves or buzzing around in fast cars, like "409," immortalized for under two minutes on the flip side of the Boys' first single and now resurrected on **Spirit**.

Something about the Beach Boys' catchy melodies and uncomplicated world view caught the fancy of America that summer, and memory will tell you that, along with the Four Seasons, no one had more hit singles than the Beach Boys. Their albums began appearing fast and furious for almost two years, all with a similar motif of cars and girls and boards and good fun. **Surfin' USA** and **Shut Down** both appeared early in 1963. Classic singles poured from these albums, most of them on Capitol's last Beach Boys reissue, **Endless Summer**. Any image that caught that ideal—the good time—fit in well, and "Hawaii," from the band's fourth album, Surfer Girl, was typical of the band's idealization of any spot where the surf ran high and the girls would coyly flash their tan lines. "A Young Man Is Gone," "Spirit Of America" and "Custom Machine" all come from the fifth album, released less than a year after the first, **Little Deuce Coupe**. The Beach Boys, in the month before John Kennedy's assassination, were one of the most popular and prolific bands in America. Whether copping Chuck Berry riffs or creating their own, the Beach Boys, and most especially chief songwriter Brian Wilson, had caught a corner of carefree America, and framed it with a unique and totally joyous musical atmosphere.

Non-serious pop: That, of course, is all critical retrospect. No one took the Beach Boys very seriously as musicians back then. "This Car Of Mine" and a reworking of Frankie Lymons' "Why Do Fools Fall In Love" from **Shut Down Volume II** were not being held up for comparison with that era's serious pop music: jazz and folk. But then, neither were the songs of the Beatles, who'd burst into the American consciousness only a month before the release of that album.

The Beach Boys' offering, in the summer of '64, was **All Summer Long**, the classic album that gave the world "I Get Around," the song that knocked the British Invaders from the top of the pops and then played tag all through the summer, with the Four Seasons' "Rag Doll" for #1 spot on the hit parade. Buyers of the album were also being charged up for the summer party by "Little Honda," "Hushabye," "Drive-In," "Do You Remember" and "Don't Back Down"—all songs that, even in the early days of Dylan, SDS, Vietnam and Lyndon Johnson, seemed somehow closer to that traditional amorphous spirit of American good will and innocence that California represented and the rest of the world admired.

As 1964 wound to a close, two more Beach Boys LPs appeared. **Beach Boys Christmas Album** was standard Christmas carols, and **Beach Boys Concert**, which included "Graduation Day," represented the last period in the Beach Boys history when Brian Wilson played with them onstage.

Brian quits the stage: "Brian wanted to leave the group the first time in 1963," his brother Carl told Circus Magazine after the Texas concerts this spring. "He chose to leave that summer. Then there were some personnel changes." Brian's replacement, a neighborhood boy, played for awhile, but eventually quit to go to dental school. Brian rejoined in 1964. "Brian started working again, kind of enjoying it," Carl said. "But at the end of '64, in Houston, he packed

Dennis Wilson: It was Dennis, the family surfer, who first suggested that the band devote itself to music that celebrated California's #1 pastime.

it in. It was too upsetting for him. He couldn't handle it: being away from home, the sound level onstage was too loud for him, all that. Houston was the last time he played as a regular member. He was hearing a lot of things and it was frustrating for him not to be able to bring them into being. He still played on the albums. No one's ever come close to him in the studio. It's always been his music."

With Brian off the road and devoting himself 100% to composing, the Beach Boys' music took off for the stratosphere. "Dance, Dance, Dance," "Good To My Baby," "Please Let Me Wonder," "When I Grow Up," and a cover of Bobby Freeman's "Do You Wanna Dance" all appear on **Spirit**, but were originally in the hit-jammed **Beach Boys Today**, an album whose cover featured the band in lovely alpaca sweaters, the West Coast style of 1965. "Salt Lake City," from the next album, **Summer Days**, was a paean to the Utah city. "Tell Me Why" and "Barbara Ann" from Beach Boys Party represent the last offerings on **Spirit Of America** from this transitional phase of the band's career.

At first there had been the band with Brian. From 1964-5, the band kept playing, while Brian wrote, and though the songs were breaking out of the car/surf/girl/fun consistency of the Beach Boys' early work, their sound remained the same. "The Little Girl I Once Knew," a single released in October 1965, was typical of the period, displaying an advancing musical sophistication, but still undeniably in the mold.

Precious 'Pet': May, 1966 saw the release of Pet Sounds, an album that

Mike Love has said,
"We're fundamentally a family unit. Brian was the overwhelming dominant creative force in the group just by virtue of his influence on his brothers, myself and his friends."

has now been released three separate times, only recently gaining the critical acclaim it deserves. Warner Brothers now owns the rights to this and all succeeding albums, but at the time, "Sloop John B," "God Only Knows," "Wouldn't It Be Nice" and "Caroline, No" all appeared on a Capitol label. Now, eight years later, they're reappearing on **Good Vibrations** this summer, thanks to the brothers at Warners. And the fact that ownership of material shifts as of **Pet Sounds** provides a convenient demarcation point between the old and new Beach Boys. Bye-bye cars and boards, hello heads and essences and music that was as thoughtful as it was beautiful. Brian Wilson began using orchestration and arrangement in a way previously unheard of in rock, paralleling, in a different dimension, the pioneering of The Beatles on **Rubber Soul**, released a few months earlier.

The story behind the shift in sound is a long one, told best by Paul Williams in his book, **Outlaw Blues**, where Brian's creative endeavors of the next year are fully explained. Suffice it to say that a masterpiece (co-produced by Van Dyke Parks) called **Smile** was due next, and it never appeared. Parks pulled out of the project and Brian, traumatized, shelved it where it stagnated. Instead, in the fall of 1967, **Smiley Smile** was released, and as far as public profile was concerned the Beach Boys went underground after the great rush of "Good Vibrations," that album's most popular track. The best example of what **Smile** might have been like was in a cut called "Heroes and Villains," now acclaimed as the strongest, and possibly grandest studio experiment Brian Wilson ever tried.

Wild Honey, released at the end of '67, was lost in the **Sgt. Pepper/Satanic Majesties Request** onslaught at the dawning of the Age of Aquarius, even though, as "Darling" shows, the Beach Boys had lost none of their punch. Only the title cut of **Friends**, "Do It Again" from **20/20**, and "Add Some Music To Your Day" from **Sunflower** (the only non-reissued Beach Boys middle period album) are represented on **Good Vibrations** to show what the Beach Boys did as the '60s turned to the '70s.

It was only with the release of **Surf's Up**, after the turn of the decade, that the Beach Boys regained the public eye. That album, again represented here by its title cut, also attracted new critical recognition: because of the LP's ties with the 1967 days through the title cut (it was originally recorded for **Smile**), critics and observers were forced to look back over the entire body of the Beach Boys' work. Luckily, that attention covered the commercial failure of **Carl and**

The Chicago Connection

"Thanks to Jim, we've been working a little at Caribou and that's just a dream," Carl Wilson said happily. "Jim" is Jim Guercio, owner-operator of The Caribou Ranch, producer of Chicago, and long-time musician's musician. He's probably as much responsible for the Beach Boys' resurgence as the re-released albums.

"We wanted some assistance in the management/direction area about a year ago," Carl explained, "and when we were playing Denver one time, Jim invited us to the ranch. We got to talking while we were there. He's always been out front about liking our music, so we asked if it would be cool with Chicago for him to assist us. We needed conscious, responsible assistance.

"We got more acquainted and then he offered to play bass with us on the road which blew our minds. We got down to business and made an agreement for them to handle our comings and goings and that's how it started. Then several months ago, I think Jim brought up the idea of the two bands playing together."

Early this year, a logistical planning session was held in Hawaii, and the reality of a Beach Boys/Chicago tour began to take shape. Everyone who touched it was charmed and enthused by the idea and now, a few months later, it seems the feelings about it were right. Chicago, of course, is touring to support their most recent album, **Chicago VIII**, and the Beach Boys, one supposes, are touring because it's summer.

Onstage, at their tour-opening concerts in Texas, the Beach Boys began the set and were joined midway by Chicago. With the famous brass blasting away, Bobby Lamm sang "Surf's Up," Peter Cetera sang "Darlin'" and then Carl Wilson sang "God Only Knows." During Chicago's set, the Beach Boys joined in for "Old Days," "Wishin' You Were Here" and "Saturday In The Park." Then, as the finale, all seventeen musicians stood onstage and delighted the mellowed crowd with "Dialogue," "California Girls," "Harry Truman," "Fun, Fun, Fun," "Feeling Stronger" and, as the closer, "Jumping Jack Flash." By the end, the co-billing seemed entirely natural, as the audience realized that both Chicago and The Beach Boys were all-American bands. Regardless, wherever they go they draw the kind of crowds promoters love and give the kind of shows the audiences of America love. And that, as they say, is the big idea.

The Passions/So Tough, and bridged the gap to the Beach Boys' last studio album, **Holland**, represented by the monumental "Sail On, Sailor." Excepting two more live albums, both considered failures by most critics, the Beach Boys oeuvre was complete. With the coming of the repackages, spearheaded by last year's **Endless Summer**, the Beach Boys' place as the quintessential American rock band was secured for all time.

Bouncing stages: "We weren't involved with **Endless Summer** at all," Carl explained, "but we do want the songs available for people. It makes you feel funny 'cause it's the third time it's been out. Then it goes to #1 and that's funky. I looked at the trade charts and thought 'My God!' It wasn't real to me. Al Coury at Capitol loves the group and he did it. We were pleased about it." So were audiences, who responded incredibly when the band re-tailored their stage set to make room for the suddenly-valid-again oldies they thought had been lost in the wash of history.

"The album was out," Carl explained, "and we like to ride the horse in the direction it's going so we changed the set. Sometimes, like at Madison Square Garden, it got scarey. The stage was bouncing. One of the light towers was shaking. But it's thrilling when people are getting off that bad. I don't want to sound corny, but we get off!"

There are still some questions, though, like the oft-asked one: is Brian Wilson crazy? Told of a conversation about Brian's state of mind, Carl was quick to reply. "My God, I can assure you Brian is not a vegetable. But that won't stop the rumors. I've heard outrageous stories about him, but he's far out. He does what he wants, when he wants."

These days he's often to be found in the studio, working with the rest of the band on a new album, their first studio set in three years, now due around November. "After we delivered the last Warners album," Carl said, "we just thought it didn't work for us anymore in the album grind, two albums a year. We decided to cruise and release an album when it gets released and it'll be an album we really like."

Then, asked about the feelings generated by this special tour, he went on earnestly. "The group feels honored that people are willing to let us participate in their lives. It may be difficult to relate to, but coming to play is very humbling. All that stuff about people being ego freaks is the biggest hype. Playing buzzes me out. It's so fascinating to make music, have the records come out, and then come out to play and discover they know about it. It's fascinating and it's wonderful."

●

CRAWDADDY JUNE 1976

CRAWDADDY

U.K. 45P
JUNE 1976 $1.00

THE BRIAN WILSON INTERVIEW
BACK WITH THE BEACH BOYS:
"I'M GOING THROUGH SHOCK RIGHT NOW"

SEX, CANNIBALISM & THE N.C.L.C.

SPIRITS OF '76:
THE DRINKS ARE ON US!

LITTLE FEAT
GENESIS
CHRIS HILLMAN

STILL WATERS RUN DEEP

A CHILD IS FATHER TO THE BAND
THE RETURN OF BRIAN WILSON / BY TIMOTHY WHITE

Well, I feel I have something to say in music, in records. What I'm trying to get across is an attitude, a feeling about staying cool and all those little things in life that put you together. I'm just saying something about them, because I feel it's needed. You walk down around and see this grim stuff and it really makes you cry. And when you cry over something it means it got to you. Do you know what I mean?

—Brian Wilson, 1976

There would be no exceptions; Fred Morgan was adamant about that.

As music instructor at Hawthorne High School, Morgan had warned his 12th grade Piano and Harmony class—especially the college-bound students—that they must complete all the course requirements if they expected to pull a final mark of 'B' or better.

Brian Wilson, a tall, timorous-but-attentive boy with wavy brown hair and a sad, distant smile, was one of Morgan's most promising pupils, despite the handicap of a deaf right ear. The 17-year-old Wilson's hearing had been damaged in an anonymous accident that occurred in early childhood, yet he was still having difficulty accepting life as a monophile. Morgan had been understanding, even allowing Brian to sit closer to the piano during class; but he felt there was no excuse for his senior slump.

Truth was, Brian had allowed his position on the varsity baseball team (he was a centerfielder) and his involvement in a rock combo (The Pendletones) to distract him from his music lessons. He'd also been spending too many evenings hanging out at the Foster's Freeze on the corner of 120th Street and Hawthorne Blvd. when he should have been home studying. Morgan wouldn't have minded so much if Brian had been an average student, but the boy had early-on demonstrated considerable musical aptitude; his knack for arranging was particularly impressive.

Nevertheless, Brian had adopted a lackadaisical attitude towards his Piano and Harmony course during the last quarter, and so what could have been a uniformly meritorious final report card was subsequently marred:

English	B
Government	B
Physical Education	A
Spanish III	B
Senior Problems (Personal Psychology)	B
Piano & Harmony	C

"Brian was the most quiet one of the bunch in his class," Fred Morgan recalls. "He was a nice boy and a good student and was fairly popular with his classmates because he had a good laugh. There was a portion of each class during which I would sit at the piano and play something, and everyone had to write down the notes. I remember Brian was very good at that; he had a quick mind.

"But I had to give him a 'C' for the year because he did not do what he was supposed to do. He did not finish his harmony exercises, for one thing. The exercises consisted of blocking in additional harmonic parts in a piece of music after the soprano part, let's say, had been supplied.

"Most important, he did not write a sonata. The major requirement of the course was to compose a piano sonata before the year was out; the project took the place of a final examination. Brian did not do a piano sonata, and so I gave him an 'F' for the project and a 'C' for the course. Instead of writing a sonata, he wrote a song called 'Surfin'.' I had nothing against the song; it was nice, but it just wasn't what I asked him for."

CRAWDADDY JUNE 1976

It is a stark, surreal tableau without a foothold in time.

Brian Wilson, 33, is seated before a handsome Hammond B-3 organ in the center of the Beach Boys' splendid, 24-track Brother Studio on Fifth Street in Santa Monica, his massive form suspended in the cold blue expanse of a giant circular stained glass window depicting our solar system which looms behind him. The air is electric with tension and Brian's thick-fingered hands are trembling so horribly they can scarcely find their proper places on the keys. Mercifully, the organ is not turned on.

"Come on, Bri," Stan Love cajoles softly. "Play your new song. Play 'California Feeling.'"

The bearded, pot-bellied man at the Hammond smiles weakly, brushes a veil of stringy brown hair from his downcast eyes and sighs with shuddersome exasperation. "Damn," he exhales, in his high, raspy voice. "I'm *so* nervous, but I *will* relax."

I hardly recognize the person before me. He bears no resemblance whatsoever to the lanky, dough-faced teenager who sat atop the bright yellow, palm-festooned pick-up truck on the cover of *Surfin' Safari*, one thin hand clutching a surfboard and the other shielding his eyes from the beach glare as he peered out at the rolling Pacific. Fifteen years and 75 million records later, Brian Wilson, the singer/composer/producer *extraordinaire* who elevated one of the most phenomenally successful vocal and musical groups in history to a permanent place in American folklore, is slumped over a silent keyboard in a soundproof room a half-hour drive from where that first album photo was shot; overweight, overwrought, and scared shitless.

"Come on, Brian," Stan continues. "Play it. It's a *great song*."

Stan Love, sandy-haired former forward with the Baltimore Bullets of the National Basketball Association and the younger brother of Beach Boys lead vocalist Mike Love, is Brian Wilson's first cousin, confidant and salaried chauffeur. He is also his bodyguard. Right now, skinny Stan, elbows on the organtop and eyes riveted on his stout responsibility, is trying his damnedest to put his pal at ease.

Since all of this is for my benefit, I decide to pitch in. "What's the song like?" I ask cheerfully, pulling up one of the folding chairs scattered about the neat, spacious room.

"I don't know," Brian murmurs. "It's got a *feeling* to it . . . there's something about it that's very *warm*. It's sort of a Bill Medley-Brian Wilson combination . . ."

Brian (far l.) at 20: "The water really scared me"

"How does the *tune* go?" I prod him gently. "What are the lyrics?"

Suddenly Brian straightens up, rolls his hefty shoulders back and shows a brave, childlike smile. "Heck," he allows. "I should . . . I should just *sing* it!"

He flicks the power switch on the organ, adjusts the volume with the foot pedal and for a split-second I don't want to hear the song. After growing up blissfully absurd to the strains of "Surfin' U.S.A.," and falling in love under the boardwalk with "Wouldn't It Be Nice" resounding overhead, I don't want to see Brian Wilson blow it, any more than I'd want to see Beaver Cleaver get beaten up or Sandra Dee take a dump.

But, as a result of a two-month long series of events too byzantine to recount, this impossible genius and myself find ourselves poised on the brink of what could be one of the bigger bummers of either of our personal lives. Brian's out to tell the world that he's still a *scientist* in the studio and I'm spending a sunny spring afternoon witnessing the first cruel rites. The two of us are shooting this pipeline together, and this time around, I'm praying he *has* that sonata.

Brian's rubbery fingers hover above the Hammond's bared teeth. Fearful, uncertain, they stiffen and he forms two chords, falters, and then begins to sing:

I was walking down the beach in San Onofre,
It was such a beautiful day.
The wind was blowing through my hair,
And the sun dances in the morning sky.
When you're driving through L.A. . . .

Ladies and gentlemen, the beach is *back*.

***

Brian Wilson is the Beach Boys. He is the band. We're his fucking messengers. He is all of it. Period. We're nothing. He's everything.

—**Dennis Wilson**

For over ten years, the eldest son of Murry and Audree Wilson has been popular music's reigning recluse, a living legend swallowed up by the shadows of Southern California with all the myths intact. Before Brian sauntered onto the music scene in the early '60s, Phil Spector had been the undisputed soothsayer of rock 'n roll studiocraft, his awesome "Wall of Sound" appearing impervious. But without so much as a by-your-leave, Bashful Brian rose up to rival the hit-making acumen of Spector and the rest of the LA music mafia with a nonchalantly uncompromising approach of his own: a tabernacle of untutored, unabashedly nasal male voices erupting in seamless Four Freshman-inspired harmonies, underscored by sneak-attack bass lines; layered, muffled percussion and a smattering of Dick Dale/Chuck Berry-flavored lead guitar offset by primitive, unorthodox rhythm chords—all of it sailing on wide-open oceans of monophonic *space*.

And the subject matter: nothing leering or lewd, just an endless summer Saturday of unfettered adolescent Americanism, replete with deuce coupes, Hondas, hamburger stands, radios blasting, spilled Cokes, shut downs, drive-in movies, amusement parks, hop scotch ho-dads and plenty of sun-tanned virginal beach bunnies that dug, *really* dug, *surfers*.

When Brian Wilson retired from public performing early in 1965 following a nervous breakdown suffered on Dec. 23, 1964 while aboard a plane enroute to a concert commitment in Houston, he was at the very height of his powers as a band leader, hit record technician and pop culture mogul. His doctors advised him that continued touring could prove disastrous to both his psyche and perhaps his good left ear, which was being over-taxed by the escalating decibels at live rock 'n' roll shows.

It was a low blow for Brian; the Beach Boys had been his creation, his window to the world. Through them he had been able to break out of his childhood shell, overcome his numbing reticence, and articulate his simple sensibilities.

He loved performing—stepping up to the microphone and singing *his* lyrics, in *his* harmonies, set to *his* music. It was more fun, more satisfaction and more human contact than he had ever dared hope for. As he was later to tell me, "It was the most amazing thing I could think of."

Now he would have to think of something else. Maybe he could bear losing his mind once in a while, but if he lost his hearing he was a dead man. "I can't fix that damn right ear, no matter what I do!" Brian would tell me in a moment of disconsolation. "It bothers me, but I can't fix it, so I have to accept it."

His concert career terminated, Brian submerged himself in songwriting, arranging and studio experimentation—not to mention hallucinogens—while his band carried on without him. Years passed and rock 'n roll changed, growing harder, heavier, more hedonistic, and then more grave. Lovely B. Wilson-produced Beach Boys records continued to emanate from some orphic source, but these too had changed. Now they were more concerned with *feelings* than *experiences*. The abandon of "Fun, Fun, Fun" and "I Get Around" was replaced by the isolation of "That's Not Me" and the rueful resignation of "I Just Wasn't Made For These Times."

Meanwhile, the bizarre myths surrounding Brian multiplied as the man grew more remote. It was rumored that he had built a sandbox in the dining room of the Beverly Hills home he occupied in the mid-'60s and placed a grand piano in it so that he could continue to draw on the beach for inspiration without ever having to visit it again. His neighbors whispered that he was a hashish head, that he lived on candy bars and milk shakes, that he would record marvelous music and then destroy the tapes, that he had locked himself in his bedroom and stayed there for six straight months—that he was *insane*. They were incredible stories, and most of them were true.

In recent years, a new crop of arcana has grown up around Brian, some of it raising the possibility that his reclusion may not be entirely voluntary. Several in his small coterie of friends outside the Wilson-Love axis grumble that Brian seems extraordinarily dependent on his family for money and mobility.

Brian's freedom of movement is hampered in part by the loss of his driver's license after he was involved in several automobile accidents. "I fucking knocked my head—got a lump on my head—on the last one," he later explained. "That was about three years ago. I haven't had my driver's license since. They took that away from me. Now I just get driven."

Stan Love apparently doesn't take Brian every place he wishes to go; on the precious few occasions he travels unescorted, he reportedly is ill-equipped. Some of his friends tell of infrequent visits by Brian in taxis for which he has to borrow money to pay the fare.

At 33: a singular charisma and a broken heart (?)

"Brian seems to have a problem getting spending money," says a prominent producer and friend, who told of several private lunches with Wilson in 1975 that ended on a humiliating note. "Brian would ask me if he could borrow $50," he alleged. "I'd always give it to him, but after a few times, I started to wonder why the hell Brian Wilson, who's made millions of dollars in the record business, didn't have any money of his own. I couldn't understand it. He told me he wasn't sure who had control over his money or even the deed to his house."

Equally puzzling are the circumstances surrounding a 1975 production deal that Brian "requested" with Equinox Records Inc., an RCA-based production company headed by Terry Melcher and ex-Beach Boy Bruce Johnston. At the time, Wilson had nothing in the works but *ennui*, and so he signed a contract with Equinox to produce 36 sides over an indefinite period of time. The generous terms included a bonus advance of $23,000 and what Johnston described as "probably the highest production royalty any producer's ever received."

Since then, Brian has worked with Melcher on only four basic tracks, among them versions of "Why Do Fools Fall In Love " and "Money Honey."

The tracks did not turn out as planned—mysteriously, Brian refused to finish them.

"He wouldn't go all the way," says Melcher. "He wouldn't even touch anything in the control booth; he acted like he was afraid to. He'd offer suggestions, but he wouldn't go near the board. He knows his reputation, so he makes a lot of unfinished records; sometimes I feel that he feels that he's peaked and does not want to put his stamp on records so that peers will have a Brian Wilson track to criticize."

Aside from these furtive stirrings, which raised more questions than they answered, Brian has remained an enigma to the handful who have periodic access to him and a phantasmal figure to virtually everyone else.

Every so often, some quick-witted shutterbug would catch a glimpse of Brian Wilson at a private party, or in the backseat of a limousine paused at a stoplight on Mulholland Drive or Sunset Boulevard. Always it was in the dead of night, and the resultant blurred photo would reveal an unkempt, sleepy-eyed manchild bundled up in a terry bathrobe and staring about blankly. As for actually *meeting* Brian Wilson, well, you had a better chance of bumping into Big Foot.

***

The Beach Boys released their inaugural single on Dec. 8, 1961 on a small Los Angeles label called Candix. "Surfin'," the 'A' side, and "Luau," the 'B' side, were two of four songs the group had recorded during September on a demo tape produced by Brian. The other two tunes, "Surfin' Safari" and "Surfer Girl," remained in the can while the company waited to see if the group, consisting of Brian, 19, brothers Dennis, 17, and Carl, 15, cousin Mike Love and neighbor Alan Jardine, had a sound worth sinking money into.

Actually, Dennis Wilson was the only member of the Beach Boys who ever adopted surfing as a hobby; Brian, the one promising people that if they could "catch a wave" they'd be "sitting on top of the world," had never surfed in his life—not even after his father Murry insisted he at least *try*, to help the group's image.

"I wouldn't go out," says Brian. "I was scared; scared of the water. It *really* scared me." Instead, Brian drew his descriptive inspiration from Dennis, the "nature boy" of the Wilson clan. "He told me stories and said it was great and I made up songs," Brian confesses.

It didn't take Brian long to get his feet wet in the studio, however. "At first my dad used to help us out in the booth," says Dennis Wilson, "but then Brian took off so fast he left *all* of us in the dust, to where the rest of us, Dad included, would just say, 'Now what, Brian? Now what?'"

Brian Wilson's first solo production was a revised version of "Surfer Girl," a 1963 hit released as a follow-up to "Surfin' U.S.A." It turned up again that September as the title song on the group's third album, an all-Brian production which marked a milestone in the industry; for virtually the first time

In concert without Brian: (clockwise) Carl, Al, Dennis, & Mike

PHOTOS BY MARY ALFIERI

in recording history, a major rock group had studio control. Understandably, Brian retains fond memories of the album and the song.

"'Surfer Girl' is my favorite Beach Boys song," he says. "I liked the melody and I liked the music. It was the first ballad we ever did; we actually recorded it before 'Surfin',' 'though we didn't release it 'til much later. We did it without knowing how; it was the first time we ever did a song like that. It was an innocent try —our first innocent recording experience."

After Brian retired from touring, the group released the *Beach Boys Today* (March 1965); *Summer Days (and Summer Nights!)* (June 1965), and *Beach Boys Party* (Nov. 1965) albums before the fateful turning point—*Pet Sounds*.

Pet Sounds was to be Brian Wilson's bid for acceptance as an *artiste*. He had become increasingly obsessed with the notion that the All-American Beach Boys, and those Liverpool interlopers, the Beatles, were locked into some strange, slightly sinister Battle of the Titans being staged on the U.S. record charts. From 1964, on, the two groups' singles see-sawed wildly in the Top Twenty, with the Beatles usually winning out. It was a situation that caused Brian some mild consternation when the British band broke big in the States, but he became downright distressed after his health compelled the retreat into the control room.

At length, he decided that, rather than slug it out single-for-single with the cockney rebels, he would contest them album-for-album with a bold new idea: the *concept*. Brian set to work and for the first time since the Beach Boys signed with Capitol, they did not release a single every three months.

"I was sitting around a table with friends, smoking a joint," Brian recalls, "when we heard *Rubber Soul* for the very first time; and I'm smoking and I'm getting high and the album blew my mind because it was a whole album with all good stuff! It flipped me out so much, I said, 'I'm gonna try that, where a whole album becomes a *gas*.'"

Pet Sounds was to be an analysis of romance, centering on the theme of a young man growing into manhood, falling in love and out again; all the while on a solitary, picaresque quest for the reasons behind his emotional restlessness. Based in part on Brian's life, it is a poignant, sometimes uplifting but ultimately dispiriting work that catalogues a succession of failed relationships. Much of the pessimism and dejection that pervaded the album's 13 selections was reportedly tied to marital problems Brian and his young wife, Marilyn, were experiencing at the time.

Prior to the release of *Pet Sounds*, Brian put out an unprecedented solo single of what was to be the last song on the lp, "Caroline, No." This burst of individualism was a reflection of Brian's growing estrangement from the touring Beach Boys and a mounting dissatisfaction with his lot in life:

Could I ever find in you again,
Things that made me love you so much then?
Could we ever bring them back
Once they have gone?
Oh, Caroline, no.

"My father used to go to pieces when he heard stuff like 'Caroline, No,'" says Dennis Wilson. "See, a lot of people don't know it, but that song was about a girl that Brian was really in love with in high school, named Caroline. He saw her again years later and it all came back to him, and he wrote the song."

Brian's joy with the single's immediate appearance on the charts turned to disgust and depression when the record hovered at No. 32 nationwide and then went into free fall. His grief was redoubled when *Pet Sounds* debuted in May of 1966; although an unqualified critical success, the album sold poorly despite the hit singles, "Sloop John B" and "God Only Knows/ Wouldn't It Be Nice." Thirteen months later, the Beatles released *Sgt. Pepper* and Brian's original vision was lost in the stampede.

"I was very proud of that album," Brian says in retrospect. "The reason we made *Pet Sounds* was because we specialized in certain sounds. I don't know how many months we spent working hard on that album to get all those different cuts just right. It was our best—the songs were our pet *sounds*.

"It was kind of a silly thing, but *Pet Sounds* just made me think that you could do a whole album that was a *bitch*; that held together and was not simply a collection of various songs. *Rubber Soul* was a complete statement, damn it, and I wanted to make a complete statement too!"

Brian Wilson rebounded in October of 1966 with "Good Vibrations," a delightful synthesis of the thematic/stylistic strongpoints of the current psychedelic wave, complete with harmonies to the hilt. While he included enough exotic instruments (sleigh bells, jew's harp, wind chimes, harpsichord, flutes, organ and theremin) to send Phil Spector packing, he sacrificed none of the Beach Boys' prepossessing airiness. It was the variegated but coherent statement he had endeavored to make with the self-conscious *Pet Sounds*. The best part was that he had managed it all in 3½ minutes, and so it became the band's biggest-selling single ever.

Whether by choice or design, Brian Wilson has not made a complete statement since. He knows it, and the Beach Boys can't bear it any longer.

For the first time since he cut "Heroes and Villains" in 1967 for the *Dumb Angel/Smile* debacle, Brian Wilson is back in the studio with the Beach Boys on *his* terms—totally in charge of his material, totally committed to the task of recording a new album; and *composing*.

***

"Well, that's it. That's the song . . ."

Brian shuts off the organ and sits back, relieved but expectant; as he dabs his forehead with his damp shirtsleeve, he keeps sneaking looks at me.

"Do you like . . . I dunno—do you *like* the song?" he finally wonders aloud, his voice loud and squeaky.

I am taken aback by the pathetic urgency of the question; devoid of any pretense to aloofness, it is the entreaty of an adolescent. I feel ridiculous in the role of arbiter of an acknowledged musical genius, and sneak my own look at Brian to make certain I didn't catch him wrong; the total exhaustion in his features is chilling. If a man could wash his face in fear—as if it were some milky, implacable liquid—surely this is the way it would emerge. I am consumed by the sensation that I am talking to a man with a broken heart. For the duration of our meeting, the feeling would never leave me again. But what about the song?

Even in its crude form, "California Feeling" sounds like the best ballad Brian has written since "God Only Knows." My first impulse is to burst forth in gushy exclamations, but instead I try to channel my enthusiasm into succinct sincerity: "I think it's a beautiful song. I think the words are great and the melody is extremely strong. It sounded very good."

There is a brief silence as Brian nods, suppressing a smile. Then he bursts into laughter. "Yeah," he beams. "It's a *good* song."

"What did I *tell* ya, Brian?" Stan chides affectionately before he also breaks up in a hearty chuckle. I feel like I am at a little boy's birthday party.

"Okay, let's do an interview!" says Brian, as if the idea just popped into his head. "Let's *wail*!"

Before I can concoct a question, the floodgates have opened: "'Palisades Park' and 'Blueberry Hill'!" he explains. "That's what us Beach Boys are working on right now! Everybody's coming in this afternoon and we're gonna do some dubdowns on those! Yep, we're trying to get back together so that we can keep our economy going. See, we don't want to go broke, and what little stuff we have to work with, well, we're trying to utilize that, because . . . well . . ."

Translation: The Beach Boys are back in the studio to sharpen their rough tapes of "Blueberry Hill" and "Palisades Park," two songs that will eventually appear on what Dennis Wilson describes as "one of three albums we're working on simultaneously to fulfill our commitment to Warner Bros. [The group's label since 1970.] It's very possible that one will be an all-oldies album," according to Dennis. "We've wanted to do one for a long time and Brian's into that. The other two could take the form of a double album of all-new material that stretches from hard rock 'n roll to these wordless vocals we've been doing that sound like the Vienna Boys Choir."

The oldies album will also include "In The Still Of The Night," "On Broadway," and "Tallahassee Lassie."

Among the original songs (all titles are tentative) are: "Ding-Dang," "10,000 Years" and "Rainbow" by Dennis; "Gold Rush" by Al Jardine; "Glow, Crescent, Glow," "Lisa" and "Everybody's In Love With You" by Mike Love, and Brian's "California Feeling," "Back Home," "Help Is On The Way" and a tune called "Transcendental Meditation":

When hustle was the name of the game,
I couldn't take the strain.
Then the Maharishi said to meditate,
It's as natural as the rain.

When Dennis Wilson talks about what "everybody" is involved in, he's referring to what he proudly calls "the original, Hawthorne-period Beach Boys." Only Dennis, Mike and Brian are on-hand for today's session; Al Jardine is over in Hollywood at a business meeting and Carl is in traction with a slipped disc. Carl's injury had occurred several days earlier in his Santa Monica home, reportedly while he was lifting a water cooler refill bottle of Sparkletts spring water.

"Carl sings the lead on 'Palisades Park,'" Brian tells me. "He did it on one take. Just as soon as he feels better, I might ask him to add more 'Let's Go Trippin'' guitar to the song, but I'm still thinking about that."

What made you decide to resume an active role in the studio?

"Well, I looked at the guys and they looked kinda sad," he explains, "They didn't look happy; they looked like something was wrong. I said to myself, 'Hey, maybe they're upset because we're not having any hit singles! Maybe they're mad at me!' I checked into it, and sure enough, as soon as we did 'Palisades,' everybody was happy again. Know what I mean?"

Brian turns toward me and smiles wanly; it is an embarrassed, painful upturn of his lips that is more the gallant gesture of an excruciatingly shy man than any demonstration of happiness. He is dressed in baggy dungarees, scuffed track shoes and a print shirt with a vaguely orange floral design that has long since been washed out. The limp, faded shirt is unbuttoned in deference to a swollen paunch which, like the rest of Brian, is pale and translucent, like the underside of an albacore.

He is not the quietly handsome man he once was; his body is rather disproportionate, the head too small atop his bloated, barrel frame, and the long arms and legs flowing awkwardly from their now-drooped anchor. Yet Brian retains a singular charisma, and when left to himself, there is a dignity in his open heart and insouciant demeanor that is striking.

His round, lightly-whiskered face is placid, practically expressionless most of the time. The action resides in his tiny eyes: One moment they reveal nothing, floating dull and glassy in their pinkish sockets; an instant later they are ablaze with a dark fire, scanning the room from side to side, up and down, in a slow, unsentimental scrutiny, as if gauging the relative worth and importance of everything present, discarding with perfect detachment what isn't useful as a tool or toy.

"Er, whose idea was it to record 'Blueberry' and 'Palisades'?" I stammer, trying to stabilize the unsettling mood.

"Oh, *I* thought of those!" Brian boasts with a vacant grin. "I sat around and thought, 'What would be good?' And it took a little time; because then I thought, 'Oh, the guys are gonna think I'm sloughing off by getting oldies instead of originals.' But now I think they agree.

"If you find the right song, and do that good rendition . . . well, when people think of my music, Beach Boys music, they think of a . . . *spirit.*"

"Your brother Dennis tells me that the group is working on three albums at once in order to fulfill its commitment to Warner Bros. . . ."

"Whew! Whoa!" he hoots, appearing startled. "Who said that? *Dennis* said that? Well, let's . . . *Hell,* the fact is we're behind commitment. And, okay, I'll tell you what happened: We got lax, very lax, slack, whatever, and we let too much time go by and now we're three albums behind." A worried look flashes across his face. "Three albums; that's a lotta albums. We could get sued, I suppose. . . ."

Brian's train of thought is interrupted by the entrance of Earl Mankey, a member of the studio engineering crew; he informs Brian that it's now 3:30 p.m. Brian had scheduled a session for 1 p.m., but didn't arrive until 2:30. Mankey says it's too late to call in the session musicians who were standing by, but says there's plenty of time to dub down the "Blueberry" tape.

"I think we should keep Mike Love's voice as the lead," Brian tells him, "and then, if my brother and Mike want to play, we'll do a track."

Stan, still leaning against the organ, mumbles something about Dennis singing lead on the song.

"What's this about Dennis doing the lead?" Brian demands.

"Oh, that's just what Carl said," Stan says with a shrug. "He thought that Dennis might want to do the lead on 'Blueberry' because he has a raspier voice."

"Beware of hurting Mike," Brian cautions. "*Really,* Stanley." Brian bursts into nervous laughter. "Boy, what is this I'm facing? The Wilsons *and* the Loves? I'm outvoted?"

"Nah," Stan says sheepishly. "You're right, Mike should stay."

Mankey moves to go, somewhat confused. Brian tells him to start playing the "Blueberry" tape and he'll be in shortly. Minutes later, the control booth is bursting with a lonesome slapback bass being goaded forward by the ghostly plip-plop of what sounds like a timbale stuck under on a dripping faucet, as Mike Love's breathless intro creeps into the foreground:

I found my thrill,
On Blueberry Hill,
On Blueberry Hill,
When I found you.
The moon stood still—

On "still," Love is joined by the rest of the group in a thunderous harmony refrain as a host of horns, guitars, drums and organ cut loose. The feel is muddy and unpolished, but the track possesses the same infectious energy that turned their original failure with "Barbara Ann" into a successful 1966 single when they redid a "live" version on *Beach Boys Party.*

Brian jumps up when he hears the music and begins walking around the studio, snapping his fingers idly and acting as if he's looking for something. He peers behind the grand piano in the corner and then squints up at the ceiling.

"Hey!" Stan calls out. "Come on back here!"

"Oh," says Brian, caught in a catnap of concentration. "Excuse me."

He dutifully returns to the organ bench, but remains distracted. I recapture his attention by asking if he's pleased with the way his two oldies are turning out.

"Hey, they sound *really* tight," he bubbles. "I like 'em both and I think they're both hits. 'Palisades Park' has an edge, though, because it's upbeat. We changed the original arrangements around quite a bit to fit our style. On 'Palisades,' we really sort of did a stock background. It wasn't a spectacular production; we did everything in one take. We wanted it to be kind of mediocre with a good beat and a simple vocal to reach people that way, because we have a little problem."

A little problem?

"Yeah. See, we used to be real *arty,* you know? And at times it only sold to a select few, but if we could just get *commercial,* I believe we could sell records; I believe it could be done. So if we could get that together, I think we could really sell—and be back in the action!"

Back in action? The Beach Boys recently tipped the scales for million-plus sales of *Endless Summer* and *Spirit of America,* two Capitol anthologies of early favorites, and they continue to be one of the most successful concert attractions in the world. Brian, however, seems mortified by these developments. In his eyes, the Beach Boys are an aimless studio band that stays on the road cranking out his aging triumphs to avoid facing up to their creative debilitation; what was once Brian's forte is now the group's greatest pitfall: hit singles.

Brian pauses, and looks away, as if reevaluating this path of thought. When he turns back, he is frowning.

"We've been off the singles chart for *eight years,*" he says, "and that's a long time not to be having any hits and stuff. So we would be really pleased if we could get something that the mass will like.

"I personally have been *long* forgotten from the writing," he states morosely. "Everybody's saying, 'You're a great writer, a real genius.' But it's been a long time and it will be a shock to re-enter. I mean, I'm going through shock myself right now."

He rifles through the pockets of his jeans and extracts a battered pack of cigarettes, lighting one hastily. He is about to resume his melancholy soliloquy when a tanned, athletic, surfer-type in overalls, sweatshirt and sneakers strolls into the studio. Dennis Wilson, his moppish hair happily disheveled, and sporting a two-day beard, flashes his good-natured grin around freely—until he spies Brian's cigarette.

Dennis *(irritated):* "What are you doing *smoking,* Brian? Huh? Listen to your voice! You're starting to get hoarse! *Jes-sus!* Don't be stupid! Put out that cigarette *now!* Take two puffs and put it OUT!"

Brian *(indignant):* No! I'll finish it and then I'll stop. I have no more cigarettes."

Dennis *(to Stan):* "Man, what *is this*? I thought you were gonna help him stop that damned smoking!"

Stan: "Hey! What can *I* do?"

Dennis: "Take the cigarette out of his *hand* and put it in the ashtray! There's too much damn smoke around here as it is! *(To Brian)* Put it out!"

Brian *(holding up the cigarette):* "When this thing reaches the butt to the filter. . . ."

Dennis: "Brian! Two puffs and then put it out!"

Brian *(voice cracking):* "What are you *talking* about? *I'm smoking my cigarette!*"

Dennis: "How many have you smoked today?"

Brian: "Four."

Dennis: "Honest to God?"
Brian (smirking): "Four packs. . . ."
Dennis (stalking off): "Jes-sus!"

Brian returns to the organ bench to continue our talk.

"What year is this?" he asks Stan.

"1976," Stan answers blankly.

"Okay," rules Brian, "so finally it's 1976 and we're still riding on our past success. I mean, I've gone on *that* for I don't know *how* long!"

"*Too* long," Stan offers. "How's that?"

"Really," says Brian with a crooked smile. "Like, okay, we'll get a song and we'll go halfway and we won't follow through. Fine. I kick myself in the ass for it and then *I* come back and try again. It's almost like a guy that gets knocked down: he has to keep getting back up until he gets himself together; that's how it works. All I care about is that I want everyone to be happy. If these sessions aren't any fun, then fuck it! It hasn't been for a while, and that's why we said, 'Fuck it!' for a few years.

"In the last two years all I ever cut, all I *ever* recorded, was skimpy little bits and pieces; little fragments," he confesses. "Something happened to my concentration—I don't exactly know what, but it weakened for some reason—and I lost the ability to concentrate enough to follow through. But that's my own problem; because of hang-ups I have.

"There's something called instinct, okay? And if your instincts start to lead you, then fuck, that's *where it's at*. And if they lead you astray. . . ." He doesn't complete the sentence.

"But you have to get a feel for *instinct* versus *opinion*," he asserts. "If you say, 'Palisades Park' and get that *feeling*—then it's straight ahead! If you don't, and start thinking too hard, well, that's what makes me retreat.

"I get too mental," he admits sadly, "and I don't think I follow my instincts as much as I should. I used to—shit, for years in a row! I mean *instinct*, I used to think them hits up one after another." He snaps his fingers rapidly. "Then I got too *thoughtful* about it and fucked up. So I suppose I have to get back on my fucking feet and trust my instincts and go with them a little.

"There's a lotta different ways to go," he tells me. "One way is very *mental*, trusting in your mind; the second is kinda going with your *instincts*, and the third would be *force*. If the first two fail, the last sets in—but that can work too.

"A lotta people use plain, sheer force to get where they want to go. Others say, 'Hey, man, this is the direction!' And they ride it. Hell, I've seen a lot of force, where you force something on somebody for their own good. You just say, 'Oh, goddamn, I *know* this is right for you!' and you can be right . . . sometimes.

"What we have to do," he decides, "is find the best ten songs we can and do an oldies but goodies thing. We could do 'Sea Cruise,' and I'd like to do 'Ruby Baby,' because I think Dennis could do the lead on that really good. We could do 'Working In a Coal Mine' too."

He sings a few bars:
Working in a coal mine!
Going down, down!

"See," Brian counsels, "The trap is, there's an awful lot of commerciality that we're exposed to, and that's intimidating. Even if the stuff isn't really art, there's something about a commercial record . . . that *special* something. We released a few good records and they bombed in the face of more commercial stuff. 'Sail On Sailor' was very arty, but it was a damn good record and it bombed. When that happens, it's a little defeating. [Actually, it was their best-selling single since signing with Warner Bros.]

"We were ahead of people in some ways during our early Warners period," Brian concedes, "but we were not commercial. I don't know if there's a real problem or not about this commercial idea; but what bugs me is to go into a studio and if I still have a defeatist mind, I say, 'Aw, it's good, but it's not gonna sell.'

"If I'm sold on the fact that we aren't gonna sell commercially, then I don't know. Maybe I've made my mind up that we're *not* gonna sell, so now I go into the studio and do it for the sheer fun of it.

"Eight years with *no* hits," he sulks. "Eight years without something the kids'll buy on *instinct*. Ahh, but look at Sinatra. Thirty-five years in this business and he can't get a hit single! Phew! Who knows what the fuck people are thinking?"

In an effort to lift his own spirits, Brian points out that "even during the Beach Boys' bad times, other people imitated us," but declines to mention any names. "I'm convinced that our thing is *very* imitatable," he says. "It's very *easy* to imitate us, so in that respect, the Beach Boys are still happening. But there's a funny thing called 'Doing your own thing.' If you're not actually projecting something of your own, it's too easy to fall down that elevator shaft, and get *panicky*.

"That's why I say it's better now to having a winning attitude. I didn't always but, by God, it works! You've got to at least think you're a winner, even if it hurts to say it!

"But since we got back from Holland we haven't recorded diddily-womp, and I don't know what the fuck for. I don't know why."

***

As far as Warner Brothers Records is concerned, the Beach Boys have been a big commercial disappointment over the last five years, and the company thinks it knows why: not enough of the Brian Wilson touch. Only time will tell whether Brian's new Norman Vincent Peale pathology will translate into hit records, but in the meantime, all the bosses in Burbank want to know is: "'Where's the product?'"

Alas, the Beach Boys have had that question mark hanging over their heads so long, what once was a Sword of Damocles is beginning to resemble a halo. As Dennis Wilson puts it: "I was talking to Brian the other day about the fact that the band hasn't released a new record in a long while and he said, 'Well, good things take time.'"

Genius at work: "What now, Brian? What now?" — STAN LOVE

***

"The best-selling Beach Boys album on Warner Brothers? That's a tough one. If you considered the *Beach Boys In Concert* album as more than a single record, well, obviously *In Concert* is the only Beach Boy album that went gold. It did not go gold because it sold enough copies to push a single-record package into the realm of a gold record, however. But because it was a double-record set and because it had a greater retail price, it went gold if you pro-rate the sales via the price and you call one of those albums 1¾ albums or 1½ albums or whatever . . . and that was the biggest-selling album."

What Dave Berson, the Executive Assistant to the Chairman of Warner Bros. Records, is trying to tell us is that the Beach Boys have managed *only one* gold record on his label—and it was a struggle. While Capitol racks up platinum awards for Beach Boys records over five years after the group left the company, Warner's catalogue seems lost at sea. To add insult to undertow, Warner-Reprise has not done as well as it hoped with the four post-*Pet Sounds* lps the Beach Boys purchased from Capitol in 1972 and repackaged on Brother/Reprise as two-record sets: *Wild Honey/20-20* and *Smiley Smile/Friends.*

"I always loved the Beach Boys image"

"The initial album, *Sunflower*, which might be the best album the Beach Boys ever recorded, did not sell many copies," says Dave Berson, "and we were very, very disappointed. *Surf's Up* was a very, very big album for us, to a large extent, I think, because Brian Wilson was still involved, but it did not go gold. The next album, the double-record set of *Carl and the Passions' So Tough/Pet Sounds*, was our worst-selling Beach Boys album."

Chronologically, that leaves *Holland* and *In Concert*. The latter was originally submitted to Warners as a single record, was rejected, resubmitted as a double album, and nearly got rejected a second time. *Holland* also was rejected once, but that's a story in itself. . . .

> Concentrating on their widely recognized obsession—technological advance—they took off for Holland where the surf's NEVER up and went through some half a million dollars settling in and arranging for nearly four tons of flying studio, a prototype for the future, to be brought from America. The evidence of the whole incredible adventure is on their new album, simply called *Holland.*
> —from a Warner Bros. press kit November, 1972

"It was Jack Rieley's idea to go to Holland," says Brian Wilson. "We met him one night when he walked into our health food store. [Brian was part-owner for a time, of a health food store in West Hollywood called the Radiant Radish. The store closed July 29, 1970, after being in operation for approximately one year.] He walked in and said, 'Hi, I'm Jack Rieley from NBC News.' And I said, 'Hi.'

"He said, 'I've got a show over at KPFK, come on over and do an interview.' So we took a liking to the guy and he joined us as a manager and a singer and songwriter; a really stimulating person. He had a deep voice.

"So after a while, we were tired of California and Jack Rieley said, 'Let's go to Holland and do some concerts!' So the band went over and stayed and did an album."

The "concert" the Beach Boys scheduled was an appearance on a Dutch TV spectacular called *Grand Gala du Disc*. After the show, the band and their families stayed on, deciding to make Amsterdam the base of operations for their European tour, and then spent several months in The Netherlands' countryside recording their fourth Warner Bros. lp. When the tour ended, they set up shop in a converted barn in rural Baambrugge and sent for Brian.

Wilson's wife and two daughters, Carnie and Wendy, made it over all right, but Brian himself was another matter. Twice he set out for Los Angeles International Airport to catch flights, but both times he decided for some unknown reason to turn back.

On the third try, Brian appeared to board the plane, but when it landed in Amsterdam there was no sign of him, save his passport and a ticket made out in his name which were found on his empty seat. After an hours-long search, he was located in the Dutch airport's duty-free lounge—sound asleep on a couch.

Brian's last three Beach Boys offerings [excepting his "Child of Winter" 1974 Christmas single] were all on *Holland* "Funky Pretty," "Mount Vernon and Fairway," a 12-minute fairytale set to music that Brian wrote while in The Netherlands, and "Sail On Sailor," which was written and recorded in Los Angeles.

Mike Love, golden-haired but irrevocably balding, and dressed in sandals, white chinos and a long woolen jacket woven in a colorful Indian design, is perched on a stool in a corner of the Brother studio, watching through a great glass window as Brian mixes "Blueberry Hill" in the spaceship-like control room. Earl Mankey, trying to be encouraging, keeps asking Bri what he thinks about "more saxophones? More echo? More bass drum? More . . .?"

Brian, stonefaced and bent over the board, is completely oblivious, sliding his fingers up and down the rows of dials, twisting this, turning that, engrossed in his favorite gambol.

"Ah *yes*," Love whispers to himself, immensely pleased by the total picture. "It's just like old times. I can remember that around 1957-'58 I guess it was, Brian had an old Rambler, and he used to come over my house a lot to hang out and sing. I was living at the corner of Mt. Vernon and Fairway in the View Park/Baldwin Hills section of Los Angeles at the time.

"You know that line in Brian's fairytale about 'distant lights'? Well, that was from my bedroom upstairs, which had a fantastic view. We had knotty pine bunkbeds built into the wall and we had a sunporch outside where we could sit out and look all over the city. We used to sleep in the bunks and I'd have a transistor radio on under the covers so we could listen to the late-night R&B on KGFJ and KDAY. You remember that part in the fairytale about the prince's 'magic transistor rado'? Well, that came from *that*.

"Brian thought up the idea of the fairytale in Holland and we all thought it was *great* how the whole thing came together. We all loved working on it, and from the start we thought it made a great little 'present' to go with *Holland*; so that's what we did. Don't you *love* it? Isn't it *wonderful?*"

About 45 minutes later, I chatted with Brian about the fairytale and he gave me *his* version of the record's development.

"The fairytale? Okay, lemme tell you. Well, we were in another country; we were in Holland, and I just sat around and drank apple sap—that's like apple cider—and just sat around and dreamed. And one night I was listening to that Randy Newman album called *Sail Away*. So I started playing the album and I was sitting there with a pencil and I started writing. And I found that if I kept playing the Randy Newman album, I could still stay in that mood. It was the weirdest thing; I wrote the whole fairytale while listening to that album. It was the weirdest little mood I created.

"I was thinking about Mike Love's house, and I just wrote, 'There was a mansion on a hill,' and then later on, in my head, I created a fairytale.

"But anyhow, so I had the fairytale, but *nobody* was ready for that. *Nobody*. I remember, Carl said, 'WHAT?!'

"Then... Oh, I know what happened! I got *fucked up*; I got *depressed*. So Carl did all the editing on it and even did part of it himself when I wasn't there. It was really a thrill; the first time we'd ever done anything that creative. I wanted it to be on the album, but they [the group] said, 'No! It's too long.' We argued and all, and I was depressed. So they finally compromised by saying, 'Okay, we'll slip it in that package as an extra record or something'...."

***

Warner Bros. was not pleased with the original version of *Holland* and rejected it, soon after it was submitted, as a "weak" album. The Beach Boys—who had dropped a personal fortune on the escapade—"freaked," in the words of one Warner Bros. employee, who added. "It was bloodshed; everybody went wild." It seems that the company had been waiting for something easily marketable to offset the *So Tough* fiasco and was unmoved by the fairytale and impressionistic cuts like Jardine and Love's 10-minute 'California Saga'—not to mention the absence of a strong single.

From here, the sequence of events takes a somewhat gothic turn.

With *Holland* in limbo and tempers flaring, a business associate close to the problem decided to contact several people near Brian Wilson in the hope that Brian either *had*, or could be induced to *compose*, a surefire single suitable for inclusion on the album. Among those contacted was Van Dyke Parks, a Warner Bros. artist who had coauthored "Cabinessence," "Heroes and Villains," "Vegetables," and other material with Brian during the *Smile* period. Parks is said to have shown up in the executive offices of Warner Bros. Records "minutes" after he was telephoned, carrying a cassette of a song called "Sail On Sailor."

The following description of what was on Parks' cassette was supplied by an extremely reliable source close to the Beach Boys (the source, who was present when the cassette was first played, requested anonymity):

"Brian [was] playing that song ["Sail On Sailor"] on the piano. It was completely different words. He's singing different words; much better words. It was one of the most curious things I've ever heard.

"It begins with Van Dyke saying, 'Brian, there's something you gotta do for me, man. I want you to sit down at the piano and I want you to write a song for me. Lyrics, melody, everything. I want you to do it right on the spot.' Brian says, 'I'd do anything for you, man, but would you do something for me?'

"Van Dyke says, 'I'd do anything for *you*, Brian.' So Brian says, 'Hey, you gotta convince me, Van Dyke, that I'm not insane.' He keeps repeating, over and over again, 'Hypnotize me into thinking that I'm not insane. Convince me that I'm not insane.'

"Van Dyke says, 'Cut the shit, Brian. I want you to write this tune right here.' And the cassette goes on for about 15 minutes. As you can imagine, there's a lot of halts in it. He's trying to do the words at the same time, too. So when he runs out of words, he stops playing and starts again."

At Warner Bros. insistence, the Beach Boys recorded what proved to be a re-written version of "Sail On Sailor," with Blondie Chaplin singing the lead. Brian reportedly had no hand in the production of the song.

***

To understand Brian Wilson, it helps to get a handle on his brother Dennis. While Brian and the others were indoors writing and singing about the surfing lifestyle, Dennis was down at Manhattan Beach *living* it.

"I don't know why everybody doesn't live at the beach, on the ocean," says Dennis with a bemused shake of his head. "It makes no sense to me, hanging around the dirty, ugly-as-shit city. That's why I always loved and was proud to be a Beach Boy; I always loved the image. On the beach, you can live in bliss. You wake up and fall out into that water, go fishing, go sailing, go...."

The rest is drowned out by a noisy flock of gulls that dip and soar in the cloudless blue sky above us. Dennis and I are spending a gusty spring day in Santa Monica Harbor, polishing the fittings on *Harmony*, a magnificent 62-foot sailboat that he rebuilt from scratch last year with "a couple of Yugoslavian guys.

"Lookit this," he orders, taking time out from rubbing a shine into one of the handrails to lick his calloused thumb and rub it against the weathered deck. "See how the grain comes out in this wood when it's wet? This is *teak*; it's made to look beautiful when it's all wet out at sea. This boat looks okay now, but it looks best when it's in action."

The boat has a lot in common with Brian Wilson.

"It took a while for Brian to get himself shipshape again, and he could still stand to lose a few pounds of gut. But I think I understand why he took off for a few years," says Dennis. "He wanted to rest and felt there was no sense living in the past. He's been through a lot of tremendous emotional changes and setbacks from taking drugs and not understanding them, among other things. Brian's a reclusive, sensitive, vulnerable guy and he was probably one of the most famous people in the world at one point. That *completely* got to him.

"But the thing I wonder about is where does Brian's creative spark come from? Not his subjects or anything, but his spark. What makes it so great for me is that I really don't know. There's a mystery behind Brian, even to *me*. Creatively, where in the fuck does the guy go? Where is he coming from?"

Dennis tosses his polishing rag into the hold and goes down into the galley, emerging moments later with a frozen cream pie that he proceeds to shovel into his mouth with a small fork.

"Brian is more reclusive now than he was 7-8 years ago," Dennis confides with a swallow and a wink. "Back in Hawthorne he had a tremendous sense of humor. He was a prankster. He used to pull the most outrageous stunts with my family!"

Like what?

"Like...." He pauses to reflect and begins laughing uproariously. "Nah, I'm not gonna tell you *that* one, but, like—like driving down the street going to school when we were kids," he snorts gleefully. "We'd be rushing to school and Brian would be drinking a carton of milk, and he'd stop and open the door and pretend he was throwing up by emptying out the whole milk carton! Or he'd stop and wait for a hitch-hiker to run up to the car and then he'd take off! Or shitting on a plate and putting it in front of my dad at *dinner*!!" Dennis nearly chokes on a hunk of pie.

"Jes-sus! He'd totally let go, and whatever could happen he'd let happen. The group started that way, setting up a stage in the garage to have funny performances. He was out front, almost in an embarrassing way. He'd be somewhere and say, 'Oh, God, I'm gonna *fart*.'"

Dennis chuckles on for a few minutes and then calls for sobriety.

"Let me say something serious," he begs. "People always thought Brian was a goodtime guy until he started releasing those heavy, searching songs on *Pet Sounds* 'n all, but that stuff was closer to his own personality and perceptions. By the time people get close to an accurate picture of Brian Wilson—if ever—he's gonna be far beyond them again, and I can dig his frustration.

"For instance; I wrote a song intended for *Holland* about Vietnam," he says. "I got the image of a soldier—me—dying in a ditch, and I ended up doing a song about it. The soldier began feeling, 'Why the hell am I here?' Then the coldness started to move up his body from his feet, to his legs, to his chest . . . until he was dead. See? It was too *negative*! How could I put that on a Beach Boys album?"

***

"The great thing is, at least *I* feel, that you can put *anything* on a Beach Boys record if you can get that *feeling*," says Brian Wilson. "I think our fans will like oldies as much as anything if we give it the classic Beach Boys touch, and I have faith in 'Blueberry Hill' and 'Palisades Park,'" he concludes, sealing the pact by downing his third consecutive glass of fruit juice.

"Boy, this stuff is good for you!" he assures as he places his glass on the counter in the Brother Studio kitchenette. "I'm trying to get everybody, Carl and Dennis and all these guys, to start taking vitamins and eating healthy foods, like I've been doing . . . lately. I'm writing a song called 'Help Is On The Way' about how people should forget about hotdogs and hamburgers and eat good food.

"I like sweet stuff, though," he admits. "When I used to hang out at Foster's Freeze, I'd get a 'Sludge' everyday; a cherry Sludge with ground-up ice. Good drink."

"Sail On Sailor": "It was arty, but good and it bombed..."

With a half-day's studio work under their belts, Dennis, Mike (and Stan) decide to take a short break, ambling into the cozy, plant-filled lounge in the front section of the "Brother Building." They are lying about on the stylish '40s beach furniture shooting the breeze when a refreshed and smiling Brian enters and sits down on the couch.

Stan: "Brian! Hey, how ya feeling buddy?"
Brian: "Okay."
Dennis: "Hey Brian. I was just telling Mike and Stan that I saw a musical in New York the other day called *The Wiz*. It's a black Wizard of Oz; the whole cast is black and the score is all soul music, man! Brian, you should go to New York for a few days sometime soon and see *The Wiz*. Hands down, it's the best musical I've seen."

Stan *(excited)*: "Brian, let's go to New York in a week or two and see the play!"

Brian *(uneasy)*: "Are you kidding! New York—that's a *lonely* place, with all those tall, dark, unfriendly buildings."

Stan: "Well, why don't you take your lonely friends with you?"

Brian: "No deal."

Dennis *(diplomatic)*: "Well, New York *can* get a little weird. When I was there last week I did a few interviews . . ."

Brian *(softly)*: "Someone should interview my psychiatrist."

Dennis: "What was that, Brian?"

Brian: "I saw a doctor today. Somebody should talk to *him*. You know what he told me? He said, 'Okay, we're gonna start on *self-nourishment*.' I didn't know what that was. He said, 'Read this little piece of paper.' He handed me the piece of paper and said, 'Read it to me.'

"It said, 'I love you.' Turns out you're supposed to read this to yourself.

"The doctor said that you're supposed to tell yourself you love yourself and you trust yourself. It's a whole, weird thing. You're supposed to read the paper three times a day for five minutes each time, no matter *where* you are, saying, 'I love you, I love you' to yourself, and all these other different thoughts; they're all written on little pieces of paper. It's supposed to be called nourishment; it's supposed to help you. It's a really weird idea.

"Heck, I lost the paper. I thought the guy was *crazy*."

***

The following morning, Brian, dressed in the same shirt he wore yesterday, the same scuffed track shoes and a pair of navy blue pants with wiggly white lines running down the outside of either leg, is jogging along a portion of UCLA's cross-country course.

Stan Love, trim and confident in a lemon-colored warm-up suit, is urging him on:

"That's it Bri . . . there's no hurry . . . enjoy yourself."

It's the first day of Brian's Stan-inspired physical fitness program and as he takes the hill, shirt-tails flapping, he does seem to be having a good time.

After the brisk run, Brian, Stan and I locate a shady spot under some pines, where my two companions hold each other's ankles while they do some sit-ups.

Brian . . . does . . . 10!
Stan . . . does . . . 11!

"You know, I dig running," Brian tells Stan as we walk back to the Mercedes. "Were you surprised I could go that far?"

"I was *very* surprised when we were coming back up that hill," Stan replies, "because coming up the hill is a lot tougher."

"Yeah!" says Brian. "Now, let's go home and get some orange juice." As we are getting into the Mercedes, Brian turns to me and asks, "Have you ever been to my house before?"

No, I tell him. Never.

"Well, I live where I've lived for the last eight years," he says. "I live in a big house with a big wall around it. . . ." ■

NEXT MONTH, PART 2: BRIAN WILSON, PRISONER OF BEL AIR? Life in a Spanish mansion with Marilyn, the kids (and Stan) and the iron gate at the entrance. Plus the truth about *Dumb Angel/Smile*: "It was destroying me!"

Made in the USA
Columbia, SC
26 June 2025